Praise for *Love Skills*

"Psychologist, couples therapist, and well-known author Linda Carroll combines deep insight into relationships with an informative and interactive approach. The hands-on and heartfelt questionnaires allow helpful realizations to float to the surface of the reader's consciousness. In sharing the answers with a partner, couples will reach deeper understanding, healing, and compassion for each other."

— **Ann Gadd**, author of *Sex and the Enneagram* and *The Enneagram of Eating*

"As a millennial, I've observed that everyone tells us to love, but they never tell us how. *Love Skills* is a candid, readable, and concrete dive into not just how to find love but how to stay in it once you've arrived."

— **Zak Dychtwald**, author of *Young China:
How the Restless Generation Will Change Their Country and the World*

"Linda Carroll brings to her book the same warm, wise, and kind presence that she does in person. A truly gifted therapist, she gives us exercises and insights that penetrate self-destructive defenses and allow us to be our better selves and ultimately more loving (and loved) partners. These are love skills to be learned — and there is no one better qualified to teach them than Linda Carroll."

— **Pepper Schwartz, PhD**, professor of sociology at the University of Washington
and coauthor of *Snap Strategies for Couples:
40 Fast Fixes for Everyday Relationship Pitfalls*

"In a landscape of rare humility and honesty, Linda Carroll weaves together lived experience and clinical wisdom into an exceptional and valuable guidebook on the intricacies of love that is both enlightening and beautifully written."

— **Peter Yarrow**, Peter, Paul and Mary

"In *Love Skills* Linda Carroll provides the map, compass, and survival kit for anyone journeying through the labyrinth of romantic love. Drawing from a range of therapeutic frameworks and tools, decades of clinical experience, and poignant field research from her own thirty-five-year marriage, Linda has distilled the wisdom of lifetimes into a comprehensive modern-day workbook full of growth-inducing to-do lists, insight-awakening questionnaires and quizzes, thought-provoking exercises, and other indispensable self-help tools for couples looking for clarity in their relationships. *Love Skills* is one of those rare, powerful books that, when used creatively and consistently, can genuinely help couples overcome common obstacles to loving and sustain a lasting bond."

— Alicia Muñoz, author of *No More Fighting* and *A Year of Us: A Couple's Journal*

"While *Love Skills* is a workbook companion to her acclaimed *Love Cycles* and is best used as a study guide to that book, it can also be a stand-alone guide to love. In addition to charts that evoke self-awareness and exercises that develop relational skills, Linda Carroll has included enough theory to illuminate the practice. We recommend this guide and the original text to all couples who want a clear path through the forest of challenges to the sunshine of a thriving relationship."

— Harville Hendrix, PhD, and Helen LaKelly Hunt, PhD, coauthors of *Getting the Love You Want: A Guide for Couples* and *Making Marriage Simple*

"A breakthrough among the confusing plethora of relationship books, this book is truly important — realistic, deeply personal, and packed not just with the wisdom of a seasoned therapist, but with real, practical tools."

— Dr. Gleb Tsipursky, CEO of Disaster Avoidance Experts, LLC, and author of *The Blindspots Between Us*

LOVE
SKILLS

Also by Linda Carroll

Love Cycles: The Five Essential Stages of Lasting Love

LOVE
SKILLS

The Keys to Unlocking
Lasting, Wholehearted Love

LINDA CARROLL

New World Library
Novato, California

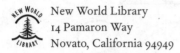 New World Library
14 Pamaron Way
Novato, California 94949

Text design by Tona Pearce Myers

Library of Congress Cataloging-in-Publication data is available.

First printing, February 2020
ISBN 978-1-60868-623-0
Ebook ISBN 978-1-60868-624-7
Printed in Canada on 100% postconsumer-waste recycled paper

 New World Library is proud to be a Gold Certified Environmentally Responsible Publisher. Publisher certification awarded by Green Press Initiative.

10   9   8   7   6   5   4   3   2   1

For
My Family, who teach me about Wholehearted Love each day,
and for
Karen Lynn Randall, who has been there for all of it

Because I prayed
this word:
I want.

— SAPPHO

Contents

Preface

People always fall in love with the most perfect aspects of each other's personalities. Who wouldn't? Anybody can love the most wonderful parts of another person. But that's not the clever trick. The really clever trick is this: Can you accept the flaws? Can you look at your partner's faults honestly and say, "I can work around that. I can make something out of that"? Because the good stuff is always going to be there, and it's always going to be pretty and sparkly, but the crap underneath can ruin you.

— Elizabeth Gilbert, *Committed: A Skeptic Makes Peace with Marriage*

An age-old idea maintains that "love at first sight" or "finding the one" is the key to a long and successful partnership. I'm sure some people have had that experience, managing to turn their first head-over-heels infatuation into a long-term successful relationship. But just as often, it leads to disaster. I speak from experience.

I was eleven when I met him: a boy with gray-green eyes and a smile so endearing I felt my breath leave my lungs. It was the pounding of my heart that helped me remember I was still alive. He had a special affectionate name for me, and to this day I have never said it out loud.

You might be thinking, "Isn't this supposed to be a serious book about relationships? Those last lines could have come from a cheesy romance novel." You wouldn't be wrong!

But I did experience that level of intensity at age eleven. He stayed locked in my psyche for twenty-nine years, and even writing about him sixty years later, I feel a tiny pang of longing. It could be the rush of chemicals that still run through my brain at the memory of him, or perhaps I yearn for those moments when I thought the euphoria I felt in his presence meant I could stay in that state forever.

Back in those days, I listened to love songs about finding The One and watched Hollywood movies that always ended with lovers walking off into the sunset. That's how the story ended: two people finding their other half and finally becoming whole.

One day, my eighth-grade teacher, Sister Germaine, had us write about the miners in the great Yukon Gold Rush of 1896. As soon as one man struck gold, a stampede of thousands followed, hoping they too would find the key to happiness. But most came back empty-handed. The few who did strike gold squandered it — and often their lives along with it. But once in a while someone struck gold! I wrote my paper comparing the Gold Rush to the search for love, arguing that finding The One was worth risking everything; love was the gold that was the key to happiness. Sister Germaine spoke to me kindly but sternly, telling me something I'd never heard before. She said, "Linda, the gold you are looking for is inside of you."

I wish I had been emotionally intelligent enough to absorb those words. Instead, my friends and I laughed in secret at the old nun who'd "never known real love" and therefore had no idea what she was talking about.

And so I became a love junkie instead. That feeling the green-eyed boy gave me was love's designer drug itself: a fluttering heart and fierce hits of pleasure.

But that "true love" didn't turn out so well. Despite my certainty that he was The One, there came a day when I discovered he had a special name for my best friend too.

For the next twenty-five years, I re-created variations of this scene with various partners, always looking for The One who would fulfill me, make me happy, and be my other half. The relationships all began with a giddy rush, then sank with a thump, and before I knew it, I was playing sad songs and reading poems about heartbreak. There was always another unhappy and inappropriate relationship waiting where the last one had left off, and then another, and still another after that. I thought the chemical rush was a signal that I should be with that next person, and I ignored the many signs trying to tell me that the people I picked just weren't right.

The morning I turned thirty-five, I felt myself at a crossroads. I didn't want the next part of my life to be a repeat of the relationship unhappiness I had experienced in the first part. So I found my way to a good therapist. I read books and went back to graduate school studying counseling and psychology, determined to uncover the roots of my disastrous history with love. Dr. Harville Hendrix and Dr. Helen LaKelly Hunt, the married couple who founded Imago relationship therapy, taught me that "familiar love" is often mistaken for "real love." It was perhaps the harshest but most valuable lesson I learned. Sometimes when we feel we've known someone forever, it's not because we were together in another lifetime or because we were meant to be together because of the alignment of the stars. It is simply that their attachment style, difficulty managing anger, or other aspects of their personality mirror those of a parent we struggled with.

One day I said to my therapist, "I realize there is no such thing as 'The One.'"

She replied, "Oh, but there is. The One you're looking for is inside of you, not outside."

The message of Sister Germaine, the old nun who "didn't know about life," had come back to me. This time, I didn't laugh. I knew my therapist was right. But I had no idea how to find The One in myself.

So a new kind of quest began. Who was I? I traveled the world, studied various philosophies, and spent many hours in contemplative practices. I asked myself many questions: Who am I? What has made me the person I am? How could I have not known I was The One, instead looking to person after person to find an answer that dwelt only inside of me? The year I turned forty, I went on a weeklong retreat aptly entitled "What Is the Meaning of *Your* Life?" There, I realized the five years I'd spent on looking within had helped me to *become* The One I was seeking.

A month later, I rediscovered a dear friend I hadn't seen in years. Tim had been on a similar path of self-discovery, and we renewed a deep and loving friendship. Slowly, it evolved into more. We took a long time to let our relationship grow into something we trusted enough to create a life together. We've now been together thirty-five years.

Of course, even after all the inner work we'd both done on our own, the human dilemma and all the struggles it brings to relationships knocked us around again and again once we came together. Still, we stayed with each other. We even gave the process a name: staying on the bronco. What bound us together — besides deep friendship and a mutual love of dogs, good books, crazy and wonderful passion, and wicked humor — was a shared belief that love and marriage are not places to hide from life. A committed relationship is a place to grow, to learn and inquire and challenge ourselves. It's a way to better know the self and, even more challenging, to practice the arts of tolerance, forgiveness, and apologizing. Relationships are opportunities to practice wholeheartedness and, in magical moments, to fully experience it.

So after years of thinking both the best and worst parts of my relationships were all about the other person, I finally realized that love is an inside job. Many of the troubles we experience emerge from conflicts we ourselves contribute to, relationship behavior we simply tolerate (and which cause silent resentments to build), and the unexamined parts of our own psyche. The health of our intimate connections depends on how we deal with our own lingering demons and on our own motivation to actually grow and change.

As a therapist, I notice these principles are some of the hardest for clients to believe. When they finally get that all of it — the good, the bad, the ugly, and the most beautiful — begins and ends within them, they experience a sense of liberation. Certainly, we are not responsible for other people's behavior and will feel pain if the people we care about hurt us, but what happens next is on us. Responding from a place of centeredness rather than reactivity will help us to choose when we need to forgive, when we need to hold to a bottom line, and when we need to face how we've helped create the conflict. Staying centered will also help us remember the unique strengths and gifts we offer in our relationships and help us select a partner who can recognize these as well.

Introduction

What makes for a good marriage isn't necessarily what makes for a good romantic relationship. Marriage isn't a passion-fest; it's a partnership formed to run a very small, mundane and often boring non-profit business. And I mean this in a good way.

— LORI GOTTLIEB, *Marry Him: The Case for Settling for Mr. Good Enough*

I made an important discovery thirty-eight years ago while working at a local agency as part of a counseling internship. I was sitting with a married couple whose love and commitment were strong, yet they couldn't stop arguing about how to manage their money. Paul saw money as a ticket to freedom and pleasure — a chance to buy the sports car he wanted, enjoy the best restaurants, and purchase the latest climbing gear. Amy, whose priority was financial security, wanted to live frugally and put away as much money as possible. Each partner was scared of the other's style. Amy was frightened of what she viewed as her husband's recklessness with the checkbook, and she worried they wouldn't have enough money socked away for the future. Paul, for his part, believed his wife was trying to leach all the fun and adventure from his life.

Their arguments were fierce and unrelenting. By this point, the blame and anger they were hurling at one another had become a bigger problem than their differences in spending styles. Even as a relatively new therapist, I could see these two weren't going to resolve their conflict by just talking it over.

Meanwhile, I was teaching a class on interpersonal communication at Oregon State University and had recently introduced my students to "pillow talk," a process in which two people discuss an issue they differ on. They begin by sitting on a pillow and stating their position. Then they move to the other person's pillow, talking about the same topic from the other's point of view. This gave me an idea. What if Paul and Amy didn't need traditional couples therapy? What if they would benefit more from the simple practices I taught in my introductory communications class?

In our next session, I suggested that Amy and Paul try the pillow-talk exercise. I asked them to describe their feelings, beliefs, and concerns about their money issue, then shift sides and describe their partner's perspective with as much conviction as they could, as though it were their own. Next, I suggested they think about how each side was right and how each side was wrong. In the last part of the exercise, I asked both partners to verbally acknowledge the truth in both positions.

Amy and Paul dove in willingly. Within a short time, I saw them make extraordinary progress. For the first time in their twelve-year marriage, they'd gained a genuine understanding of what it was like to be the other person. Although they still didn't agree about money, something between them had softened; they were gentler with one another and had fewer arguments. Over time and with practice, the couple learned how to allocate money in a way that at least partially accommodated both of their needs and how to be a little more tolerant of their partner's different way of doing it. Despite their ongoing disagreement, they managed to stay connected. In short, they were developing and honing their love skills.

The truth is, most couples don't lack love; instead, they lack the skills to communicate compassionately while hurt, upset, or holding a different perspective. It's usually the way we manage our differences — not the differences themselves — that causes pain.

Improving your communication skills is a familiar concept in the work world, but we tend to practice it less often in our love lives. After all, most of us "fall in love." "Falling" doesn't require competence, intention, or practice. It just happens. The necessary elements of a healthy relationship — making time to be together, pleasure in pleasing and listening to one another, acceptance of differences — come naturally at the beginning of a relationship. But over time, as the dopamine high of infatuation fades, we begin to experience our differences in a new way. Increasingly, they feel painful, more glaring, and sometimes impossible to navigate. We start to think something is terribly wrong. We may believe we've "fallen" out of love and conclude that we've chosen the wrong person.

The heart of my teaching — and the heart of *Love Skills* — comes from the Love Cycles model, which explains that relationships develop in predictable stages, each of which presents its own challenges. With knowledge, commitment, and practice, we can usually work through these challenges, even when they initially feel insurmountable. Contrary to conventional wisdom, people don't meet, fall in love, overcome a few trials, and then live happily ever after — nor do conflict and dissatisfaction between partners necessarily mean a couple is headed for Splitsville. According to the Love Cycles model, lasting love develops in five stages: The Merge, Doubt and Denial, Disillusionment, The Decision, and Wholehearted Love.

Amy and Paul were stuck for a long time in the Disillusionment stage and were almost ready to give up on their marriage. With just a few skills, they were able to find their love for one another again and move on to a new and happier stage of their relationship.

The Merge

Doubt and Denial

Disillusionment

The Decision

Wholehearted Loving

Love Skills will teach you how to stay connected even when you're feeling hurt, angry, or distant. You will acquire a tool kit to navigate the thorniest issues and learn how two imperfect people can love one another as perfectly as possible.

The Case of the Dirty Dishes

Over the three decades that I've worked as a therapist and couples coach, I've participated in countless training programs and acquired numerous certificates and degrees, but my primary source of knowledge — especially when it comes to the cycles of love — is my own thirty-five-year marriage.

When Tim and I began our relationship, we never expected that the qualities we most loved about each other would become the ones we were most determined to change. I was infatuated with Tim's strong moral compass, his idealistic commitment to living a meaningful life, and his reliability. He, in turn, was charmed by my spontaneity, my bubbling enthusiasm for life, and my relaxed attitude toward time and money (my motto: "Don't sweat either; there will always be more"). We had no idea this initial magic was a euphoric but temporary state caused by a biochemical cocktail. We had no clue we were in Stage One of the Love Cycles model: The Merge.

Five years after we rekindled our relationship, he had sold his veterinary practice and his boat and arrived at my house with a well-packed trunk filled with clothes, books, and two silver candlesticks from his grandmother. We got married and adopted our dream child: an Alaskan malamute we named Sylva. We had pulled it off: we were together forever now. We believed we were off to Soulmatesville and a lifetime of magic and wonder.

But that's not what happened. Instead, within a short time, I began to see his reliability as rigidity, his moral compass as self-righteousness, and his idealism as ridiculously naive. He began to accuse me of being impulsive and financially irresponsible; on dark days he reclassified my enthusiasm as infantile, pie-in-the-sky optimism. We argued over everything: how to celebrate Christmas, how to spend money, and — the original power struggle — how to do the dishes. I didn't know it at the time, but we were entering Stage Two of the Love Cycles model: the Power Struggle, also known as Doubt and Denial.

When Tim and I first met, I was living in an old New Zealand farmhouse. We met in a sheep paddock and immediately began to talk easily and with a sense of familiarity, as though we'd known one another forever. He'd followed me inside to the kitchen, still talking, where I began to wash dishes. After watching me for a moment, he asked why I was washing them "excessively" under hot water before putting them in the dishwasher. Lightly, I countered that even the best dishwasher wouldn't remove all the food. He grinned while informing me that I was "wasting hot water."

At the start of our relationship, we thought the other's dishwashing practices were charming, however misguided. We teased each other about our differences and laughed about them good-naturedly. But once we started living together and washing the dishes daily, side by side, we quickly moved from annoyed to exasperated to righteously indignant. It may sound like a small and even silly problem, but it quickly escalated into a major one. At first, we tried to win over the other with somewhat calm logic, but before long we were hurling insults at one another. The dishwashing problem encapsulated a situation in which the qualities we loved about one another had become the very traits that drove us crazy.

The conflict came to a head one night when we had dinner guests we barely knew. After Tim and I cleared the table, we started to load the dishwasher and quickly spiraled into a spiteful argument in front of them. We went so far as to individually present our own dishwashing points of view to our guests and demand they be the judges. Our voices were hard, unyielding, and self-righteous. Our guests looked stricken. At that point, our problem had nothing to do with the dishes and everything to do with our intensely negative reactions to each other's differences. Blame and anger had become our default strategies in the face of conflict, and now we were performing them in front of other people.

We walked away from the dispute feeling hurt and angry. Both of us began to wonder whether our relationship was the biggest mistake of our lives. This is a classic symptom of Stage Three of the Love Cycle, when disillusionment sets in and connection is replaced by ongoing disenchantment.

Here's the good news. Today, Tim and I generally stay out of each other's way when one of us does the dishes, and we (usually) end up laughing when we bump heads over this. Tim still does them wrong in my opinion, and he feels the same about my style. However, I no longer show him dried dishes that have some nasty pieces of food stuck on them to prove my point, and he has ceased leaving statistics about wasting hot water on my dresser.

How did we get there? After an unusually vicious argument with Tim, I reflected on the craziness of it all. I remembered Amy and Paul from my counseling internship and how something as simple as the pillow-talk exercise had helped them. Like Amy and Paul, my husband and I needed love skills.

When I told Tim the story of Amy and Paul, he got it — to my great relief. We didn't want to lose each other. Yet neither of us had the slightest idea how to escape our agonizing arguments. So we set out to learn. That's when we entered Stage Four — making a decision to stop the pain. We began to seek a new relationship road map while letting go of the old one, which had insisted that in the face of differences someone had to win — and therefore someone had to lose.

Tim and I attended relationship workshops all over the country. We participated in Dr. Lori Gordon's renowned PAIRS psychoeducation program in Washington, DC, which teaches that all couples have unresolved issues — about ten on average! — that are resistant to change. The key to relationship happiness is learning conflict-management skills that preserve love and respect. We also trained in Imago relationship therapy with Dr. Harville Hendrix and Dr. Helen LaKelly Hunt, who teach couples how to use arguments and differences as opportunities for healing and growth. We soaked up all we could from educators, psychologists, and interdisciplinary teachers about how to make a relationship thrive, how to manage differences productively, and how to discover empathy when it seems impossible.

Wanting to share all we learned with others, I created a curriculum that included the best information, skills, and practices from our finest teachers. Once Tim and I learned how to manage our own conflicts and move toward mutual compassion and, eventually, delight (at least most of the time), he and I began to teach a Love Skills class to other couples. The program, which we've taught for the past twenty-five years, draws from many sources: my longtime counseling work with couples and individuals; our training with the pioneers of interpersonal therapy; wisdom found in ancient mythology, poetry, music, and spiritual traditions; and, of course, our own marriage.

When we started the Love Skills class, I began by teaching long workshops and added weekend seminars for individual couples later. Currently, I travel around the country offering two-day intensives that combine love coaching and psychoeducation for individual couples and families, and I also work online with people around the world. Passing my knowledge on to others has brought me great joy. I have been amazed and heartened at how education and coaching can free people from destructive patterns and help them rediscover a relationship filled with mutual love, understanding, compassion, and just plain fun.

For Tim and me, learning love skills was an enormous undertaking. We practiced, failed, and tried again. Each of us worked hard on taking responsibility for our own parts in the conflict — the stubborn need to be right, the underlying triggers stemming from events in our past, and our individual personality traits that tended to escalate our disagreements. Practicing acceptance, learning to be kind to one another even when we were upset, and letting go of self-righteousness made a huge difference in the texture of our relationship. Eventually I could feel us softening, just as I'd witnessed with Amy and Paul. We still disagreed, but most of the time we remained openhearted in the face of conflict.

We also experienced a second, surprising benefit: in the process of healing and enhancing our relationship, we were becoming healthier, more wholehearted human beings. Each of us developed more self-respect, needed less validation from one another, and could manage our differences without feeling threatened or seeking to make the other wrong.

Gradually, our relationship became easier and warmer. To our astonishment, we were even able to recapture some of the earlier magical chemistry of Stage One. Meanwhile, our *friendship* also deepened. As we continued to replace our endless arguments with more acceptance, humor, and generosity, we moved into Stage Five, Wholehearted Love. Although we are not able to stay there all of the time, it is the "home base" we go back to again and again.

Love Skills will teach you the very best of the skills we learned that got us through the earlier stages of love. With the right tools, practice, and patience, you can get there too, time and time again.

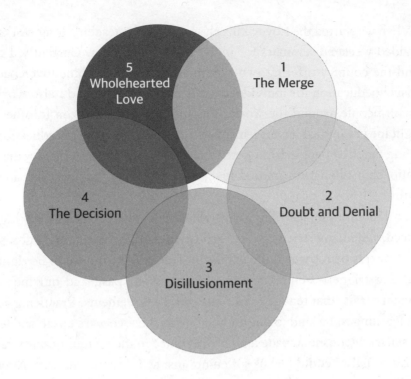

A Crash Course on Love

Here's the truth about intimate relationships: the conflicts you face right now may never disappear. You and your partner may always hold different perspectives about child-rearing, money, the best vacation spots, and how to properly clean the bathroom. But the good news is, the ways you manage these differences can change profoundly. As you develop the emotional and interpersonal skills described in these pages, your conflicts with your partner will become less painful and destructive — and your relationship can begin to thrive again.

This workbook is a companion to my first book, *Love Cycles: The Five Essential Stages of Lasting Love*. This first book describes the five stages of intimate relationships in detail, illuminating the behaviors associated with each stage and strategies for successfully navigating them. This companion manual, *Love Skills*, is a practical guide to help you design your own tool kit for creating and maintaining a loving relationship. It's a do-it-yourself version of the Love Skills program that you can use at your leisure. Consider it a self-exploration guide, one you can work with either alone or with your partner.

These pages are filled with information, exercises, activities, self-assessments, and other tangible tools to help you understand where you are in your relationship cycle now and how to foster the self-awareness, communication, conflict management, and empathy you need to weather all of love's seasons.

Awareness comes first. This workbook begins by helping you to answer critical questions about your relationship and yourself. For example: Why do I try to change the very qualities in my partner that most charmed me at the outset? Where did easy loving and juicy sex go? Does it make sense to start all over with someone else? How do my personality type and family history affect my view of myself and others?

This book then offers specific, effective solutions to the most common struggles that couples face — both the small troubles and the more serious dilemmas of communication gridlock, betrayal, and seemingly intractable differences. I will provide a clear map for moving forward with these issues and address how to most productively approach arguments, including the importance of establishing connection before dealing with conflict. I will also offer several types of quick, well-researched practices to help keep love alive and thriving during all five stages.

A key message of many of these lessons is "The wave is not the ocean" — that is, the times that feel intolerable between you and your partner do not mean the conflict is an all-encompassing, permanent state. There will always be another wave, another opportunity. When you know how to navigate the storms, conflict can lead to understanding and even closeness that makes your relationship even better than it was before. In most cases, the Love Skills process will help you to rediscover the original promise of your relationship and offer you a road map for traveling this rewarding and challenging path.

Before you get started, keep one rule in mind: don't make this book another war in your relationship. Anything can be used as fodder for a fight, even resources meant to assist and enrich. If you invite your partner to accompany you on this journey, make sure both of you are involved only as much as you want to be. A partner's half-hearted or begrudging attempt to mend a relationship may only end up opening more wounds.

If you have a reluctant partner, then do the work for yourself. I believe one person's growth can often initiate change in both people; if not, it will lead you into your own wholehearted best self. As I said, awareness comes first. With any relationship work, the vital first step is to become more aware of our own not-so-healthy behaviors — perhaps our hair-trigger reactivity, a reluctance to forgive, or a tenacious need to be right. Once we understand and acknowledge our own role in our relationship challenges, we can use this awareness to begin to practice more thoughtful and loving behaviors.

This process is neither quick nor easy. Love is a feeling, intense and joyful. But the practice of loving another person is hard work — the work of a lifetime. And of course, some relationships present more challenges than others. As we begin to learn about our own needs, some of us may find that changes in ourselves resulting from this process actually create more distance in our relationship. If this happens, this book will help you take the healthy next steps forward.

How to Use This Book

Love Skills can be completed individually, by a couple, or a mixture of both. Although this is a book about relationships, a significant portion of the work must be done by each person alone first — after all, all couples are comprised of two separate people, who each come with their own unique set of past experiences, ways of thinking, and areas for growth. (*Differentiation*, the fact that we are two individuals who are both separate and connected and not half of a whole, is a key tenet of wholehearted love, which you'll soon learn.) If you choose to work on this book together with a partner, you can complete the individual exercises alone and then share your findings with each other; many activities include specific instructions for ways to share. You may each want your own copy of *Love Skills*, so that you can do the readings separately and have your own space to complete written exercises. Or you may choose to share one copy of the workbook and write responses in separate notebooks.

Of course, there are many couples-specific exercises throughout this book as well. If you're working on the program alone, you can invite your partner to join you for specific joint exercises you want to try, or you can simply read through them on your own to glean the knowledge and then move on.

Love Skills is crafted to be accessible, relatable, and easy to understand no matter where you are in your self-development and relationship journey. That said, it's no walk in the park. Completing these exercises, particularly with a partner, will push you to confront raw emotions and difficult experiences from your past, and it will require you to treat yourself with honesty, patience, and compassion. That vulnerability may come easily for some and feel challenging, upsetting, or even threatening for others. Move slowly. Be mindful of your partner's limitations and your own.

Importantly, this book is not intended as a replacement for therapy. It will not heal domestic violence, serious breaches of trust, or severe psychological wounds. In cases of depression, addiction, affairs, trauma, and/or abuse, always seek the help of a professional.

An ideal time to use this workbook is during moments of inner quiet, when your mind is open to growing and learning. But it can also be helpful in times of relationship trouble or when you want to address bumps and snags in a largely satisfying connection. Some may gravitate toward the book out of natural curiosity and a desire to demystify the concept of wholehearted love, while others might dive into the Love Cycles approach as part of a larger ongoing effort to more consciously sustain an important relationship.

There's no "right way" to use this manual. You might set aside a single evening for you and your partner to dig into a handful of exercises relevant to your particular relationship, or the two of you may decide to return to the material once a week to delve into the program gradually. Alternately, you might prefer to explore every section and activity on your own and complete small portions on a daily basis. Feel free to delve deeply into the sections that particularly intrigue you, jump from chapter to chapter, or regularly return to the same instruction page because it's the one that really works for you. If you get stuck on something or if it's simply not clicking with you, move on to another section.

Finally, remember that the guidelines contained in these pages are just suggestions. They're based on decades of experience and training, but they are not a science. Love never is. Although all relationships may journey through the same cycles, every union is unique, and the people within them are constantly changing. The particular skills that work for some will not work for all, and the skills that work sometimes won't work all the time. Choose the exercises that create positive movement between your souls. Save the rest for when the seasons change.

The Quest for Wholeness

In addition to reestablishing intimacy with our partner, we will explore the barriers and the bridges to becoming wholehearted as individuals — a necessary personal journey we'll each need to take alone in order to eventually access a place of wholehearted love together.

As you move through this book, never forget that we are in this world to become more whole ourselves. Although our intimate relationships can be a powerful catalyst for the development of that wholeness, it is our connection with ourselves that matters most, no matter how much we might love another. This isn't about indulgence or self-preoccupation; it's about being determined to become the best human we can. Renowned vulnerability researcher Dr. Brené Brown describes wholeness (or wholeheartedness) as having the courage to be imperfect, embracing our story as the right journey for us no matter how difficult it may be, practicing empathy for ourselves and others, and authentically connecting with those around us. All of this book's teachings on love are grounded in developing and deepening these qualities.

The truth is, the quest to create a thriving relationship is inextricably intertwined with the individual's quest for wholeness. In her book *Broken Open: How Difficult Times Can Help Us Grow*, Omega Institute founder Elizabeth Lesser tells us, "When there is nothing left to lose, we find the true self — the self that is whole, the self that is enough, the self that no longer looks to others for definition, or completion, or anything but companionship on the journey."

A New Way to Love

A few decades ago, when people began to talk about "soulmates," unconditional love was considered a permanent state of being rather than an ever-evolving one. Many of my clients wonder if their relationship problems stem from not feeling "in love with" their partner all of the time; instead, they sometimes feel bored, annoyed, or outright fed up. Based on inaccurate beliefs about the normal progression of relationships, many people feel that if they have conflicts, power struggles, and times of unhappiness in their relationships, they have failed.

The Love Cycles model encourages us to see those troubles as normal seasons in a long-term relationship. I am optimistic that some of us are beginning to move toward this more generous, compassionate, and realistic view of what healthy relationships look like — one that is less linear and more cyclical. Falling in love is never a straight line to "happily ever after." Like all parts of nature, we go through seasons of change, renewal, darkness, and light. Always remember that temporarily losing our way or failing to respond with our best selves to a challenging interaction is simply a reminder that we're all human. We have the opportunity to heal ourselves of old wounds that began long before we met our partner and to grow into our best selves emotionally and spiritually.

By following the guidelines in this book, we can learn how to keep our inevitable relationship troubles from overwhelming us (because they really don't have to) and make the times between the trouble as rich, delightful, and loving as possible.

Where Am I — and Where Do I Want to Be?

Tremendous growth happens when couples learn to "swim in anxious soup together." This means learning to tolerate anxiety for growth, rather than moving to control and manage one another or collapsing and complying in order not to threaten each other.

— Ellyn Bader, at a 2018 Couples Conference in Oakland, California

Before you can start learning any new love skills, you first need to understand why you're doing this at all. When it comes to improving your relationships, what is the ultimate goal?

In the Love Cycles model, which outlines the five stages all romantic relationships go through, the final stage is Wholehearted Love. But there's no real end point in this journey: everlasting love is an everlasting journey. Most couples will need to make repeated treks through all five stages, continuing to learn and grow together with each cycle. If and when we arrive at the fifth stage, however, our relationship is at its healthiest and most rewarding. Although we don't stay in Stage Five permanently, we can find our way back to it with greater ease each time we drop into an earlier stage, and we stay in that fifth stage for longer periods of time.

Wholehearted love is more than just loving someone with all you've got. It means loving from a place of *personal* wholeness and with a full recognition of your partner's wholeness. There are three elements of wholehearted love: mindful self-awareness, relationship skillfulness, and care and nourishment of the relationship.

WHOLEHEARTED LOVE

Mindful Self-Awareness

Relationship Skillfulness

Care and Nourishment
of the Relationship

The first step is to assess where you are on the journey toward wholehearted loving — right here, right now. The quiz below will help you understand each of the three elements of wholehearted love and how well you practice each one.

I will ask you to retake this quiz at the end of the book, and I think you'll be surprised at all you've learned. If you're willing to thoughtfully consider the ideas in *Love Skills* and try out most of the exercises, I'm confident you'll find yourself in a very different place by the time you finish the book.

Wholehearted Loving Quiz

This exercise should be completed individually. If you're working with a partner, share your results after you've both finished.

Rank yourself on a scale of 1 to 5 for each item based on the definitions below. After each section, add up the scores to get your total for that section.

The usefulness of this quiz relies on your self-awareness and honesty with yourself, so be as truthful as possible.

1 = This is never true for me
2 = This is rarely true for me
3 = This is sometimes true for me
4 = This is usually true for me
5 = This is almost always true for me

Mindful Self-Awareness

Until you make the unconscious conscious,
it will direct your life and you will call it fate.

— C. G. JUNG, founder of analytical psychology

Mindfulness is a meditative practice of paying attention to the moment in a nonjudgmental way, and self-awareness is your capacity to observe and reflect on your inner world of thoughts and feelings. Mindful self-awareness allows you to tolerate the discomfort of self-reflection, to turn reactivity into responding, and to develop self-care practices to support your wholeheartedness. Being mindfully self-aware means understanding yourself and committing to being the best version of yourself.

Score

1. I don't usually get worked up about little things. _____
2. I know which parts of my personality are "challenges," and I've learned to embrace them without engaging in destructive behaviors. _____
3. When I'm upset, I'm able to be compassionate with myself. I don't beat myself up when I'm already down. _____
4. I have ongoing practices that support my ability to stay mindful. _____
5. I value my relationships with people besides my partner; I have a community that I'm able to give to and receive from.

6. I like my sense of humor and often laugh at myself. _____

7. I'm not embarrassed or ashamed of being vulnerable, although I am discriminating about where I show it. I share it with appropriate and supportive others. _____

8. I'm an introspective person, and I reflect on why I think, act, and feel the way I do. _____

9. I value the quality of generosity and work to develop it in myself. _____

10. I understand the impact my history has on my current life. _____

11. I'm comfortable being alone as well as being around others. _____

12. I feel that I'm living close to the values I hold dear. _____

13. I care deeply about my partner but know that the most important part of my well-being depends on the relationship I have with myself. _____

14. I understand the general makeup of my personality: whether I'm an introvert or extrovert, what my go-to defense mechanisms are, which environments I mesh well with and which ones to avoid, and what motivates me and what deters me. _____

15. I make my own mental, emotional, and physical health a major priority in my life. _____

TOTAL SCORE _____

Relationship Skillfulness

Relationship skillfulness refers to your ability to use specific skills to resolve conflict and express appreciation, affection, and compassion. Most prominently, this includes the ability to communicate both your positive and your negative emotions in ways that enhance your relationship. There is an art to sharing both your vulnerable and your loving feelings, while also being able to express your negative feelings in a way that preserves your connection. Relationship skillfulness also includes being able to openly receive your partner's feelings — both the loving ones and the difficult ones.

1. I easily use "I statements." _____
2. I take responsibility for my part of the trouble. _____
3. I'm empathetic when listening to others. _____
4. I don't seek out arguments or problems with the things people say or do (I don't badger, provoke, or nag). _____
5. I attempt to understand someone's perspective before making judgments about their words or actions. _____
6. I make an effort to repair my relationships when there is strife. _____
7. I don't think I'm always right, and I'm willing to admit that. _____
8. I'm comfortable being vulnerable with people who are close to me. _____
9. I set clear and healthy boundaries, not too rigid but not too loose. _____
10. I know how to complain without criticizing. _____
11. I'm able to forgive and apologize. _____
12. I recognize nonverbal cues in others. _____
13. I practice being an attuned listener, and I rarely interrupt others because I truly want to know what they have to say. _____
14. I'm aware of how my body language and facial expressions may come across to others. _____
15. I recognize when I'm getting defensive about something and consciously calm myself down, so I can have thoughtful and healthy conversations. _____

TOTAL SCORE _____

Care and Nourishment of Your Relationship

When you take the time to nourish and care for your relationship, you make it a priority to create time to talk, experience new adventures and pleasures, give gratitude and gestures of intimacy, and seek guidance from professionals when you encounter the inevitable bumps in the road.

1. My partner and I have similar values and respect the ones that are different in the other.

    _____

2. Although we may have had nasty arguments in the past, we've learned from them and continue to discover more about how to argue in healthy, productive ways.

    _____

3. I don't let our disagreements get in the way of loving my partner.

    _____

4. I want to treat and respond to my partner with the most loving and mature part of me.

    _____

5. There are times that my partner discloses more (or less) than I do or can. I feel a little uncomfortable with it, but I also know we are different people and that it's okay.

    _____

6. I appreciate when my partner is honest with me, even if it's not always what I want to hear. I know that my partner would only say negative things about our relationship if there were important problems we needed to repair.

    _____

7. I recognize that communication about our issues needs to happen early on and be done in a productive way. I don't build up resentment, "sweep it under the rug," or resort to pettiness.

    _____

8. We are affectionate: holding hands, kissing, and cuddling are a regular part of our relationship.

    _____

9. I can count on my partner to usually listen and help me with my issues — my partner never turns me away without a justifiable reason and a promise to get back to me soon.

    _____

10. I take time to honor our relationship daily, whether that's giving my partner an amorous hug and/or kiss, saying a sincere "I love you," performing an act of gratitude, intentionally reserving time in my schedule to devote solely to my partner, or some other way of letting my partner know that she or he is special to me.

    _____

11. Although our sex life may not be what it was when we first started dating, we both make it a point to keep passion and novelty alive in the bedroom and give each other feedback on what we each like and need sexually.

    _____

12. We make a point of talking things out face-to-face rather than over email or text.

      _____

13. Having fun is a major component of our relationship — we love taking on adventures together.

      _____

14. My partner and I both seek to learn about and accommodate each other's preferred "love languages" (receiving gifts, quality time, words of affirmation, acts of service, or physical touch).

      _____

15. We laugh together often, but jokes at each other's expense or about a known sensitive area are off-limits. If we cross that line, we apologize.

      _____

TOTAL SCORE   _____

Reflections

The sections with the highest total scores are the areas in which you already have a high degree of skill. Below, list your skill sets (Mindful Self-Awareness, Relationship Skillfulness, and Care and Nourishment of Your Relationship) in order, beginning with your strongest one, then your second strongest, and finally where you are most challenged. The great news is, all of these practices can be learned over time — and even an area in which you got your highest score can be improved.

#1:

#2:

#3:

Keep these results in mind as you move throughout the rest of this book. Every exercise will help you get closer to one of these three qualities of wholehearted love — sometimes several at once.

Let's move now to understanding the Love Cycles model.

The Love Cycles

2

We have to be whole people to find whole love, even if we have to make it up for a while.

— CHERYL STRAYED, *Tiny Beautiful Things:*
Advice on Love and Life from Someone Who's Been There

It's easy to absorb the romantic tales of novels, films, TV, and other media and conclude that all intimate relationships reliably progress from the initial juicy moment of meeting, to giddy infatuation, to a series of small trials and tribulations, and finally to a quietly blissful state of happily-ever-after. It makes for a satisfying and comforting story, but it's not how real life operates. The truth is, love is a journey without a final destination throughout our lives. We shouldn't expect that at some point in some particular relationship, we'll look back at the obstacles we overcame and exult, "That's it! We're here! We made it!" It's difficult to see in advance, but beyond wherever you are now another hurdle awaits.

But we *can* manage these hurdles. Learning more about them and equipping ourselves to respond to them effectively is a crucial part of sustaining a rewarding long-term relationship.

In the Love Cycles model, intimate relationships move through five stages: The Merge, Doubt and Denial, Disillusionment, The Decision, and Wholehearted Love. Imagine these stages not as stepping-stones to a final outcome, but rather as a series of seasons that we move through in an eternal cycle. No matter how glorious a summer may be, a cool autumn breeze will eventually blow through that will one day give way to icy winter. Likewise, even the harshest of winters will melt away in time. The fresh breath of spring always returns.

Although people experience these cycles differently, the skills and road map are useful for everyone. The journey to wholehearted love is never a straight or easy line. That said, I have certainly seen those who begin their relationships with a lot of self-awareness and wisdom already gleaned from their lives, having already experienced the cycles of love enough times to know how to pass through the earlier stages more quickly. We can all get to this place. As we do this work, we will learn to move through the tougher stages with more ease, grace, and kindness, and we will find ways to hang out longer in the bountiful stage of Wholehearted Love — and maybe even dip back into the deliciously sensual moments of Stage One.

Stage One: The Merge

In Greek mythology, Cupid — the god of desire, eroticism, and affection — dipped his arrows in a special love potion that caused innocent targets, when struck, to fall into a mad passion for the next person they saw. As it turns out, this tale accurately reflects the biochemical changes in our brains that both trigger and maintain infatuation. In 1979, psychologist Dorothy Tennov coined the term "limerence" to describe the state of mind that occurs when our brains are flooded with a cocktail of hormones and chemicals that includes pleasure-inducing dopamine and endorphins, aphrodisiacs such as phenethylamine (also found in chocolate), and oxytocin, which promotes empathy and bonding.

The Merge is the initial sweeping romance that consumes a couple. The passion and chemistry of this first stage are what we customarily associate with the concept of love — all-encompassing joy in the presence of our partner, utter fascination with the other's personality and life story, and insatiable mind-blowing, deeply connected sex. We feel we've found our "perfect match," a person who seems eerily similar to ourselves and for whom we can check off all the boxes on the list of characteristics of our envisioned ideal partner. Our emotional brain drowns out our rational one as we give ourselves over to the delicious pleasures of infatuation.

In this stage, partners always want to be together, communicate constantly when apart, and believe their love can see them through whatever challenges life may bring. Just as the infant merges with the mother and cannot tell the difference between itself and another, and just as the new mother lives in constant awareness of her newborn child, so it is with new lovers. Boundaries melt away, and the sense of "we-ness" is paramount and intense.

And have you ever noticed that this first stage of love also makes you feel better about yourself? The magical new person in your life seems to bring out the best in you. You've never been so spontaneous, so witty, so warm, so sexy, so open! You marvel at your new capacity for compassion, patience, and generosity. Your whole being simply glows.

Some couples may skip the infatuation stage, establishing a relationship of companionable and caring friendship without the fireworks. For the majority of couples who do experience The Merge, the glorious intensity may last anywhere from several months to a few years, although some pairs find the ecstatic free fall lasts just a few weeks before giving way to judgment and disappointment. Here's what I know for certain: there's no straightforward path from that initial biochemically induced plunge down the rabbit hole of infatuation to the kind of mature committed love that will last a lifetime.

Stage Two: Doubt and Denial

For some partners, doubt creeps in slowly, like a gently rising tide. For others, it can strike suddenly and powerfully, like a bolt of lightning. However it occurs, a realization dawns on the couple that they're not entirely "perfect" for each other after all. In this second stage, they start to realize there are more differences between them than they first thought. And as soon as they feel the first stab of doubt, they anxiously try to deny its existence. Even when partners acknowledge their differences, they tell themselves they will eventually be ironed out — or that they're no big deal in the first place.

As all of this unfolds, the special magic of The Merge starts to subside. You're no longer compelled to spend every moment together, no longer mesmerized by each other's presence, and no longer as willing to bend over backward to make the other happy. You may start to show more critical, irritable, or unattractive parts of yourselves. One or both of you might start to air small grievances, only to be met by knee-jerk defensiveness or even retaliation. Arguments start to arise more frequently, affection dulls, and alone time begins to feel restorative rather than intolerable. Sex may become less frequent — or at least less passionate — now that the novelty is fading and the "love chemicals" in the brain have begun to subside.

At this point, partners may think, "It used to be so easy!" and "Why can't he (or she) see things the way I do?" And most disconcerting of all: "Have I chosen the wrong person?" If you're experiencing these kinds of thoughts and feelings, it may indeed be a signal that you're with the wrong person. But, just as likely, it's a manifestation of the emotions that naturally arise during this second stage of the Love Cycle. Though painful, the death of illusion permits us to move closer to the possibility of real, abiding love. It's the great paradox of relationships. As romance recedes, we can learn to steer through difficulty in ways that deepen the relationship rather than damage it.

I call this the "silent stage," because it's the step in love's journey that partners rarely discuss directly. We find ourselves smoothing over differences and fearful of broaching them with our partner, let alone our friends and family. We stay silent because we don't want to admit our relationship isn't the perfect haven we once believed it to be.

Stage Three: Disillusionment

The Disillusionment stage is the winter season of love, one that may feel like the end of the road for some couples. The power struggles in the relationship have come fully to the surface; the issues the couple have consistently shoved under the rug are now glaringly obvious. Some people become perpetually vigilant, on edge, and ready to fly into battle at the slightest provocation. Other couples might quietly move apart over time, putting less and less energy into maintaining the relationship and investing more outside of it. They begin to make separate lives in the places that matter most, sharing less and less with one another about what really matters and practicing "the art of nice" without much depth.

At this juncture, our original experience of passionate love is a distant memory. The "I" reemerges, a state that feels a lot safer than our former blissful experience of "we." Dark thoughts might even enter our heads, ones we may share with others: "I'm not sure I love my partner anymore," or "My husband has turned into someone I don't know," or even, "I think I married the wrong woman." Even if we don't frame our differences in such a dramatic fashion, we experience a sense of growing distance and estrangement from our partner.

Other couples may experience Stage Three not as a time of questioning their commitment to the relationship itself, but rather as a strong message that things need to change or that the original contract their relationship was built on is no longer relevant. For example, these messages might be the product of life transitions. Perhaps who we were in our twenties is not who we have become in our thirties, forties, or fifties, and that transitional process becomes disruptive to the relationship and can cause intense alienation.

Whatever shape the Disillusionment stage takes, at this point life feels unpleasantly predictable. We're having the same fights over and over again — or not communicating at all about anything that's actually important, avoiding all the possible places of trouble. Where we once saw the best in our partner ("He's so confident and reasonable!"), now we see the worst ("He's so controlling and out of touch with his feelings!"). Perhaps we even witness our own unappealing qualities — and then turn around and blame our partner for them. Bad moods abound. We may resort to behaviors that are unhealthy and deeply hurtful to our partners and ourselves — lies, betrayals, and sexual transgressions. We may find ourselves fantasizing about an old love, a current colleague, or even that cute pizza-delivery guy.

Stage Four: The Decision

Finally, you reach a breaking point. Nearly every relationship hits what I call "the wall" — the stage where the differences, challenges, and negativity between partners feel unbearable.

For many couples, this decision is about staying or leaving. You're utterly worn out. Emotional breakdowns — crying fits, screaming, or slamming the door and leaving the house for several hours — are commonplace. You and your partner retreat into self-protective behaviors and emotions: emotional shutdown, remoteness, and indifference. Maybe you even find yourself telling your friends and family things like, "I can't do this anymore." Sex is rare, nonexistent, or takes place exclusively after arguments. You may feel ready for an enticing new beginning with a new person. Other couples' successful relationships feel like grim proof that yours is unsalvageable. Singlehood starts to seem better and better, compared to remaining in this dysfunctional, energy-sapping arrangement.

Some couples face a different kind of decision that isn't about whether you're walking out the door. This stage is called The Decision for a reason: something isn't working, and it's reached the point where you desperately need a change. What you do next will likely determine whether your relationship thrives and moves in a new direction or you become resigned to status quo.

Many couples decide to separate when they reach this level of estrangement. Some opt for living parallel and distant lives: living together but no longer seeking intimacy, emotional support, meaningful sex, or personal growth from each other. In this case, polite indifference often becomes a coping strategy. Others peacefully accept the living of parallel lives, perhaps coming together for family occasions and even supporting each other, but neither partner is hopeful for deeper intimacy. Still other couples simply stay as they are, playing out the same tired battles over and over without any willingness to change or leave.

Even if we do successfully extricate ourselves from what can feel like a doomed relationship, it's a mistake to fail to fully explore the difficult lessons of this stage. If we don't come to grips with our own role in the relationship's conflicts, we'll likely choose the same kind of person next time and re-create a similar story. In addition, committing to learn from our experiences in this stage can help us to leave the relationship without bitterness and blame. We might even be able to become a little more tolerant, emotionally intelligent, and wholehearted in the process.

Sometimes, when I am working with a couple at this stage of the Love Cycle, especially when there is a lot of hurt and many messes to clean up, I suggest they consider that "the marriage is over." After a moment's pause to let the concept sink in, I continue: "So how about making a new marriage, keeping what worked and changing the parts that you've outgrown or weren't healthy to begin with?"

If both partners decide to fully embrace their commitment to the relationship and their own healing, *that* decision may lead them to the fifth and final stage of the cycle.

Stage Five: Wholehearted Love

Reaching the stage of Wholehearted Love requires the hardest work of all: true individuation, self-discovery, and acceptance of imperfection in both our partner and ourselves. Wholehearted love recognizes there's no such thing as a "perfect match." It acknowledges both the inevitable differences between the self and the partner as well as how one's own actions contribute to the relationship's challenges. We're no longer looking at problems with an intention to blame but rather to understand, take responsibility for, and courageously address our own challenges. In acknowledging and exploring our own imperfections, we learn to accept those of our partner, rather than fruitlessly insisting that our partner be the one to change.

In essence, we lean into discomfort instead of running from it. That means we no longer avoid difficult conversations, but instead face them head-on with an open heart. We learn to listen carefully, even when our partner voices an opinion we find threatening. At the same time, we no longer view alone time as an escape from the other person, but rather a healthy way to replenish the self — and consequently replenish the relationship as well.

And sex? Sometimes it's wonderful. Sometimes it doesn't quite work out — and we learn to laugh or shrug about what is less than perfect. Always, it's an ongoing candid conversation between both partners to ensure mutual satisfaction.

Importantly, the stage of Wholehearted Love doesn't merely mean a calm, mature acceptance of what is. To the contrary, it can be a thrilling adventure in which we rediscover some of the joy and passion of The Merge. Although we may not recapture the dopamine-fueled bliss of the first stage, we begin to play together again — to laugh, relax, and deeply enjoy each other. Together, we might create art, plant a garden, travel, develop community, and share work and family life in new ways. And throughout, as we work toward greater maturity and connection, we rediscover new aspects of ourselves and our partner that allow us to fall in love all over again.

Once we know how to live comfortably in this stage, we can fairly quickly return to stability even when we fall out, without necessarily having to travel through every stage each time. No one can stay in wholeheartedness all of the time, but we can live here for longer and longer stretches.

The Love Cycles model offers a concrete method for practicing mindfulness within our relationships. It encourages us to identify and grapple with our innermost thoughts and feelings about our partners and accept the ever-changing nature of love. Once you pinpoint where you and your partner are in the cycle, you can pause, breathe, and begin to thoughtfully address your relationship challenges. In the next chapter, we'll get started with that process by figuring out which stage you're currently in.

Which Love Cycle Stage Are You In?

Romantic Love sticks around long enough to bind two people together. Then it rides off into the sunset. And seemingly overnight, your dream marriage can turn into your biggest nightmare.

— HARVILLE HENDRIX, *Making Marriage Simple:*
Ten Truths for Changing the Relationship You Have into the One You Want

It is possible, even likely, that you may see yourself in a different Love Cycle stage than your partner does. It's normal for two people to see their relationship in different ways.

Let's Find Out

Take the following quiz to find out which stage you are in.

Love Cycles Quiz

This exercise should be completed individually. If you're working as a couple, come together to share your results at the end after doing the quiz separately.

Rank yourself on a scale of 1 to 3 for each item based on the definitions below:

1 = This doesn't apply to me at all
2 = This somewhat applies to me
3 = This definitely applies to me

Stage One: The Merge

Score

1. I feel as though I could be with my partner all the time, and when we're not together, I miss my partner terribly. _____

2. My partner and I can talk for hours and never get bored. _____

3. I tell my partner things about myself that I rarely, if ever, tell anyone else. When I do, my partner doesn't pull away. _____

4. My partner seems to accept me with all of my flaws, and I accept my partner's. _____

5. I don't get as much sleep now that we're dating — just thinking about my partner fills me with energy! _____

6. I think my partner may be my perfect match, even though we haven't been together very long. _____

7. I always take longer to get ready before meeting up with my partner. I *need* to look my best! _____

8. Our sex life is fantastic — we make love more frequently and enjoyably than I have with any previous partner. _____

9. My partner is so attractive that I could stare at him or her for hours. _____

10. We have fun no matter what we are doing — even normally boring things like grocery shopping or cleaning. _____

11. My partner brings out my generosity; I'm happy to spend money on him or her. _____

12. With my partner, I'm willing to try things in the bedroom that I've never done before. _____

13. Anytime we are relaxing, I can't help but cuddle. _____

14. My partner likes a lot of activities I've never tried, but I'm really interested in getting into them too. _____

15. We like to "sext" and send sexually suggestive messages to each other…even during the workday. _____

16. I'm seeing my friends less often because I want to prioritize love right now. _____

17. I almost feel guilty when I think about flirting with other people (which happens rarely). If I had dating apps and/or files, I've deleted them. _____

18. I want to know *everything* about my partner. _____

19. After a date, I replay every moment in my head. _____

20. I love to talk about my new partner with supportive friends and family members. Sometimes, even my partner has to remind me to talk about things other than our relationship. _____

TOTAL SCORE _____

Stage Two: Doubt and Denial

Score

1. I'm more critical of my partner than I used to be. Even if I don't actually say I'm annoyed, I'm sure my tone and facial expressions communicate my disapproval. _____

2. More and more, my partner is criticizing me for just being me. _____

3. I need my own time sometimes; being around my partner can get on my nerves. _____

4. I don't tell my friends or family about my concerns with my partner, because I'm sure we'll move past them soon. No need to alarm my loved ones. _____

5. It's time for me to reconnect with some of the friends I put on hold earlier in our relationship. _____

6. Sometimes I really want to argue with my partner, but then I remember how happy we are, so I decide that whatever's bugging me really isn't *that* big of a deal. _____

7. When my partner complains about something small, like a mess I've made or something I've forgotten to do, I tend to take it as a personal insult. I feel defensiveness creeping in. _____

8. Some of the things my partner does are just silly. Why isn't my partner more rational about things — like I am? _____

9. I sometimes worry we disagree too much, but when I see other couples arguing, I feel a lot better. After all, we aren't nearly as miserable as they are! _____

10. Our sex life is decent, but I keep waiting to feel the kind of passion I once did. _____

11. We aren't "sexting" each other nearly as much as we used to. In fact, our texts aren't even flirtatious. _____

12. There are times I wonder if I chose the wrong partner. But I know that's just me being overdramatic. _____

13. Our communication isn't working the way it used to. I feel like we need to "spell things out" to each other now rather than understand them intuitively. _____

14. I think about being single more often — and sometimes even wish I were. _____

15. I feel like our libidos are out of sync — either my partner wants more sex than I do or vice versa. _____

16. I'm less likely to spend a lot of money on my partner just for fun; now I only do so on special occasions. _____

17. I'm more likely to flirt with someone else now, just for fun and to see what else is out there. _____

18. I find it hard to comfort my partner when they are upset over something I personally think is no big deal. _____

19. I still think my partner is attractive, but no longer irresistible. _____

20. I pretend to like things my partner is interested in, and I'm a bit worried I'll never actually enjoy them, even if we do them together. _____

TOTAL SCORE _____

Stage Three: Disillusionment

Score

1. Premeditated romance is rare between us — date nights, random gifts, and other gestures of love aren't things we do for each other anymore. _____

2. I seldom feel as though I'm the number-one priority for my partner. _____

3. Right now I just need to make sure that *I'm* emotionally safe and happy, with or without my partner. _____

4. Nothing new is happening in our relationship, and it's driving me crazy! We're tediously predictable in our interactions and routines. _____

5. I don't do everything I promise my partner I'll do, but it's not that big a deal. My partner just takes it too personally. _____

6. Though I feel guilty about it, I think about cheating to get some novelty and zing in the bedroom — even if it's just one time. _____

7. The only time sexual passion returns is after we fight. _____

8. I've secretly gone through my partner's phone, laptop, social-media accounts, email, drawers, pockets, and the like to see if I find anything suspicious. _____

9. I am committed to my relationship, but the way we are together doesn't work as it once did, and I don't know how to change it. _____

10. I'm high-strung around my partner and feel I need to walk on eggshells. I feel as though I can't do anything the way my partner wants me to. _____

11. We keep fighting about the same thing! We think we've finally settled the issue, and then — *BAM!* — it flares up again. _____

12. We are two very different people. I'm shocked I didn't see it when we first got together. _____

13. I seldom hold back my criticism of my partner. _____

14. I don't think my partner and I have the same moral standards, which makes me think less of my partner. _____

15. I'm starting to doubt we can last. _____

16. I think I still love my partner, but I'm not 100 percent certain. _____

17. I spend a lot of time in my life with people and activities that matter and don't share much about them or include my partner in them. _____

18. My life is starting to become more separate from my partner's; we make plans without considering each other, and the time we spend together is more convenient than intentional. _____

19. We don't compliment each other anymore. I can't recall the last time my partner called me smart, attractive, sexy, or funny. _____

20. Saying "I love you," "I miss you," and "I want you" have pretty much disappeared from our vocabulary. _____

TOTAL SCORE _____

Stage Four: The Decision

Score

1. I'm completely worn down from all of our fighting and bickering. _____

2. I barely recall why we fell in love. _____

3. I just can't do this anymore; something has to change. _____

4. The only times I have strong emotions toward my partner are when we're arguing or when I'm emotionally breaking down. _____

5. I speak critically of my partner to friends, family, and sometimes even new acquaintances. _____

6. I feel that the cons of staying in this relationship outweigh the pros now. _____

7. I fantasize about being single or being in a happy relationship with someone else. _____

8. I play out and rehearse our "breakup talk" in my head. _____

9. I've never been lonelier, even though I'm in a relationship. _____

10. There are times I don't even *like* my partner, and I wonder if that will become the new norm. _____

11. Most things I'd prefer to do alone or with a friend rather than with my partner, even important stuff like making big purchases or getting career advice. _____

12. I'm not sure what the next step in our relationship is, and to be honest, I'm not sure I care. Whatever it is, it just needs to happen soon. _____

13. When I see other people in happy, healthy relationships, it makes me sad. It reminds me that mine is neither happy nor healthy. _____

14. I can't help but look for the flaws in my partner. I never give my partner the benefit of the doubt, and I'm not sure he or she even deserves it. _____

15. I care about my partner, but sometimes I'm indifferent to the deeper things we shared. _____

16. I think I lost myself in this relationship. I need to be my own person again rather than just being part of a couple. _____

17. We don't even argue with passion anymore. We just give up. _____

18. Going to events or social gatherings together feels like a facade; we tend to take part in separate conversations. _____

19. Most of our conversations are essentially small talk now — that is, if we're talking at all. _____

20. The tension and animosity in our home is almost palpable. I feel weighed down in my own house. _____

TOTAL SCORE _____

Stage Five: Wholehearted Love

1. I recognize that my partner and I are separate people and that we have to accept each other for who we are. _____

2. I'm almost always open to having difficult conversations about "us." _____

3. When we talk, I actively listen and seek to understand my partner's point of view, even if I don't fully agree with it. _____

4. Silences between us aren't filled with tension, nor do they necessarily indicate an issue between us. _____

5. I'm comfortable being myself around my partner. _____

6. My self-worth isn't determined by my relationship. _____

7. I acknowledge that I may have idealized love in the past, but now I see that love is more than passion, sex, and novelty. Love is also about kindness, companionship, and collaboration. _____

8. I realize that our relationship will continue to ebb and flow. Someday we'll have an argument again, but what matters is how we approach and handle the argument. _____

9. We've had very tough times together, but I now see that we were able to build a stronger relationship from those experiences. _____

10. I want to treat and respond to my partner with the best and most mature part of me. _____

11. When we spend time apart, it doesn't feel like a threat to the relationship. _____

12. I'm not anxious when I don't hear back from my partner right away. Instead, I feel connected and content when I see a returned call, text, or email. _____

13. Our love is not a distraction from my work life or social life. _____

14. I'm comfortable being with my partner around friends and going to social gatherings together. Sometimes we talk to different groups of people at the same event, which feels perfectly okay. _____

15. My partner is always going to have certain behaviors that annoy me, but they don't prevent me from appreciating the great partner I have in life. I'm now able to cope well with those small annoyances. _____

16. When there's an issue, I seek to understand how I contributed to it, rather than focus entirely on what my partner did wrong. _____

17. We have a comfortable daily communication style, and we make each other laugh. _____

18. I'll introduce my partner to new things I like or find interesting, but I'm not offended if my partner isn't as interested as I am (and vice versa). _____

19. We are affectionate, maybe not as much as when we first started dating, but we regularly hold hands, kiss, and cuddle. _____

20. We tell each other "I love you," but we don't feel obligated to do so. _____

TOTAL SCORE _____

Results

Add up your total score for each section. Whichever section you have the highest score in represents the stage you are probably in. If you receive similar scores for more than one section, then you may be in between stages.

Stage One	Stage Two	Stage Three	Stage Four	Stage Five

The next chapter will guide you through what to do now that you know which stage you're in.

Can Each Person in a Couple Be in a Different Stage?

Remember, couples experience the stages individually; one person might be in The Merge while the other is in Doubt and Denial. Individuals themselves may fluctuate between stages close to one another. For example, people may go back and forth between the first two stages, fluctuating between rapture and denial because they're reluctant to let go of the promise of perfect love. People who've reached the fifth stage can fall back into The Merge, and then go through the difficult power struggle stages before eventually getting back to Wholehearted Love.

Right now it is important for you to keep this discussion positive. If either of you feels resistant or tense while discussing your relationship stage, let it go for now. As you work your way through *Love Skills*, you will learn some new ways to talk and listen, so you can revisit this later on when you have learned more about sharing together.

Now What?
Navigating Your Stage

In real love you want the other person's good. In romantic love, you want the other person.

— MARGARET ANDERSON, founder, editor, and publisher of *The Little Review*

One of the greatest gifts we can give ourselves is mindfulness. To be mindful means to gently bear witness to ourselves in the moment — physically, mentally, emotionally, and spiritually. Too often we're so swept up in what's happening to us, how we feel about it, and what to do to change it that we fail to fully experience these internal currents. Consequently, we react without real awareness of what's actually driving our choices. When we learn to observe our feelings, thoughts, and experiences without reacting to them — and without trying to judge, analyze, or deny them — we become less attached to our dramas and less swept up in our moods. We are more able to take a step back and make the wisest possible decisions that blend heart, head, and instinct.

Now that you're aware of which stage of the Love Cycles you're in, this chapter offers you specific focus areas for surviving and navigating each stage. This process will require constant mindfulness. Go slowly in order to avoid reacting. Practice a more thought-out, slower response while you look at the stage of relationship you may be currently experiencing. I recommend you follow these steps:

1. Read the material on each stage in the preceding chapter.
2. Go through the suggestions for the stage you are in. Circle or underline the suggestions that apply to you. You should also read through the other stages as well, so you're prepared for when you shift to another stage and understand what your partner is going through if he or she is in a different stage than you are.
3. Think about how you might implement the ideas you've underlined. Commit to starting with the ones that are easiest for you.
4. Later, add some of the more challenging ones, which I call stretches.

Stage One, The Merge: Do Not Trust Only Your Heart

Beware of the fantasy of permanent bliss that this stage wraps you in. The first stage of love is perhaps the most euphoric and sensation-intense of them all. But that spectacular spike in feel-good neurochemicals can overpower common sense. The main problem people face in this stage is believing their feelings are the true and lasting barometer for the relationship. People ignore red flags, differences, and plain old logic. ("It doesn't matter that he's had seven wives, doesn't speak to any of his eleven children, and can't hold down a job! I love him. Plus, he's changed. He promises *our* relationship is forever.")

In spite of Western culture's message that "all you need is love," touted in every imaginable media, this is a time when you need to access your rational self as much as your emotional self.

Here's your Stage One to-do list:

1. Be mindful of your heightened emotions. By all means, enjoy this stage to the fullest — this is the stuff that makes courtship so delightful

and intriguing. There's no need to forgo these joys. Just be aware that you're in a trance — a victim of Cupid's magic potion. Take time to step back and observe your emotions and behaviors; ask yourself whether they're objectively rational. Ask a trusted friend for a candid opinion about your relationship. Awareness is key. (Journaling is a great way to foster this mindfulness.)

2. **Don't make any permanent moves.** Because you're not in a rational state of mind, you may regret moving in, getting engaged, or making big joint purchases with your partner. Wait a while — I recommend a year or two — until the haze of this stage has faded.

3. **Tell your partner you need to go slow in making major decisions.** Pay close attention to your partner's reaction. Is it respectful, or does your partner push you in a particular direction?

4. **Actively question whether this person is the best match for you.** Investigating your new relationship in this way doesn't mean you're sabotaging it, nor does it make you a doubtful, wavering, or uncaring person. It simply keeps you grounded and helps you make decisions that are best for both of you in the long run.

Stretch

1. **Write down all of the reasons this may not be a great match.** Here is a hint. We all bring our own troubles to a relationship. If you cannot identify the ones your new lover brings, you are too far under love's chemical spell to make any sensible decisions.

2. **Make an objective list of qualities you want in your life partner.** For you, how important is a sense of purpose, humor, humility, loyalty, and flexibility in an intimate relationship? How important is a willingness to take responsibility for one's behavior and engage in the emotional work you'll need to do together to develop and nurture wholehearted love? Be as tough-minded as you can here. Does your list match up with the qualities of the person you're dating?

3. **Become aware of your partner's relationship history.** Listen carefully to how your partner talks about family and former partners. Watch

how your partner manages conflict and acknowledges — or fails to acknowledge — personal mistakes.

4. **When others note red flags, pay attention.** Don't get defensive. Do your best to listen openly to the perspectives of those who care about you.

Stage Two, Doubt and Denial: Don't Let Fear Get the Best of You

The transition from Stage One to Stage Two may feel like a creeping cold, or it may feel like sudden food poisoning. You have arrived in the power struggle. As my mentor Dr. Harville Hendrix says, The Merge feels like "We two are one"; Stage Two is more like "We two are one, and I am the one!" But don't panic. What your relationship is going through is not necessarily unhealthy, and it's not likely terminal. Infatuation isn't meant to last forever. We fall in love, but we don't fall into good relationships. Like it or not, we have to work at them. They take practice, patience, and intention.

Here's your Stage Two to-do list:

1. **Understand that power struggles are a normal relationship process and not the end of love.** Research shows each couple has a handful of irresolvable issues, and the difference between couples who thrive and those who don't make it is how they *manage* those issues. Learn to fight fair, making use of the core communication skills (found in Chapters 9 through 12) and practicing the daily gestures of caring behavior (Chapter 13). Those go a long way to counter the power struggles you'll inevitably face.

    Ultimately, most arguments are about disconnection rather than the actual topic you're arguing about. For example, let's say one of you wants to live in the city while the other longs for country life. Objectively, you have a disagreement to work out. But the real pain creeps in when both of you become so entrenched in your positions that you become sarcastic, mean-spirited adversaries who place winning above all rather than teammates trying to work out a problem together. The first priority is to treat each other with care and respect. If you fail to do that, "winning" the battle will be a hollow and damaging victory.

At the same time, it's vital to recognize the difference between healthy disagreement and unhealthy control issues. In the former, we hold genuinely different points of view on something — how to do dishes, how much to disclose about our relationship to other people, how much time to spend together or apart — and are willing to consider the other's viewpoint. In the latter situation, we insist on our own way and can't let go of our need to dominate the situation.

2. **Keep up the loving behavior.** It's like putting money in the bank. When Cupid's potion has worn off, the real work of love begins. You'll need to regularly check in with your partner about what's going on in your relationship, bestowing on him or her the sustaining gift of affection and reaching for your higher self in the face of conflict. Don't stop expressing care, kindness, and goodwill even as you start to encounter major differences and arguments.

Think of three ways to be generous that don't compromise you, even when you are disappointed or angry. Examples may be filling your partner's car with gas, cleaning up after dinner when it's not your turn, or genuinely wishing your partner a good day when you part company in the morning. Do these often, whether you're feeling good or bad about your relationship on a given day.

3. **Learn your love languages.** According to bestselling author Dr. Gary Chapman, everyone has a particular way they most enjoy receiving love. There are five so-called love languages: tangible gifts, quality time, words of affirmation, acts of service, and physical touch. (You'll find a full guide to the love languages in Chapter 13.) Spend some time with your partner figuring out which love language each of you most needs and start to incorporate this knowledge into your everyday interactions. If your partner values words, make a point of telling him how you appreciate and care about him. If you most love quality time, make sure your partner

knows, so that she can devote more attention to the date nights you cherish.

Remember times you have expressed caring in your style (maybe with a gift or with words in a text or email), and it wasn't received in the way you hoped it would be. Think about times your partner has reached out to you in their caring style (maybe by doing the laundry or putting air in the tires), and you discounted this as not heartfelt enough. There's no need to do anything about this other than observe with loving-kindness that most of us "give what we want to get" and mark this as something to learn from.

4. **Ask yourself if you are staying on your own mat.** In yoga, we're taught the importance of "staying on our own yoga mat" — not concerning ourselves with how well (or badly) other participants are holding their poses. The teaching translates beautifully into our relationships: instead of pointing an outraged finger at your partner when problems arise, work on understanding your own triggers (triggers can be seen as automatic stress reactions stemming from our past experiences).

Stretch

1. **Acknowledge your triggers.** As you begin to understand how you're responding to your partner's actions — and how you yourself may be contributing to conflicts — bring up these areas of tension with your partner and focus on your own experience. (Example: "I realize I get hurt when you want to spend time alone. I know that's a trigger for me.") Ask your partner for help instead of launching into criticism.

2. **Acknowledge the ways you try to grab power in your relationship.** Think about the ways you push your viewpoint on your partner, try to get your way, and discount the other point of view as childish, unreasonable, or just plain wrong. Can you acknowledge when winning becomes more important to you than playing fair?

Stage Three, Disillusionment:
Clear the Air and Create Space

During The Merge, the brain notices only the positive and avoids anything that challenges that view. In the Disillusionment stage, by contrast, the brain zeroes in on the relationship's deficiencies and disappointments. If something goes right, the brain slides right by it. Things are still terrible. The end is near!

As in Stage One, in this stage of Disillusionment you must remember that what you're experiencing isn't the whole truth. Take steps to "de-smog" your vision, all the while taking good and gentle care of yourself.

Here's your Stage Three to-do list:

1. **Nurture the relationship even as you stand your ground.** As frustrated and sluggish as you might feel, now is the time to devote even more energy to your relationship. Make time to enhance your communication and connection skills. Try to reframe your thinking to see trouble as an opening to understanding, empathy, and a closer connection with both yourself and your partner. Importantly, don't stop practicing goodwill. For example, my husband has made me a latte every morning for the entire length of our marriage. Some mornings, he brings it to me with a kiss; other mornings, he gives it to me silently. Once in a while, he puts it way over on my dresser rather than the nightstand, so I have to reach for it. But come hell or high water, that cup of latte is there every morning.

2. **Stop pushing problems under the rug.** Of course you're exasperated by repetitious and fruitless arguments; understandably, you'd rather just stay grimly silent than get into another heated exchange with your partner. Too often, we avoid dealing with our issues not out of apathy, but out of fear that speaking up will trigger even greater mutual hostility. However, the opposite is more often true — a lumpy carpet leaves much to trip over.

    It's absolutely essential to learn how to listen to our partner's grievances and speak up about our own. In healthy relationships, there are no lumps hidden under the rug; instead, we should manage conflict in a timely way that ensures problems aren't shoved underground, where they can fester and develop into ugly lasting resentments. Pay particular attention to the DTR exercise in Chapter 13 as a simple and effective way to manage these inevitable annoyances.

Stretch

1. **Practice affection when upset.** Can you feel angry and be aware that something isn't working that you need to talk about — but still go to dinner and a movie together? Try holding hands, expressing appreciation, or celebrating your partner's success even during an unresolved power struggle.

2. **Create boundaries without closing your heart.** By this stage, you're often interacting with your partner from a chronically defensive position. "You're pissed off that *I've* done *this*? What about all the times *you've* done *that*?" Instead of trying to one-up your partner, explore the possibility of creating limits and looking after yourself without closing your heart. What would that look like? Can you say no to something and still be kind? "At the moment I'm not comfortable having dinner with your colleagues, because we are going through such a tense time. I really want to support you in your new job, so let's talk about it in a few months after we get through this."

3. **Acknowledge your part.** As power struggles between you and your partner mount, practice the counterintuitive move of turning your attention away from your partner's transgressions and toward your own role in causing the rift. Use this difficult period to develop this self-reflective response to conflict. For example, "I know my own sensitivity to feeling abandoned made it even harder for me when you decided to have lunch with your friend Saturday and not hang out like we planned." There's always a way of making a piece of conflict about you without denying your partner's role.

4. **Protect yourself.** Never forget that your negative emotions arise for

a reason. They often signal when something's wrong, whether the issue is minor or serious. If you are in danger — for example, if your partner is physically abusive — take immediate measures to protect yourself and your family. Don't be afraid to ask for help. If there are issues of addiction, untreated depression, or an undisclosed affair, it's essential to get outside support.

Stage Four, The Decision: Do the Work

You're at a crossroads. If something doesn't change, you'll have to leave the relationship. The "right" decision cannot come from me or any book. It can only come from within, after you take the time to truly understand what's become dysfunctional in your relationship. You will need to align the information in your rational brain, the feelings in your heart, and the instinct in your gut to make the best decision about the relationship.

Even if you're on the brink of walking out the door, I encourage you to take the time to pause, breathe, and try to understand what went wrong before you leave. Sometimes people are stuck in the power struggle, and once they work to get unstuck, they can restore their love. Even if this isn't the case, spending time figuring out what happened will help to ensure you don't end up in the same type of relationship in the future, repeating the same painful unworkable patterns.

Moreover, you *can* leave a relationship wholeheartedly — and all of us should strive for this when we're heading toward a breakup. In the short term, it may feel more satisfying to sling blame, but ignoring your own culpability and hurting your partner on the way out will cost you your own well-being in the long run. Saying goodbye is always painful, but to be able to wish your ex-partner well and to acknowledge your own part in the breakup will free you from repeating many of the same patterns. (We'll talk more about wholehearted breakups in Chapter 15.)

Here's your Stage Four to-do list:

1. **Prioritize self-care**. You're in a fragile place right now, so taking care of yourself — even more than usual — is your top priority.

Eat well, exercise regularly (even if all you can manage is a short walk), meditate, pray, or take an art class. Reinvest in hobbies that make you feel good, such as music or reading, and dedicate time to being with your friends. Find a therapist, life coach, or support group. These activities will take you out of your negative context and help you to gradually reconnect with your essential aliveness.

2. **Understand your role in your relationship's deterioration.** We're all human, which means we all have unhealthy patterns and ways of protecting ourselves that aren't mindful of others' pain or the trouble we cause them. Sometimes a small change on your part can have an almost magically positive effect on the relationship. For example, try expressing a few words of appreciation for something positive your partner has done, even though you may be feeling disconnected most of the time.

3. **Slow down.** Don't let impulses and knee-jerk reactions rule you. Before reacting, give yourself time to fully register your needs and desires. For example, you may think you want to leave your partner when what you really want is to escape the pain of a stagnant relationship or a seemingly never-ending power struggle over the same infuriating things. If you can give yourself enough "break time" to soothe yourself and regain some measure of calm, you can begin to assess whether there's something to salvage from your troubled partnership. Stay aware and deliberate. Leave the room, call a friend, or do some yoga or other exercise.

Stretch

Trust the process. If you're not sure what to do next, then practice patience. Let go of the outcome until it becomes clear. In the meantime, just keep doing the work — investigating your own feelings, acknowledging your contributions to the problems, and identifying your true desires. The answer will emerge.

Stage Five, Wholehearted Love: Keep Practicing

First off, congratulations! If you've arrived at this stage, you and your partner are in a deeply rewarding place of caring and connectedness. That isn't to say Stage Five comes without challenges. Like deep meditative awareness or the perfect yoga session, wholeheartedness is a joyful experience but not a permanent one. It's a place we can sometimes contact and live from, no question. But for every one of us, wholehearted love is an ongoing practice that demands daily intentions, daily actions, and daily choices.

Here's your Stage Five to-do list:

1. **Practice, practice, practice.** All the skills you've developed as you've moved through the other stages — grounding yourself in reality, addressing conflicts directly, creating healthy boundaries, and investing in doing the work — are the same skills that will keep you on the path to wholeheartedness.

2. **Nourish yourself.** Wholehearted love requires both partners to continually sustain their own wholeness, in addition to meeting the needs of the relationship. In many ways, the relationship itself is a tool for cultivating each individual's own personal growth. Remember to continue investing in your own passions, self-care rituals, self-exploration, and inner work, whatever that might mean for you. Gently encourage your partner to do the same. Help each other grow into better versions of yourselves in all sectors of your lives.

3. **Relish the journey.** Humor, playfulness, and spontaneity will be your friends in this stage. Use them freely as you continue to learn and expand with your partner. Be ready to laugh at yourselves, as Tim and I do when we suddenly realize we're having the same ancient, ridiculous argument about how to do the dishes. For us, the difference is that it's now about a 1 on the scale of annoyance rather than a 10. Chapter 16 explores the bridges toward wholehearted love, and I urge you to take some time to explore them.

4. **Know that there will always be new challenges.** Hurdles are not signs something is wrong. Living life, even from a place of whole-heartedness, is like walking through a labyrinth. You find detours, twists, and turns, and just when you think you're near the center, you come across another detour you didn't expect. Sometimes, though, when you think you are a long way from where you want to be, the obstacles disappear, and you are there.

As in a labyrinth, we can walk part of the way with another person, but we must also walk by ourselves. Sometimes, the path opens for two; other times, it is only wide enough for one. Whole-hearted loving is as much a commitment to that path as an individual as a commitment to the relationship.

Centering the Self

Understanding the five stages of the Love Cycle and how to navigate through the painful and limiting ones can help you transform a good relationship into a great one. This framework can help everyone — from those starting a new relationship with the intention of avoiding some of the sinkholes of the past to those in a committed partnership with long-standing conflicts they haven't been able to resolve as yet. It will help you re-create the trust, humor, and intimacy that first brought you together and teach you that conflicts — even the hardest ones — don't need to take away love. In fact, you can use them to deepen your connection, heal your own historical wounds, and expand your empathy and insight.

Ultimately, the entire point of the Love Cycles philosophy — in a relationship and in all of life's cycles — is to continually move ourselves toward a state of wholeheartedness. It involves developing deep, mindful self-awareness and self-compassion as well as a willingness to work on the parts of ourselves that are small-hearted, closed-hearted, or brokenhearted — behaviors that stop us from accessing generosity, vulnerability, trust, and joy in our lives.

In relationships, wholeheartedness also means practicing the art of differentiation: understanding your partner is not you and accepting that you have no control over the other person's choices. As intimate as we may feel at times, we are not one another. Even so-called soulmates who spend decades in love will eventually part, if not through life's challenges, then through death. That means true wholeness cannot come from another person. It must come from within.

In the chapters that follow, you will learn skills to help you realize your full potential and that of your intimate relationship. An important side benefit is that these skills will also help you better navigate other vital relationships in your life, including, most importantly, your relationship with yourself.

How Did I Get Here?

If we hope to preserve our loving connections over a longer period of time, we must become more aware of the impact that our family traditions have on our lives. Powerful forces within our family begin to shape our sensibilities and sensitivities from the earliest days of our development and continue to exert enormous control over the way we think, feel, and behave throughout our lifetime.

— JOHN JACOBS, psychiatrist and author of
All You Need Is Love and Other Lies about Married Life

"Who am I?" It may be the oldest question in the world. It was written on the walls by our earliest cave-dwelling ancestors and sung in ancient ballads, and the edict "Know thyself" was carved on the Temple of Apollo in Delphi. Almost two thousand years later, William Shakespeare told us, "This above all: To thine own self be true." The journey to understand the self drives the deliberations of philosophers, the musing of poets, and the endless chicken-or-egg debate among psychologists about whether we are formed by nature or by nurture.

For some people, the answer is simple. "It's just the way I am," said the Brooklyn cabdriver when I commented on his kindness in giving a homeless man a free ride to a health clinic. Conversely, "It's just how I was raised," said my client in response to his wife's question about why he didn't want the family dog in the house. "Dogs belong outside."

Understanding who we are and how we got this way is essential to the success of our connections with other people because, at the end of the day, relationships are an inside job. Your past and the forces that have shaped you go on to shape how you love and where you struggle. When you understand these forces, you can begin to work on changing the ones that get in your way.

Nature versus Nurture

A healthy relationship requires a lot of yielding and bending as well as establishing and honoring healthy boundaries. Understanding what's inherent in our character based on biology ("nature") and what is learned from our lived experience ("nurture") can help us to more skillfully develop the flexibility that is a necessary part of relationships — and manage sensitivities that may be hard or impossible to change.

Our personality, our physical appearance, and possibly even qualities such as generosity, jealousy, and introversion have genetic components, whereas other qualities are developed by being in certain environments. The interaction between the two forms much of our personality. For example, a child with an introverted temperament who grows up in a home where that temperament is respected learns to manage it much better than an introverted child who grows up being shamed for not being outgoing enough.

It's Just the Way I Am

Some parts of our makeup are undeniably inherited; they are, indeed, "just the way we are." But we must be mindful of how we use that explanation. Are you familiar with the Bowling and Richey song "That's Just the Way I Am," made famous by Tammy Wynette? In this song, she tells her partner that she cannot help expressing her loving feelings for him, even when his friends are nearby.

And if this embarrasses him, he needs to remember that she can't help it. As Wynette croons, "Mmm, that's just the way I am."

This doesn't give her lover much room to protest if he feels uncomfortable, for example, when they are having dinner with his very formal family and she throws her arms around him, kisses him intimately, and says how much she loves him. After all, it's just the way she is!

EXERCISE: "It's Just the Way I Am!"

List three personal examples that fall into the category of "That's just the way I am." They could be particular personality traits, go-to behaviors, or strong likes or dislikes. If working with a partner, complete this exercise alone first; then come together to share if you wish, though it isn't necessary.

1.
2.
3.

After you've created your list, consider whether you think you were born with each characteristic (if so, write "nature" next to it) or you learned it at some point in your life (if so, write "nurture" next to it).

Now write down three personal examples of "That's just the way I am" that you have learned to manage in new and more self-loving ways. For example, you may be inherently impatient and have found ways to increase your patience. Perhaps you are disorganized but have learned new organizational skills that help you stay more on top of things. Or maybe you are shy and have developed social skills that counter your basic shy personality.

1.
2.
3.

Understanding our basic nature, exploring the ways we were affected by our upbringing, and learning how we can adapt and grow through our own self-nurturing are all essential to learning love skills.

What Do We Really Know?

Many people see themselves as born introverts or extroverts. And it's true that some of us come into the world with confidence, while others are shy. Some are born pessimists, and others wake each morning with a song in their hearts. Some people are called "natural leaders," while others are labeled "dreamers" from their earliest days.

Yet we change. We outgrow our childish fear of the dark. We develop into new versions of ourselves once we leave our parents' homes, exploring new ways of dressing and eating, and getting tattoos. We go through phases of obsession with a particular musician only to look back years later and wonder, "What was I thinking?" We shift our values as we gain new information about the world around us, changing our diet, habits, or ways of viewing family customs. We attend a seminar or read a particularly moving story, feel something shift within us, and call the experience "transformative" when we emerge.

We may never know exactly how we became the people we are today; it continues to be one of life's great mysteries. But as individuals, we can identify parts of our personal histories that may be contributing to our current sense of self and use that knowledge to transform our lives.

This process of self-reflection and self-analysis is essential to the health of our important relationships, which will constantly challenge us and often demand that we adapt, adjust, and grow. Seeing ourselves clearly — both who we are now *and* how we got here — is a vital step toward offering our best selves to our partner and building a relationship that is capable of succeeding in the long term.

In this chapter and the next, you'll find a series of exercises to help you sort out "the ways you are" from "the ways you learned to be" by exploring your family history. This will give you the opportunity to identify the strengths you want to enhance and the challenges you want to find ways to manage. First, you'll complete assessments and exercises designed to help you understand yourself in relation to your family history. These will help you gain a more objective understanding of your answer to the "Who am I?" question. They'll also encourage you to examine family stories in new ways and to understand the most influential people in your life through a different lens. You'll review, and possibly redefine, the messages you internalized during your childhood, thinking this is "just how things are."

Then we'll explore your personal experiences, which are the basis of the stories you tell yourself about your lovability (the right to be loved) and your ability to depend on (and be depended on by) important people in your life. These experiences form our beliefs about attachment, one of the essential components of how we create and maintain adult relationships. It's important to know where we were nourished and supported — and by whom — and where we were neglected and wounded. Without that knowledge, we will re-create the same stories in adulthood.

Our personal experiences also help us to understand our negative reactions to seemingly insignificant events (like when our partner forgets to buy the spinach), somehow believing these small stumbles are evidence of our lack of importance and worth. We tend to choose partners who bring out the most vulnerable parts of us, but healing is possible once we recognize our triggers and develop new ways to manage our old inner stories about ourselves.

As you work on each exercise in the following self-exploratory chapters, remember to be mindful. We all have beliefs about who we were, are, and are capable of becoming. At the same time, each of us has many blind spots. For many of us, exploring our personal history breaks some foundational family rules: "Don't look too deeply," "Don't ask questions," or "Just look on the bright side." As you explore each of these tools, remember that mindfulness begins with self-compassion rather than self-judgment, including any self-recriminations you might have about looking deeply into stories that may have been off-limits or even forbidden to explore. Go slowly and be patient with yourself.

For all the ambiguity that surrounds the eternal question "Who am I?" there is one thing I know: we have the power to shape the answer. Regardless of our "default" selves, we can make conscious choices to change and expand ourselves. Starting from who and where we are now, we can create new versions of ourselves.

EXERCISE: Creating Your Family Tree

If you don't know history, you don't know anything.
You are a leaf that doesn't know it is part of a tree.

— MICHAEL CRICHTON, author, screenwriter, and film director

To start exploring your family history, draw your family tree. Using a piece of paper at least 8½ by 11 inches, make a diagram that shows you at the bottom and your parents directly above you connected by a line. Draw a box for each person and write the name inside each box. Above the boxes that represent your parents, write the names of their parents, their grandparents, any siblings, and subsequent marriages or partnerships of your parents. Try to go back at least three generations, or even farther if you can locate the information.

Here's a sample basic family tree:

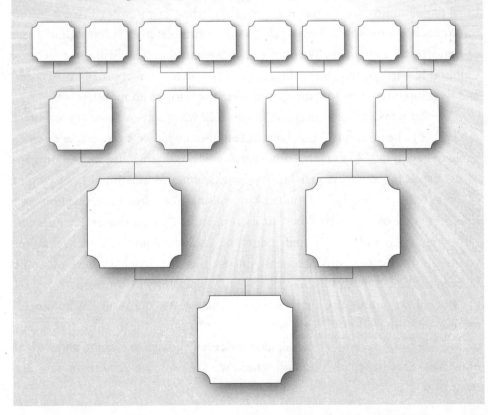

If you wish, you can signify men with a square, women with a circle, and other genders with a star. When writing the names of couples, stay organized with genders by keeping all the men on the left side and the women on the right. If there are same-sex parents involved, select a specific symbol to signify the members of the couple. In the case of same-sex parents, adoptions, and other nontraditional family structures, be sure to also include the biological parents when possible — this will create more branches of your tree to research, but all of the information will be valuable, as all of these various parents may have had some influence on who you are now.

You can also extend the family tree outward by including your siblings with you beneath your parents and any spouses or partners, plus any children.

The Genogram

We all have histories that deeply shape our personalities and behavior as we grow up. You can dig deeper into the relationships and connections between the people in your family using a genogram, which is a more detailed graphic representation of a family tree that can be helpful in assessing old family patterns. Though based on the idea of a family tree, a genogram can help you see your family story in a new way because it includes much more information about family members, their relationships, environmental influences, pivotal events, health issues, and the impacts on their lives, offering a deeper understanding of the events and personalities that have shaped you. According to the genogram website www.genopro.com:

> [Genograms] contain basic data found in family trees such as the name, gender, date of birth, and date of death of each individual. Additional data may include education, occupation, major life events, chronic illnesses, social behaviors, nature of family relationships, emotional relationships, and social relationships. Some genograms also include

information on disorders running in the family such as alcoholism, depression, diseases, alliances, and living situations. Genograms can vary significantly because there is no limitation as to what type of data can be included.

As children, we perceive our family through the eyes of a child, noticing who cheered us on and who was unkind or oblivious to our needs. We often see our family and the story we tell about it as though it is a frozen snapshot. Genograms give us a broader, dynamic view of the hidden factors at play in our upbringing, and they humanize our parents and grandparents as we discover more about the difficulties they've faced as well as their achievements. As a result, they help us understand ourselves in relation to the stories we've grown up believing, which of course go on to affect our important relationships.

Ted, a former client of mine, grew up with a father who did many of the "right things." He was a soccer coach, a PTA parent, and a professional who took his son to work to show him off. Ted recalls knowing his dad was proud of him, but at the same time, his father seemed distant and preoccupied. Sometimes Ted would see him sitting in his living room chair staring blankly, often for hours. There were whole days when his father didn't talk to anyone. The young Ted felt that, although his father showed up for him physically, he wasn't really interested in Ted — and even that his father didn't love him. In fact, he told me, he couldn't remember his father ever saying those words to him.

I suggested we create a genogram together, even though he said he knew his family history well and "there's not much new to learn." We went back two generations, creating a visual map that included some historical events of his family as well as writing down some personal characteristics of his parents and grandparents (see next page).

I noticed his father had been in the military for two years before Ted was born. I asked Ted about it, and he thought his father had been somewhere in Southeast Asia, but his dad didn't talk about it. By the time we created the genogram, Ted's father had passed away, so he asked his mother about those two years. She reacted nervously, throwing her hands up and saying, "Your

TED'S GENOGRAM

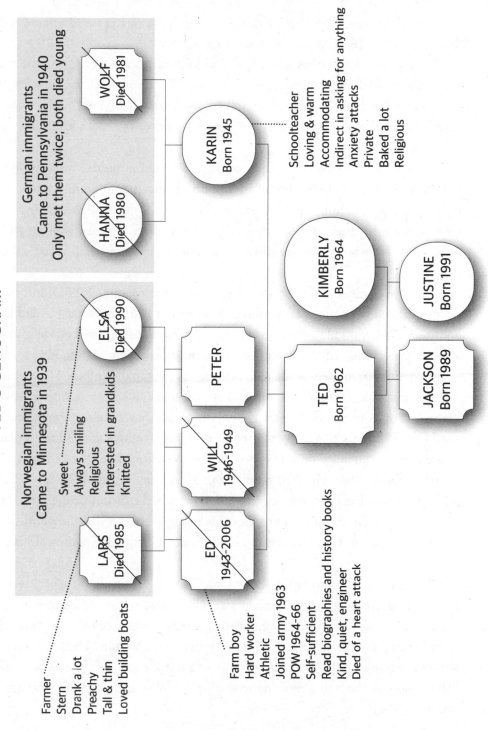

Norwegian immigrants
Came to Minnesota in 1939

German immigrants
Came to Pennsylvania in 1940
Only met them twice; both died young

WOLF
Died 1981

HANNA
Died 1980

KARIN
Born 1945

- Schoolteacher
- Loving & warm
- Accommodating
- Indirect in asking for anything
- Anxiety attacks
- Private
- Baked a lot
- Religious

ELSA
Died 1990

- Sweet
- Always smiling
- Religious
- Interested in grandkids
- Knitted

LARS
Died 1985

- Farmer
- Stern
- Drank a lot
- Preachy
- Tall & thin
- Loved building boats

PETER

WILL
1946–1949

ED
1943–2006

- Farm boy
- Hard worker
- Athletic
- Joined army 1963
- POW 1964-66
- Self-sufficient
- Read biographies and history books
- Kind, quiet, engineer
- Died of a heart attack

KIMBERLY
Born 1964

TED
Born 1962

JUSTINE
Born 1991

JACKSON
Born 1989

father decided it was best to let sleeping dogs lie, and I certainly agree with him. All that mattered is that he came back alive."

So Ted asked his father's brother. Ted told me he'll never forget the moment his uncle drew a deep breath and said, "Ted, your dad was in a POW camp in the Vietnam War. He never talked about what happened, and we never asked. But we knew it was bad…You know, we never talked about things that were hard."

He hesitated a moment before saying, "We had a middle brother, Will. When he was three, he drowned in a pond on my grandparents' farm, and nobody mentioned him after the funeral. I remember my mother crying a few months after he died, and our dad said, 'Karin, there is work waiting to be finished and two boys who are still alive and need your attention. What's done is done.'"

Ted was a physician with firsthand experience treating PTSD, but he'd never realized his father had suffered from it. On learning what his dad had endured, Ted was able to see his father's tremendous resilience. He gained a new appreciation of the love his father must have felt for his kids to put as much effort into them as he did, despite his personal demons. He realized that his dad's background, growing up on a Minnesota farm in a stoic Norwegian farming community, had taught him that emotions were not something to spend time with; there was always work to do, and feelings didn't have a place in the rural community he was raised in. He was astonished that he had never heard of the brother who had died and tried to imagine what the loss of the middle brother had been like for his dad, who was the oldest of the boys. His father didn't have the skills to express his inner pain, and like the good farm boy he was, he did what needed to be done and kept the difficulties of his life on the inside.

Looking at his mother's background, Ted saw a similar story: She was raised by parents who were German war refugees who had settled in Pennsylvania, where they had a watch repair store. Her parents worked day and night at the store, and the family lived in an apartment above it. He remembered once asking his mother why her parents had left Germany, and she had said, "We don't talk about that time in the world, Ted. We need to get on with living our lives now."

As a result of their backgrounds, neither of his parents had the ability to manage whatever his dad had lived through as a POW, and their early adaptation of "getting on with it" and "not looking back" would not have helped them gain the skills needed to be able to share anything about it. After his father had died, Ted recalled his mother looking at a photo of his dad as a young man in a military uniform on the day of their wedding. Ted asked, "Is that Dad?"

His mother replied, "Not the dad you knew, Ted. That man didn't come back from Vietnam."

When Ted asked her what she meant, she laughed nervously and said, "Oh, don't get nosy now. It didn't mean anything. Let's get on with the Sunday meal."

Understanding a little of his parents' story also helped Ted feel empathy, not just for his parents and their lack of ability to deal with loss, but also for the little kid who still lived inside him because, like all children, he had believed *he* was the cause of his father's remoteness. The genogram helped him gain understanding and compassion for everyone in the story and gave him a new determination that his kids would not be left wondering who he was. He dove deeper into his own therapy to remember his early years and formative experiences, including the painful ones, and to learn how to recognize his feelings and then to talk about them.

EXERCISE: Creating Your Genogram

The directions for making a genogram can be found in many places on the internet. Here are two that I have found useful that are available as of this writing. As you will see, your genogram can be as complex or simple as you choose; I do encourage you to put in enough time to include the primary people and their most important relationships, events, occupations, personality traits, and health/behavioral issues.

www.genopro.com/gcnogram
en.wikipedia.org/wiki/genogram

You will need your favorite pens, perhaps a cup of tea or coffee, some old photos that will bring stories to mind (be sure to look on the back of the photographs, as people may have written things at the time they were taken), and a comfortable place to sit and spread things out. Approach the process in a spirit of openness.

As you answer the questions throughout this and the next chapter, keep your genogram nearby. You can add any new information you discover to this graphic representation of your genetic and historical past. As you work through these chapters, you may start to identify ways in which your family's history has influenced your beliefs about life, love, and who you have thought yourself to be.

Family Stories

At the beginning of this process, people sometimes claim they don't know much about their family history. What you *don't* know tells you something right away about family secrets and rules about disclosure. Sometimes parents fail to share their history, because they're cut off from their original family or feel shame or sadness. That immediately gives you information about family rules.

If you don't know some of your family stories, perhaps someone else does. Older close relatives, distant cousins, and the people who raised you (if not your biological parents) can often lead you to other people who do know parts of the story. Many people, especially as they age, are eager to tell their family tales. Be sure to ask those outside your immediate family. It can also be helpful to identify the historical events that surrounded your upbringing and that of the two or three generations before you. Events such as immigration, war, recessions, and financial dramas within the family, early deaths, divorce, mental illness, and great successes may affect many subsequent generations through passed-down attitudes and beliefs.

Many of us don't question some of our most strongly held convictions. We don't question our attitudes about money, loyalty, or family, perhaps because they've been instilled in us over generations and presented as facts rather than opinions. But many ideas held as facts were formed under completely different circumstances, when they may have even been important for survival — such as when our immigrant ancestors were fleeing from religious or political persecution.

Some invisible loyalties stretch through generations and have little to do with objective reality today. These stories are inherited and accepted as true merely because "things have always been that way." Some of these may be mundane, everyday beliefs. For example, a man prepares a pot roast for dinner by cutting off both ends. His wife asks, "Why do you cut the ends off?"

"That's just how it's done."

"*No*," she says, clearly annoyed. "You put the whole roast in; otherwise, you lose juice."

The man retorts, "No, you cut the ends off because they are often too dry, and it makes for a juicier roast."

Later the man remembers the argument while visiting his mother. He asks her why she cuts off both ends of a roast before cooking it. She says, "I always had a small oven and small pans, and it didn't fit any other way."

So much of what we do and how we do it, as well as the associated feelings of "rightness," originates from once functional practices that are no longer relevant. Yet we often defend our way as the "right way" without actually knowing the facts behind what we're defending. We might be following an old script we didn't even write for ourselves. However unimportant the belief may seem — like the pot roast example — it can contribute to a power struggle in our relationships.

The purpose of understanding your three-generational history is to become conscious of many of the factors that have contributed to your beliefs and worldview and to open up some space to make new decisions. Which family scripts do you wish to continue, and which do you wish to let go? Understanding this information becomes essential when you are creating a life with someone else who has his or her own set of beliefs and worldviews.

Although some of the old family rules made sense a century ago, many of them don't fit with current life. First-generation children of immigrants often struggle with the clash between the social norms in the culture around them and family norms based on the past. If your family came to this country because of religious or cultural persecution, you needed to be careful whom you talked to, because sharing family business of any kind could have been life-threatening. If near starvation was a real possibility, spending money for a vacation would have been preposterous. If housing or food was scarce, having a family pet could have taken precious resources from the people in the family who were just surviving. The rules get passed on as though they are "truths" rather than appropriate guidelines from a particular situation in a different time.

In this next phase of exploring your history, you'll look at the stories of the people who came before you, many of whom have had a significant, though often unseen, influence on who you think you are. Going back two or more generations may give you a sense of where some of your family's ideals, judgments, fears, and resilience came from.

When you were a kid, did you ever play the game "Gossip," sometimes known as "Telephone"? You whisper a phrase or a quick story to the person next to you. That person then whispers it to the next person, and so on. The process repeats, often many times, until the last person who hears the story says it out loud. The discrepancies between the first and last messages are often dramatic. Family history is similar: many of the stories you've heard may differ significantly from what actually happened.

EXERCISE: Your Family History

Answer the following questions about your family. Be sure to use the names of your ancestors and current family members in order to clearly link stories to specific people. If you want to get extra fancy, use some colorful highlighters and markers to color-code the stories in order to connect them to specific people on your family tree. If you don't know some of the answers, consider asking your family members or look at old photo albums or other pieces of family history.

1. What do you know about the parts of the world your ancestors came from? Did they emigrate from another country? Why did they leave their homeland? Adventure, poverty, religious persecution, opportunities, love? What were their journeys like?

2. Did any join the military? Were they involved in a war? How did they talk about the experience, or were they mainly silent about it?

3. How did economic pressures affect your family? How were they impacted by the Great Depression and subsequent recessions? Were there stories of rags to riches, or riches to rags?

4. Did anyone in your family suffer serious medical or psychological conditions or illnesses? Were there early deaths of parents or children? How did the family cope with these difficulties and losses?

5. Going back two generations, who were the stars and who were the black sheep in your family's mythology?

6. Did your family have a religious tradition? If so, did it have a positive influence, a negative influence, or somewhere in between? Did it change through the generations?

7. Were there divorces, illnesses, deaths, stepparents, or adoptions in the family?

8. Is there anything else unique, special, troubling, or inspiring about your family history going back through the generations?

EXERCISE: Your Family Themes

What are the themes in your three-generation map? Make a list of the themes that are relevant to your family story and explore the attitudes and ideas that might have come from these experiences. Are any of these themes playing out in your life now?

Some common themes include:

- Love (love lost, love found, unrequited love, forbidden love, lack of love)
- Death and loss, grief and shock, people (often children) left behind, coping and resilience
- Looking for the true self, which often means defying tradition, making decisions about leaving home, and rejecting customs
- Power, money, and managing its gain or loss; corruption, integrity, and exploitation
- Survival against persecution, abuse, loss, famine, or disease
- Heroism in the face of adversity
- Prejudice, racism, genderism, or bullying
- War, relocation, loss, survival
- Illness, depression, addiction, medical trauma, accidents
- Resilience, creativity, courage, and surviving against all odds

Stories from Your Past

6

Stories are compasses and architecture; we navigate by them, we build our sanctuaries
and our prisons out of them, and to be without a story is to be lost in the vastness of a
world that spreads in all directions like arctic tundra or sea ice.

— REBECCA SOLNIT, *The Faraway Nearby*

In his play *Fences*, August Wilson tells the story of Troy Maxson, a garbage
collector who lives in Pittsburg in the 1950s with his wife, Rose, and their
son, Cory. When Cory is recruited by a college football team, Troy refuses
to sign the permission slip, and an argument ensues. Cory finally confronts his
father with a question about why he never liked him. Troy answers, "Liked
you? Who the hell say I got to like you? What law is there say I got to like
you?"

Cory sees a heartless parent who doesn't like him or believe in him; eventually, they get into a physical fight fueled by a young man's bitterness toward
a father who seems cruel and dismissive. As the story develops, we discover

Troy was once a talented baseball player who couldn't progress in his career because black players weren't allowed in the major leagues until 1947. The impossibility of his dream broke his heart.

From his son's perspective, Troy was an unkind and discouraging father. But a closer look reveals the story of a man who didn't want his son to experience the heartbreak he'd endured. Although it was now a generation later and a black man may well have had the chance to succeed in football, Troy was not thinking rationally, but rather reacting to the old story as he had known it. Troy's behavior toward his son was harmful; that doesn't change even with understanding. But if Cory could have known Troy's reasons, he might have realized that his father's rage and discouraging words were never about Cory himself.

Doing the work of learning the strengths and struggles of your family can free you to understand some of the painful events of your own history — and to recognize that messages that may have led you to believe something was wrong with you *were never about you*. Instead, these painful events sprung from old unresolved pain your family members were carrying. These beliefs will play out in your current relationship until you become aware of them; then you have a choice to change the patterns.

For example, let's say Cory marries a woman who is by nature a person who doubts things will turn out well. One day he enthusiastically tells her he is in line for a significant promotion at work. She says, "Well, don't get your hopes up too much." What do you imagine he hears? He might think, "Part of her personality is to be cautious, so I won't personalize that," or he might think instead, "Why doesn't she believe in me? She doesn't think I can do anything right." Most probably his history will steer him toward the latter, interpreting his wife's caution as another strike against his self-worth.

Our family relationships provide our first model of how to interact with those close to us. How love, connection, and conflict were managed become road maps we may not be aware we're following. We may intentionally change some of what we experienced, or we may reproduce it. Either way, many of us unconsciously pass on to our own families many of the ways we learned to interact — the healthy ways and not-so-healthy ones.

In this chapter, you'll take a closer look at your earliest life experiences (and the people involved in them) to continue understanding how you got to be the way you are and what patterns you no longer want to perpetuate in your relationships today.

Finding Balance

As a therapist, I look for two red flags when people talk about their childhood: "It was all terrible," or "It was all perfect." Following either statement, I always look for an "and." In other words, a personal weakness can be the flip side of a personal strength — or vice versa. Below are examples of using the "and" to describe a realistic view of one's parents.

> "My father was tough on me, *and* he was a dearly loved school principal, capable of showing tenderness to his students in a way he couldn't at home."
>
> "My mother wasn't particularly warm, *and* she had tremendous wisdom, which still helps me daily."
>
> "My sister was so clever that she inspired me, *and* I grew up in her shadow."
>
> "My grandmother was the most unconditionally loving person I ever knew, *and* it was tedious to care for her and listen to her describe her ongoing anxiety about whatever could go wrong."

Our genogram allows us to see our fallible family members more objectively, as the complex human beings they were (and are), and our childhoods as the imperfect experiences they were. When we do that, we can learn volumes about our own strengths and struggles.

A Closer Look at Your Parents

Now it's time to take a closer look at the two people who likely have had the strongest influence on who you are today.

EXERCISE: Understanding Your Parents

Answer the following questions about your parents. As in the previous chapter, if you don't know any answers, consider asking other family members. It can be very illuminating to have these conversations and can help you connect more deeply with the people you are talking to. If you had same-sex parents, stepparents, unknown parents, grandparents involved in parenting, or other parental figures in the home when you were growing up, adapt the questions to reflect your family situation.

1. How did your parents meet? Was there a love story, a beginning brimming with hope and affection — or not? What do you know about this?

2. When you were born, what was happening in your parents' lives?

3. Did your parents already have kids, or were you the first? What was it like to grow up in your birth position?

4. What do you think your father would say was his greatest joy and his biggest disappointment?

5. What do you think your mother would say was her greatest joy and her biggest disappointment?

6. How did your parents show affection, argue, and reconcile after an argument?

7. How did they speak about each other when they were not together?

8. What was one of the main things you learned about life and what to expect from your mother?

9. What was one of the main things you learned about life and what to expect from your father?

10. From watching your parents' relationship, what did you learn to think love was?

The Impact of Siblings

Sibling relationships have often shaped people's self-concept even more than parental relationships. Sarah's sister, Julie, was eighteen months older than she was. Julie had little time for Sarah; in fact, she blatantly ignored her. Sarah was constantly trying to be more acceptable to her big sister. But her gambits never worked; Julie ignored Sarah's repeated invitations for connection and thoughtlessly threw away the little gifts she gave her. Sarah concluded it was all her own fault. Julie appeared superior to her in all ways — prettier, smarter, more popular — and her rejection seemed to be proof that Sarah was deficient.

Consequently, Sarah often felt inadequate and longed for acceptance from friends, mentors, and older women in general. Whenever a woman reached out for friendship or complimented her at work, Sarah couldn't believe the gesture was sincere. She remained self-doubting and isolated.

One day, when Sarah was in her forties and visiting her sister, she worked up the nerve to talk about their shared family history. To Sarah's surprise, Julie welcomed the conversation. When Sarah asked what Julie remembered about their childhood, Julie revealed she'd been so deeply depressed as a kid that she remembered little from that time. Sarah persisted, sharing her feelings of rejection and her belief that she was somehow unacceptable to her sister. She was stunned when Julie said she'd always seen Sarah as a happy kid with a free and adventurous spirit and had been jealous of *her*.

When Sarah came to therapy, she said to me, "In some ways, my life has been about loyalty to a story that was never even real."

EXERCISE: Sibling Interactions

If you have siblings, including half siblings, adopted siblings, or foster siblings, answer the following questions about your immediate family.

1. How important were your siblings in your life? Why were they important — or not so important? Describe your early relationships with each sibling.

2. Were there any special alliances or conflicts between siblings that had an impact on you?

3. When you or your siblings needed help, what did you do? How did your parents (or perhaps your siblings) handle children's requests for help?

If you do not have siblings, describe how your life was affected by growing up an only child. Be sure to identify the strengths and the challenges.

Stories We Tell Ourselves

Like Sarah, we all have stories we tell ourselves about who we are, how others see us, and why things happened the way they did. Many of these stories become our life narratives; we replay old scenes and fill in the blank spaces based on how we've interpreted our early experiences. Further, we assign meaning to new experiences based on our history and edit out information that doesn't fit into the familiar narrative.

When I was teaching a college class on interpersonal communication, the first thing I would ask my students to do was to write their interpretation of the following event:

You are walking down a street near campus, and you see someone you went to high school with coming toward you. You look up and are about to smile when they cross the street, not looking at you. This is because . . .

Then I would ask them to finish the story. The answers always varied widely. The person crossed the street because:

"She never liked me to begin with."
"He was always a snob in high school."
"She is depressed."
"He just found out he has an incurable disease."

Very few people would say, "She didn't see me," or "I don't know."

As humans, we have a strong need to make sense of what is happening, and to do that, we fill in the blanks. We will always try to make sense of our lives through a narrative, an inner story that we are continuously creating and editing.

As children, we look for reasons to explain painful events, usually blaming ourselves. Then we carry these meanings forward into adulthood, repeating messages such as these to ourselves:

"I'm not as good as..."
"My needs are special."
"My needs aren't important."
"I'm on my own."
"Something is wrong with me."
"I can't get it right."
"It's not safe to make mistakes."

The truth is, most of the painful events we suffer are not in fact personal; we don't cause our father's anger, our mother's anxiety, or our sister's rejection, but we often *feel* as though we do. These stories have profound effects on our lives and our relationships. They influence how we see the world and make decisions about everything from how we spend money to how we realize — or abandon — our dreams. Our stories also wield enormous influence on how we react to our partner.

Sarah, who felt invisible next to her sister, Julie, became a very competent and well-loved community-college biology teacher. Her partner, Sam, was also a teacher in the same field, and one year he won an award for "Teacher of the Year." To other people, Sarah expressed her pride in Sam and his award, but inside she told herself this was proof she was always second best.

A mindful attitude can help us pay attention to the ways we explain painful, disappointing, or even happy events to ourselves through the old clouded lens of childhood conclusions. When you experience an event and find yourself telling yourself something about it that diminishes you in any way, make an effort to:

1. Notice the story behind it.
2. Allow the story, and observe it with curiosity, not judgment.
3. Write down the emotions the story evokes when you tell it to yourself.
4. Finally, ask yourself if there are alternate explanations for why the event took place or why someone responded to you the way you think they did.

Affection and Connection

Over twenty years ago, researchers at the University of Nebraska and the University of Alabama discovered six key traits of strong families. They found these families:

- Express appreciation and affection.
- Have a strong commitment to each other.
- Spend rewarding time together.
- Manage stress and crises effectively.
- Have a sense of spiritual well-being with common values and ethics.
- Have effective, positive, and respectful communication patterns.

EXERCISE: Patterns of Affection and Control

Looking at the six qualities above, assign a number from 1 to 5 for each quality, with 1 being the weakest and 5 being the strongest, as a measure of how strong that trait was in the family you grew up in.

Below are more questions to help you look more deeply at patterns of affection and control. Try to be fair and objective as you respond to each question. It's not about whether you liked family members, had issues growing up, or agreed with everything they did. Instead, it's a chance to look objectively at the patterns and ways of being you learned early on that may be helping or hindering your current intimate relationship.

1. Did family members express affection for each other through physical affection, gifts, words, or other means? Describe the ways they did or did not do this.

2. Did they keep their promises to each other and support each other in times of both trouble and triumph? List some examples of support and/or nonsupport.

3. Did they interact as a family within the greater community? If they did, describe where and how those interactions took place (in the extended family, church community, or larger social connection). If they kept more to themselves than engaging in wider contexts, describe what that was like.

4. How did they manage inevitable times of crisis, loss, and trouble? Did they reach out beyond the family? Were there therapists, religious leaders, elders, or other guides they turned to?

5. How were values, ethics, and life's mysteries treated within the family? Did you grow up in a religion? How did your family manage difficult passages such as death? (Again, this is not a question about whether you agree with or participate in the religion you grew up with, if there was one.)

6. Was communication valued? Were you encouraged to form your own opinions and express them? Write about how people did or did not express feelings, manage conflict, and show affection for one another.

7. How did family members handle apologies and forgiveness? Were there grudges and grumbling about one another without directly dealing with the issues, or were there more direct ways of handling inevitable conflicts? Describe how your mother and father each handled these issues.

8. What strengths did you take from your family?

9. In which areas and how do you want to do things differently in your current relationships?

The Power of Attachment

I'm going to tell you three true stories.

First story: A woman is sitting on a park bench in a garden with a boy about four years old. The boy sees a rose lying on the ground, picks it up, and hands it to his mother. She takes it, smiles, and thanks him. Then she says, "But why don't you ever say you love me?"

What is one lesson this boy is learning about reaching out in love?

Second story: A family is sitting in a restaurant when their three-year-old daughter drops her stuffed giraffe and begins to cry. It's obvious she is very tired. Her mother picks up the giraffe, wipes it off, and hands it back to her. The girl throws it on the floor again, still crying. The mother gets it again, and this time the child screams with all of her might. At this point, her father's face turns beet-red. He pounds the table and yells, "Stop crying, or I will give you something to cry about!" When the child cries even harder, her father grabs her roughly under his arm and marches out of the restaurant.

What is this child learning about managing upsetting feelings?

Third story: A seven-year-old has his heart set on getting a special teacher for second grade. His mother tried her best to help this happen, even writing a letter to the principal. On the first day of school, the boy comes home devastated. He got a different teacher, the one who all the kids said was the meanest. His mother flies into a rage, stomping around the kitchen and calling her friends to complain about how much she pays in taxes and how her rights are being violated because her son has gotten a terrible teacher. A neighbor comes by, and the two women talk until dinner about how the world is "going to hell in a handbasket." Nobody speaks to the boy until he asks his mother, "What does 'going to hell in a handbasket' mean?" She snaps, "Mind your own business. Go out and play." His feelings about his teacher are never discussed.

What is this boy learning about support?

If you asked any of these parents if they love their kids, they would say, "Of course!" They buy them car seats, take them to the dentist, and go to great lengths to give them the bike they want most for their birthday. But again, love is only a feeling, while a healthy relationship is a set of skills. These parents certainly felt love, but none of them showed skill. They each provided the kind of care they could, likely in the way that was shown to them.

Skillful loving is different. A skillful loving parent knows how to help children calm down when they are upset, they don't become angry when their children get angry, and they don't allow their own distress to trump the children's. In other words, they have mastered a lot of the qualities of emotional intelligence (which we will have a closer look at in Chapter 12).

EXERCISE: Your Stories

Think about some true stories of your own.

A struggle story: In one paragraph, recount a family experience that was painful and full of struggle, an event that shows how one or both of your parents responded to you in a time of distress.

A happy story: In one paragraph, recount a memory of a positive family experience. Focus on an event that exemplified your own strength, your resilience, and being supported in a way that made you feel loved and understood.

Attachment Styles: Islands, Waves, and Anchors

In psychology, the idea that the way we connect with others today mirrors the ways our earliest caregivers showed us affection as babies is called attachment theory. Developed by psychologists John Bowlby and Mary Ainsworth in the late twentieth century, the theory posits three main attachment "styles": avoidant attachment, anxious attachment, and secure attachment. Personally though, I love the way psychotherapist Stan Tatkin describes these styles in his book *Wired for Love: How Understanding Your Partner's Brain and Attachment Style Can Help You Diffuse Conflict and Build a Secure Relationship*. Originally his book described three kinds of people in this world: Islands, Waves, and Anchors.

Islands are people with an avoidant attachment style; they generally had absent or unavailable caregivers as children. As adults, Islands tend to live self-sufficiently in their own worlds. Islands:

- are often seen as remote and emotionally unavailable by their partners.
- don't ask for help when they're distressed.
- feel overwhelmed when their partner wants too much from them and manage this by distancing.

Waves are people with an anxious attachment style; they're people who usually grew up with inconsistent caregivers and could never really know whether their support system would be around or available on any given day. Waves become adults who:

- splash around looking for a landing place in the form of a relationship they can cling to.
- can be seen as "overly expressive" about needing a lot of closeness, usually wanting more than another person can provide for them.
- are pursuers in the relationship, always noticing if their partner is pulling away or not responding and then going after their partner for connection.

Anchors are people with a secure attachment style. They had consistent, loving, and attentive caregivers growing up. Anchors:

- are both secure in themselves and available for intimacy.
- collaborate well with others, are dependable, don't feel intruded upon when pursued, and don't feel abandoned when on their own.
- can both calm themselves and be comforted by others.

However, in a later article about diagnostic categories Tatkin noted:

Most of us do not neatly fit into categories or classifications. In *Wired for Love* terms, think of yourself as being "anchor-ish," or "island-ish," or "wave-ish." And this "ish-ness" can be understood to be state-related (temporary) rather than trait-related (permanent), such as, "Last night I behaved in a wave-ish manner," or "You can be island-ish sometimes," or "I tend to be more anchor-ish in this relationship than ever before."

I hope this clears up the question of "what am I," to which I say we are all mostly "ishy."

The Two-Step

In their adult relationships, Islands (those who are "island-ish") avoid connection, while Waves (those who are "wave-ish") pursue it. Together, they do a predictable dance often called the Two-Step, in which Waves constantly move closer to their partner in a bid to avoid abandonment, which prompts the Islands to instinctively pull away to avoid feeling engulfed. This distancing behavior makes Waves feel even more alone, and the beat goes on. When the partners lack awareness, the steps of this dance become increasingly dramatic over time, and the reactions become more painful.

However, there is good news: our original attachment style is not our destiny. With awareness and committed skill building, both people can become Anchors, more securely attached to each other and more secure in themselves. The chapter on conflict, Chapter 15, will show you why this is called a "loop" and how to break free of the Two-Step.

EXERCISE: Your Attachment Style

You can find many quizzes online to help you determine your style, but many people know on an intuitive level which one they are. Answer the questions below.

1. Which of the three attachment styles best describes you? What qualities of that specific style feel most familiar?

2. When you were growing up and felt sad, scared, or angry, did you typically single out one parent as a source of comfort? How did that parent respond?

3. Do you think it's acceptable to have needs and be vulnerable with others? In what ways do you offer care and in what ways are you cared for? Are they done with equal ease and safety?

4. Can you describe ways the Two-Step has played out in your own important relationships? Is there an imbalance between one person's need to be close and the other's need to be more self-sufficient?

5. What skills could you develop to help you become an Anchor?

Reflections

Write down five things you have learned from this section on attachment styles:

1.

2.

3.

4.

5.

JOINT EXERCISE: Sharing Family Stories

Once you and your partner have completed the exercises in Chapters 5 and 6, find a time when you won't be disturbed or preoccupied. Agree on an amount of time you'll spend on this exercise, and try to stick to it.

Sit facing each other and tell your family story to each other, starting from the earliest generation to your parents. If you're the listener, be sure to hear and respond without judging, critiquing, or analyzing. Notice similarities and differences in the stories of your families — the themes and the coping strategies for the common struggles of life.

There are many ways to share your family history:

- Read it to your partner, tell it more informally, or draw it.
- As a playful stretch, share your genograms and family stories with each other as though they're great novels. You are the main character. Who were the difficult characters, and how did you grow as a result of the challenges you faced? Who were the helpers, the ones who encouraged, believed in, and supported you? What were the most significant conflicts and the attempts to resolve them?
- Tell your story as a myth or fairy tale. For example, it could begin, "Once upon a time, a child was born in a city by the sea." Tell the story as though you were not the main character, but rather the narrator of a human story of love and trouble, strife and victory, despair and hope. Sometimes this helps you distance from your usual way of telling the story and see it in a new light.

How Our Past Plays Out Today:
The Imago Vision of Relationships

The Latin word *imago* means "image." A model of couples therapy developed in 1980 by Dr. Harville Hendrix and Dr. Helen LaKelly Hunt, Imago relationship therapy is built around the concept that your feelings and experiences from childhood reappear again throughout your adult relationships. For example, if you were constantly neglected, shamed, or criticized by your parents as a child, you'll likely often feel those responses coming from your partner as an adult.

But as you work to uncover these childhood wounds, you can begin to recognize when you're being triggered by those wounds rather than by what's actually happening in your relationship. And importantly, your partner can learn to be aware of these trigger points, be more empathetic toward you, and try to avoid behaviors that poke unnecessarily at your tender spots. And you, of course, will learn how to do the same for your partner.

EXERCISE: Understanding Your Imago Match

This exercise is borrowed from Dr. Hendrix and Dr. Hunt's Imago work with their permission.

Fill out the divided circle below. In the left side of the circle (A), list all the positive character traits of your mother, father, significant siblings, and any other people who influenced you strongly when you were young. Put the positive traits of all these people together (don't group them according to individuals). Describe the traits with simple adjectives or phrases like *kind, warm, intelligent, religious, patient, creative, always there, enthusiastic, reliable*, and so on.

In the right side of the circle (B), list all the negative character traits of these people. This might include terms like *abandoned, ambivalent, angry, odd, tense, violent, servile, tightwad*, and so on. Remember, often a weakness is a strength overdone. Understanding how this trait affected you is not as important as identifying the trait.

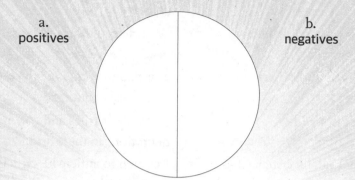

a.
positives

b.
negatives

In the circle, underline the three best traits. Circle the three worst traits. Next, complete the following prompts:

c. The thing I didn't get — the one thing I wanted most as a child — was:

d. The negative feeling or thought that I had over and over as a child was:

e. List the reoccurring frustrations you had as a child, followed by the ways you responded:

Examples:

Frustration	Response
Mother was depressed	Tried to comfort her and not upset her
No attention from my older brother	Was a pest — teased him

Felt inferior to older siblings	Resigned myself to being inferior, compared myself to others, didn't compete directly
Mother was overprotective	Would keep things to myself, became secretive
Father was authoritarian	Learned to comply with resentment, resent authority
Chaotic homelife	Looked for rules and concrete definitions in the world
Felt continually criticized as a child	Learned to anticipate criticism (even when it wasn't there) and quickly make it the other person's fault

Frustration	Response

EXERCISE: Your Unfinished Business

Use your answers to the previous Imago workup to fill in the following.

1. I have spent my life searching for a person who has these traits (insert answers to a):

2. When I am with such a person, I am troubled by these traits (insert answers to b):

3. I wish that this person would give me (insert answers to c):

4. When my needs are not met, I feel (insert answers to d):

5. As a result I often respond in this way (insert answers to e):

Sharing

Sit face-to-face with your partner and take turns reading your last page out loud. Is there anything familiar here? Does your "unfinished business" reflect what goes on in your current relationship? Consciously avoid making judgments or criticisms about your partner's responses in the exercise. In these times of sharing, you are not just exchanging information; you are learning how to become safe for one another. Acceptance and empathy are the tools of safety, and these exercises are where you can practice those skills. What news did you discover from this?

EXERCISE: Reimaging Your Partner

Find a photo of your partner as a little kid, a photo that expresses what you love most about your partner. Is your partner funny, adventurous, brave, curious? Carry it around in your wallet, save it on your cell phone, or put it on your fridge — somewhere you can see it every day. Use your understanding as an anchor to hold on to your empathy and understanding, tools that can lessen your own reactivity to your partner, which comes from your own childhood story. Ask your partner to find a photo of you and engage in the same process.

Because a lot of the patterns are in our unconscious mind, the goal of Imago relationship therapy is to align the unconscious with the conscious through practices that help us understand those patterns and create empathy for both our partner and ourselves. Through exercises to help gain insights, such as "Your Unfinished Business" and "Reimaging Your Partner," which you have done in this chapter, the power struggle can become a doorway to a more wholehearted love.

Who Am I Now?

The Enneagram

The purpose of the Enneagram is not to put you into a box, but to help you identify the limitations of a box you may already be in, and to give you guidance on how you may break free and develop beyond it.

— DALE RHODES, Director of Enneagram Portland

We have been exploring the impact of our family history and the stories we tell about ourselves — stories that feel like "truths" rather than old beliefs that aren't necessarily accurate. Once we have a good handle on how our past affects us, we can start to understand ourselves through the lens of our personality as we continue to address those big questions: Who am I? Why do I do what I do? Why am I so different from others? In other ways, why am I so similar to others?

The Enneagram

Personality systems are helpful tools in understanding the legitimate differences between us. Assessments like the Myers-Briggs Trait Inventory and the

DISC Assessment are often used at couples retreats. They provide ways for partners to see how each individual responds differently (or similarly) to life, conflict, problem-solving, and issues of motivation.

For me, the most beneficial of these personality systems is called the Enneagram. I've been using it in my Love Skills classes for many years. Long after taking this class, many couples and individuals have reported back to me that the Enneagram has been an enormously helpful tool in helping them see each other's differences as valid and valuable. They learned an essential lesson: we are not wrong for being different from our partner — and our partner is not wrong for differing from us.

Based on ancient wisdom and spiritual and philosophical traditions from Christianity, Islam, Judaism, secular thinkers, and Greek philosophy, the Enneagram is a geometric figure — a nine-pointed star within a circle — that maps out an in-depth description of nine types of personalities. (The Greek word *ennea* means "nine," and *gram* means "a written symbol.") Some researchers believe they've identified variations of the Enneagram in texts from four thousand years ago. Since then, extensive research and modern science have converged to demonstrate the validity and accuracy of Enneagram tests as a tool for understanding human behavior.

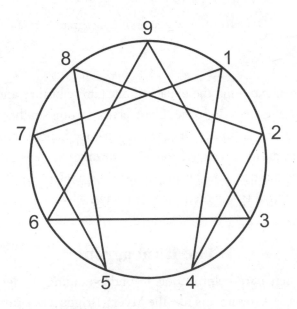

The system describes nine distinct patterns of thinking, feeling, and sensing, named by a simple numeral from One to Nine. The word *pattern* is used there very intentionally — each of the personality types is not a single, standalone character strategy, but rather a map of several. All nine types are interrelated, and we have elements of all of them within us. Although one of those types emerges as our dominant everyday coping strategy, we tend to shift into one of the other strategies in times of stress and yet another one in times of healthy growth and relaxation. For example, someone who is a Two uses the Two strategy in times of normalcy, becomes an Eight in times of stress, and becomes Four in times of relaxation. Your personal Enneagram type is defined by this three-point pattern.

On some level, we think everyone else is like us, subconsciously assuming that we all look at the world through the same lens. We're shocked when we find ourselves in a relationship with someone we respect and care about — a romantic partner, a friend, a family member — who doesn't see everything the way we do. Many of the disagreements within a relationship stem from a core underlying question, one we may not be consciously aware of: Why aren't you me?

Though we may consciously realize the question is absurd, it fuels our frustration with others surprisingly often. Why wouldn't you want a surprise party with 150 people when I would love it if you did that for me? Why wouldn't you want to plan the next adventure while we are still on this one, like I do?

Wholeheartedness means not just finding wholeness in ourselves but also embracing it in others. It requires us to recognize that simple but difficult truth: you are not me.

Accepting our partner's otherness not only offsets our hurt and anger in the face of our inevitable differences, but it also nourishes the foundations of our important relationships. We all ache to be seen and validated for who we are. We usually feel the other person "really gets us" in the beginning stage of a relationship. This exploration will help you "get" one another again in a new and deeper way. Exploring your Enneagram types will help you to understand each other's worldview, the places where you get stuck, and the gifts you bring to one another and to the larger world. Through this process, you will likely take your differences less personally, develop more tolerance and compassion for each other's differences, and laugh at yourselves more easily.

EXERCISE: Your Enneagram Type

Your Enneagram type can be difficult to determine, because many of the types share similarities. A handful of online and book versions of the test offer the highest-quality testing methods and thus the most accurate results. I recommend seeking these out to explore which Enneagram type fits you best. (Look in the Resources section at the end of this book for suggestions.) Take one or even a few, and have your partner take the tests as well, even if he or she is not working through this book with you. (Having knowledge of each other's types is invaluable.) Then return here and fill in the information below to begin learning how this profound system works.

1. The Enneagram test shows me as a _____ type.
2. I took more than one test, and some also show me to be a _____ type.
3. Here's what seems true about that description of me:

4. Here's what doesn't seem true about that description of me:

5. According to the Enneagram test, my partner is a _____ type.
6. Some tests also show my partner to be a _____ type.
7. Here's what seems true about that description of my partner:

8. Here's what doesn't seem true about that description of my partner:

9. Other observations I have made so far include:

Using Knowledge from the Enneagram

Knowing our type doesn't justify excusing our negative behaviors by saying, "Well, I'm a Three! That's just how I am!" The Enneagram does not describe our permanent attributes, but rather our habitual tendencies as well as our potential for growth. The purpose of the Enneagram is not to create a limiting box for ourselves or our partner, but rather to identify our unconscious patterns and learn how to break free. In other words, the whole point of the Enneagram is for you to be able to identify and *grow out of* unhelpful behaviors and to fully appreciate the strengths and possibilities your type offers you.

Below are brief descriptions of each Enneagram type, how our dominant patterns affect our relationships, and practical strategies for avoiding unhelpful patterns for both partners. If you're curious about the strengths and challenges that specific pairs of types experience, I recommend two books: *Are You My Type, Am I Yours? Relationships Made Easy Through the Enneagram*, by Renee Baron and Elizabeth Wagele, and *Sex and the Enneagram: A Guide to Passionate Relationships for the 9 Personality Types*, by Ann Gadd. (In Chapter 14, which is all about sex, we'll come back to the Enneagram and look at how our personality types can affect our sex lives as well.)

Type One: The Idealist

Also called the Reformer or the Perfectionist. Ones are highly ethical, responsible, trustworthy, conscientious, and dedicated to improving themselves, others, and the world. At their best, they are inspirational moral heroes with the capacity to imagine and work toward their ideals.

However, Ones can also be judgmental, inflexible, and controlling — toward themselves, others, and situations that fall short of their exacting standards. They are often self-critical and sensitive to criticism and want to be seen as a "good person," but their "perfectionistic" standard is often out of reach.

Tips for you in your relationship: As a One, it's important to recognize that you can't control other people's perspectives or behaviors. Your partner's differing point of view may be as valid as your own. Instead, focus on enjoying the present moment with your partner. Notice what's going well. Develop curiosity and compassion for your partner's objections rather than instantly responding defensively. The more you can appreciate yourself and accept life's imperfections, the more easily you can roll with the fallibility of others.

Tips for partners: Those who are in a relationship with a One should do what they can to help their partner embrace imperfections as a natural part of being human. Encourage Ones to go easy on themselves and reinforce their goodness. Be aware of their sensitivity to criticism and be careful to express feedback as complaint about a specific behavior rather than judgment about their core selves. Make them laugh. Beneath a serious and perfectionistic exterior lies someone who, when they allow themselves to let go, is full of humor and love of life.

Type Two: The Giver

Also called the Helper. Twos are relationship-oriented and other-oriented. They're the empathetic, supportive, nurturing types who are always available to lend a helping hand and express their affection. At their best, they are altruistic and unconditional in their loving.

However, Twos' drive to be seen as generous and caring stems from a belief that their value depends on what they give. As such, Twos can become knee-jerk people pleasers and are sometimes intrusive in their insistence on helping. They often forget to take care of themselves or to acknowledge their own needs.

Tips for you in your relationship: Remember to take care of yourself while taking care of your partner. Don't let your own needs fall by the wayside, because people who aren't nourishing themselves will eventually break down under stress. Ask your partner what he or she really needs and what behaviors constitute "going overboard" — for both you and your partner. Finally, don't deny your partner the gift of looking after you. Work on increasing your ability to experience the joy of receiving as well as giving.

Tips for partners: If you're in a relationship with a Two, be attentive to your partner's needs. Twos will often ignore their own well-being in order to nurture you. Gently remind them that you can take care of yourself and encourage them to do the same for themselves. Encourage them to say "no" more often, and celebrate them when they do. Always express gratitude for their generosity, care, and support, while reminding them that you also care deeply about who they are and what *they* need.

Type Three: The Performer

Also called the Achiever. Threes are all about personal success and accomplishments. They're goal-oriented, full of energy to "do," and usually competent in whatever activities they pursue. They are optimistic, and their favorite word is "done" (with a check mark). At their best, they are authentic and inspirational, infusing their "doing" with heart.

However, Threes' focus on status and external validation stems from a core belief that their value is based on being a successful and efficient "doer." This means Threes can be workaholics, inattentive to their own and others' emotions, and overly adaptive to others' expectations. They can also be overly competitive and vain.

Tips for you in your relationship: Make sure you're not ignoring your partner's needs because you're so bent on achieving your own goals. Additionally, a relationship is not a conquest, nor is it about performing or being the "best" partner ever. Don't push problems under the carpet in order to look good. Spend some time fostering your connection with your own emotions and focus on creating an authentic connection with your partner. You don't need to impress your partner; you just need to be real. Your real work is understanding your strengths as a "human being," not a "human doing."

Tips for partners: If you're in a relationship with a Three, encourage your partner to be attentive to his or her emotions and to feel free to express them to you. Show Threes that you care about who they are, not just what they've accomplished or how superbusy they are. Because Threes tend to be very concerned about their careers and achievements, remind them to slow down and experience the value in having fun without needing to complete a task or attain a goal. At the same time let them know you are proud of them and their accomplishments.

Type Four: The Romantic

Also called the Individualist. Fours are extremely expressive, introspective, and creative people who feel things deeply. They seek meaning and depth in a relationship. At their best, they have tremendous resilience and can often turn their struggles into truly inspirational art, music, and other soulful expressions that touch others deeply.

Fours experience a sense of value by being unique, but they can also be dramatic and prone to melancholy. They're preoccupied by a sense of longing, and their attention often goes to what's missing in their lives, such as lost opportunities or someone else's relationship that seems better than their own. Because they tend to focus on what they don't have, they often find themselves disappointed and envious of others.

Tips for you in your relationship: You're likely to be frequently caught up in your feelings. This is not necessarily a bad thing, so long as you regularly step back and observe what is going well in your life in addition to what may be lacking. Identify whether you are telling yourself a familiar, sad story that's outdated. You're probably great at sharing your emotional state with your partner, but make time to ask about your partner's own. Your partner may not be as in touch with or as interested in feelings as you are, but ask anyway. In your quest for the extraordinary, remember that all relationships go through "ordinary" periods. It doesn't mean something between you has gone wrong.

Tips for partners: Fours are typically impassioned about their feelings, so make sure to acknowledge and honor them. Show Fours that you really "get" them by not minimizing their longing for what is missing — but don't take it personally. You can better appreciate their sensitivity, creativity, and emotional honesty when you know how to step back a little. Gratitude practices may serve you both well.

Type Five: The Observer

Also called the Investigator. Fives are cerebral, curious, and independent. They tend to stand back and observe, choosing to remain private and focused on accumulating knowledge. They love information and are often experts on many topics, enjoying their discoveries of uncharted territories. At their best, they are visionary pioneers that project competence, clarity, calmness, and deep wisdom.

When stressed and vulnerable, they may revert to feeling a basic fear of being helpless and overwhelmed. This is why Fives want to understand everything and often isolate themselves from people. Fives do not easily get in touch with or express their thoughts and feelings, but they most definitely have them.

Tips for you in your relationship: Don't be afraid of emotionally engaging with your partner: your discomfort or reluctance to be open doesn't necessarily mean that it's unsafe to do so. Push yourself to share more personal experiences and feelings, and learn to pick up more emotional cues about what's going on with your partner.

Tips for partners: Recognize that Fives need space, so don't take it personally. Allow them their alone time and accept when they choose not to offer their views or needs. At the same time, find small ways to show them that their feelings matter to you and that it's helpful for *both* of you to be in the know when it comes to matters of the heart. Pay attention to their gestures of caring. Remember that their feelings run as deep as your own.

Type Six: The Loyal Skeptic

Also called the Loyalist. Sixes show deep commitment to their partner, friends, and beliefs. They are warm, playful, and reliable, with great humor. They are the bravest of the brave; honest and reliable, they expect no less of others.

Sixes are also cautious. Their attention tends to go to perceived threats and what might go wrong. This can create suspicion, inflexibility, and an ambivalence toward authority. On the one hand, they want to believe in an authority to be safe; on the other hand, they will question and doubt it. They prepare for the worst in an attempt to gain a sense of safety and security.

Tips for you in your relationship: Remember that everyone experiences insecurities, even though you may feel them more than others. When you become aware of your suspicions about your partner's attention, ask yourself if it is your default distrust rather than actual evidence that is causing the doubts. Find as many ways as you can to feel compassion for your doubts and worries. Develop your own sense of empowerment, and trust your full range of feelings. There is no way to be safe! The authority (i.e., the power) has to come from within!

Tips for partners: If you're in a relationship with a Six, be consistent and deserving of your partner's trust. Follow through on promises, because breaking them will set Sixes off on a dark path. Be aware that they tend to be uncertain and suspicious, so disclose your actions and feelings amply, perhaps more than you naturally would. Don't be alarmed by their doubts; instead, learn to understand where they're coming from, and don't necessarily take them personally. Appreciate your partner's loyalty and reliability.

Type Seven: The Epicure

Also called the Enthusiast. Sevens are playful, energetic, and productive. At their best, they are exciting visionaries with ideas that can bring joy and adventure to the people around them.

Sevens believe life has endless possibilities — but the people around them constantly limit their potential. In reaction, Sevens can become pleasure gluttons, slurping up exhilarating experiences and exhausting both themselves and those who are trying to keep up with them. They also feel a lot of anxiety, and their pleasure seeking is often an attempt to avoid feeling it. Their chase to find the next thing can also be unfocused and impulsive and then cause them to be depleted by their nonstop activity.

Tips for you in your relationship: Restlessness is normal for you, so don't assume that your longing for something new is evidence of problems with your partner. What are some things you can do to reignite some excitement in your relationship? Remember too that all your new ideas and planning may be anxiety-producing for your partner. Reassure your partner it's your creativity at work and that you don't expect all of your ideas to come to fruition.

Tips for partners: Don't be surprised by your partner's tendency to plan the next great adventure before the two of you have finished the one you're currently experiencing! Greet your partner's never-ending ideas with interest and patience, without feeling you need to say "yes" to every plan. Also remember that Sevens' abundant optimism can hide their vulnerability and their fear of slowing down and feeling their feelings. Give them a lot of space and comfort to express their fears.

Type Eight: The Protector

Also called the Challenger. Eights are powerful and intense personalities who tend toward leading and protecting others. They are confident and strong and often use their strengths to address issues of social justice and to protect the vulnerable. At their best, they are magnanimous, courageous, and heroic.

However, these same strengths can be used to control, intimidate, and create confrontations. They believe the world is unjust and thus seek power, sometimes to an unhealthy degree. If they don't vigilantly control and protect, they fear being harmed or controlled by others. They often deny their own limitations and can take on risky situations because they appear to be (and sometimes think they are) fearless.

Tips for you in your relationship: Remember, there's power in vulnerability and tenderness. It takes strength to reveal your true emotions and to let others see this part of you. Practice paying attention to the impact of your strong personality and learn how to use this power wisely. Practice acknowledging (and trusting) when your partner knows what's best for him or her without your input or actions. Be careful of a tendency to take on challenges that may be frightening to others, and practice letting others take charge sometimes.

Tips for partners: Eights can be wonderfully protective partners who make you feel secure. But don't let their strength of personality keep you silent or submissive; stand up for yourself and stay firm about your point of view. If they're being too overbearing or confrontational, make sure they know how their words and actions are affecting you. Remain calm and use "I" statements, so they don't feel attacked. You don't need to tell them to constrain themselves (that can be a uniquely stressful experience for Eights), but do encourage them to embrace softness. If they are trying to control your behavior, you can clearly ask them to stop. Don't forget that under their bravado is a lot of vulnerability. Give them a safe place to express it.

Type Nine: The Mediator

Also called the Peacemaker. Nines care deeply about avoiding conflict and keeping the peace. When they are at their best, their ability to embrace many points of view can lead them into situations where they can help to heal challenging conflicts.

Although Nines tend to be easygoing, adaptable, and stable, at times they veer into being overly complacent, indecisive, or even stubborn, which can be a reaction to bending over backward to keep the peace. Nines can often preoccupy themselves with small, inessential comforts rather than addressing troubling issues head-on, and they tend to say "yes" when they mean "no." At core, they fear not being loved or valued, so they avoid any perceived trouble by dodging conflict.

Tips for you in your relationship: Remember that you don't need to go along with everything your partner does or wants just to keep the peace. If you disagree or feel upset by your partner's words or actions, speak up. By constantly sweeping everything under the carpet, you're only pushing the problems off to a later date, allowing tensions to pile up and eventually explode into something that may seriously damage your relationship. Acknowledging and valuing your own thoughts and feelings and addressing problems directly are what keep the peace in the long run.

Tips for partners: Make a habit of directly inquiring about Nines' needs and desires, since they may not regularly express them. Nines infrequently acknowledge their anger directly, so if you sense stubbornness or passive aggression, ask about it up front. Give them space to air their frustrations. Appreciate their capacity to see the big picture and to hold many points of view.

EXERCISE: The Enneagram Worksheet

The Enneagram is a tool that awakens our compassion for people just as they are, not the people we wish they would become so our lives would become easier.

— Ian Morgan Cron, *The Road Back to You:*
An Enneagram Journey to Self-Discovery

Here are some questions to help you look at yourself and your relationship through the Enneagram lens. If you're working as a couple, complete this exercise individually first; then come together to share your answers. Remember, this worksheet is about respecting all perspectives as being true. Practice listening without criticizing, judging, or taking another point of view personally.

1. When I think of my Enneagram type, something that makes sense to me in a new way is:

2. The potential strengths I bring to my relationships include:

3. When I'm stressed, some of the ways I'm difficult to deal with are:

4. When I think of my partner's Enneagram type, something that makes sense to me about my partner is:

5. One of the strengths of my partner's type that I appreciate is:

6. One of the challenges of my partner's type for me is:

7. When I think about when we first met, one of our differences that attracted me to my partner was:

8. One of the ways our types conflict is:

9. One way we can become a better team is:

We have expectations and make assumptions in our relationships, thinking our partner sees the world the way we do. Understanding the differences between our type and our partner's type reduces those troubling assumptions and offers insight, compassion, and curiosity about each of us.

No combination is either blessed or doomed any more than the Enneagram is your destiny. If two people are healthy, then any combination will have gifts and challenges. Two self-aware people are the best types of people to be together, so congratulate yourself for doing this work. In the next chapter, we're going to continue the process of developing deeper self-knowledge — and we're also going to add to it the skill of revealing our true selves to other people.

Discoveries
and Disclosure

8

When people say, "If love takes work, something must be wrong," I want to climb the walls! Of course love takes work. Put two people, even two really compatible people, under the same roof, add a couple of jobs, kids, and some in-laws, and the fairy tale just got a whole lot trickier. Happily ever after means searching — again and again — for the beauty amid the mess.

— Dr. Alexandra Solomon, psychologist and writer

Shortly after I met my husband, now forty-five years ago, we were at a party. I remember little about that party except for one experience. Tim and I began a casual conversation about dogs, and he asked me to tell him about the dogs I'd loved. What a great question! I started telling him about the whole pack — from Skipper to Schmoo — when I was struck by something extraordinary. This man was *really* listening to me.

Although I don't remember what he was wearing or where we were sitting, I do remember that his head was slightly tilted and he was leaning forward, intently, as though there was no one else in the room. The more he listened, the more I talked — and the more vulnerable I became. Our conversation moved past the names and breeds of each dog to how important each of them was to me.

Finally, I turned the tables on Tim and asked the same question. He answered deeply, thoughtfully, and with a lot of feeling. I found myself listening as intently to him as he had to me, but I also began to feel very uncomfortable. Although we had come to the party with other people, the intimacy between us was palpable. After a few minutes we parted and returned to the partners we had arrived with, but *something* had clearly happened between us that evening.

It would be another ten years before that "something" turned into a relationship and, eventually, a marriage. But the seeds for the intimate connection had been sown that night. Each time we met after that, we would immediately fall into a deep conversation, each of us asking and telling, as though we each found the other to be the most fascinating person we'd ever met.

In 2015, the *New York Times* published an article entitled "To Fall in Love with Anyone, Do This." In it Mandy Len Catron described a 1997 lab experiment in which a group of strangers were randomly paired off and told to ask each other a series of thirty-six personal questions. After answering the questions, they were asked to look into each other's eyes for four uninterrupted minutes. According to the article, one of those couples married six months later. The *Times* writer tried the experiment herself with someone she'd just met, and they ended up dating for two years. The story instantly went viral as a formula for falling in love.

Although I don't believe in magic formulas when it comes to the human heart, I think Dr. Arthur Aron, the psychologist behind that widely publicized experiment, did capture at least two essential ingredients for fostering love: self-disclosure and deep listening. In the paper that described his study, Dr. Aron wrote, "One key pattern associated with the development of a close relationship among peers is sustained, escalating, reciprocal, personal self-disclosure."

When we first fall for someone, we spend a lot of time *telling* and *listening*. Whether it has to do with our darkest memories, how we feel about sex, or our enduring love for canine companions, we're eager to *tell* and *listen*, which could explain why I felt a little uncomfortable during that first conversation with my now husband. As we gain insight into each other's inner workings and begin to trust one another, that vulnerability creates a sense of intimacy, which is one of the key building blocks of love.

Unfortunately, for many couples, conversations become more of a workaday habit than an attempt to genuinely connect with one another. After being together for a while, we begin to think we fully know who the other person is. We tell ourselves we've heard this or that story umpteen times, and we inwardly turn off. We stop listening and sharing what really matters to us.

This chapter's three topics — personal values, self-contemplation, and eye gazing — will help you get back to that place of discovering each other, all the while continuing to discover yourself. The first two topics and their accompanying exercises are designed to encourage some fresh revelations about yourself, allowing you to further explore the core question "Who am I?" The third and final section, which is specifically for couples, introduces you to the most delicious, shockingly connective element of Dr. Aron's famous intimacy experiment: eye gazing.

As you move through the solo activities, embrace a reflective state of mind and allow yourself to feel uncomfortable at times. When it's time to share, keep the following tips in mind.

For the Speaker

1. Speak slowly and use bite-size sentences. You may feel compelled to ramble, but try to stay as concise as possible to help your partner follow your train of thought.
2. Stay connected with your listener, maintain eye contact, and convey your appreciation for your listener's interest in you.

For the Listener

1. Remember that the intimacy-building powers of self-disclosure only work when, as the listener, you are active, responsive, and engaged in the conversation.

2. Imagine that you've never met the speaker before and see if you can find yourself learning something you didn't know about the person.

3. This part of the exercise is about your partner, not you. Quiet your mind and place your entire focus on your partner. Maintain eye contact, and make sure your partner knows that he or she is worth taking the time to listen to fully and without distractions.

4. Never, never interrupt your partner. To facilitate this, you may want to put a time limit on each person's sharing — say, fifteen or twenty minutes.

Remember, going deeper within yourself and sharing your experience with your partner can create genuine closeness, no matter how long you have been together. Be humble, curious, and open.

Personal Values

Like many of you, I was taught values by my family, culture, and education. These values were presented as beliefs that all "good people" held, and they were sometimes explained using confusing clichés. Each Friday in my fourth-grade classroom, the bushy-eyebrowed priest Father Jenner would give us a "little talk," warning us of a wide range of possible sins. For example, we were not to think "bad thoughts," nor should we lie or be impolite to our teacher. Each time he wrapped up his fifteen-minute lecturette, he would start to leave, pause, look around the room at each of us, and then say darkly, "If the shoe fits, wear it." I worried that if I didn't confess to these sins, whether or not I had committed them, I would be denying that the shoe fit and not telling the truth. Another cliché comes to mind as I write this: "catch-22."

My parents created rules and rewards to reinforce their values, but we never had thoughtful discussions about how any *one* value can mean something different to different people. As I grew older, I discovered my relationship with my values was complicated and subject to change. I also began to meet people who claimed to have values similar to mine but whose behavior was the exact opposite of mine.

When I was seventeen, my cousin asked me to be the maid of honor at her Episcopalian wedding. I was thrilled — until I talked with my Catholic parish priest about it. In no uncertain terms, he told me it was "not acceptable" for me to walk through the doors of any church that wasn't a Catholic one, even for a family ceremony. "It would be a serious sin," he said. When he told me this, a lump formed in my throat, my heart began to pound, and I felt nauseated.

I spent the rest of the day walking the streets of San Francisco alone, rushing past the graffiti-painted North Beach coffeehouses, smelling the fresh catches on the boats coming into Fisherman's Wharf, and glancing through the windows of stores selling exotic spices, squawking chickens, and glittery gifts in Chinatown. After several hours of turmoil, I felt my own truth emerging: I would disobey the priest. My love for and loyalty to my cousin was what mattered most to me. Once I made that decision, my distress melted. A sense of peace settled into my body. I had been through the experience of a "values collision" and chosen the value that was truest for me.

Alongside the values we're taught in childhood, we hold personal values that are part of our unique nature. When two sets of values conflict, as they had for me, we may have to set aside what we were taught to discover what is true in our hearts. In fact, one of the most stressful things about becoming an adult can be realizing we hold ethical standards that are different from those of our family. Moreover, these personal values can change over time. As we embark on a new career, for example, we might value financial or job success over finding a romantic relationship or having a family. But as we get older, we may reverse those priorities. Throughout our lives, we're always developing and changing.

To make things even more complicated, values aren't one-dimensional ideals. Words like *loyalty*, *integrity*, and *fairness* can describe multiple ways of feeling and acting. Here are two examples.

Zac and Bella both valued animals and loved to care for them. They decided to raise chickens for their eggs and for the pleasure of getting to know these interesting creatures. For their safety, Bella wanted a solid cage to lock them in at night. Zac, however, felt the chickens should be free to sleep in the tall apple tree in their backyard, and he refused to lock them up — even after some of the chickens were killed by raccoons. Each partner believed the other was interfering with the animals' essential well-being.

Grace and Joseph agreed that caring for children and preparing them for life was a vital shared value. But they never talked about what each partner *meant* by this. When they had kids together, they found that for Grace "caring and preparing" meant lots of music lessons, art classes, and dance recitals. Joseph insisted that kids should be allowed to find their own fun and interests in order to develop creativity and independence.

Every decision we make, including who we date and how we behave in a relationship, is influenced by our personal values. The better we understand our most important ethical beliefs, moral codes, and ideals, the better able we'll be to choose a compatible life partner.

Do you believe in family loyalty? Do you believe in generosity? Does this mean that if one of you has a disabled family member, you will help support them, both financially and in everyday practical ways? What about a family member who can't hold a job? Would it be okay for that person to live with you for a time?

Most partners will say they value their intimate relationship — and they mean it. But for one person, valuing the relationship might mean learning all they can about how to make relationships enriching. For the other, it may mean a lot of sex, praise, and gifts.

Begin by exploring your own values in the following exercises.

EXERCISE: Exploring Your Values

If you're working with a partner, complete the following exercise independently first. Afterward, follow the instructions below to help share your answers with one another and discuss how your common values — and your differing ones — play out in your lives.

Here is a list of values people may *think* they share, but often define differently:

Achievement	Fame	Optimism
Adventurousness	Friendship	Peace
Authenticity	Happiness	Play
Authority	Hard work	Pleasure
Autonomy	Helping others	Popularity
Balance	Honesty	Purpose
Beauty	Hope	Recognition
Boldness	Humor	Religion
Challenge	Influence	Resilience
Cheerfulness	Inner harmony	Respect
Community	Integrity	Responsibility
Compassion	Joyfulness	Security
Creativity	Kindness	Self-respect
Curiosity	Leadership	Spontaneity
Determination	Learning	Trustworthiness
Environmentalism	Love	Truth
Exploration	Loyalty	Wealth
Fairness	Making a difference	Wholehcartedness
Faith	Openness	Wisdom

From the list above (and feel free to add others), circle the five values that are most important to you. Write them in the left-hand column on the next page. For each value, list next to it two very different ways that people who share that value might behave, as shown in the three examples below.

Most Important Values	Possible Behavior of Someone Who Shares This Value	An Alternate Possible Behavior of Someone Who Shares This Value
Teaching your kids to love music	Requiring that they take music lessons	Taking them to concerts often

Maintaining good health	Attention to diet and exercise	Regular doctor visits and lots of supplements
Making a difference in the world	Recycling carefully and biking when you can instead of driving	Joining civic groups or starting a non-profit for a cause you believe in
1.		
2.		
3.		
4.		
5.		

Reflections

1. Can you remember a time when the values you were *taught* to believe in conflicted with one of your personal values? Which values conflicted?

2. Which of your top five values did you learn during childhood and which did you develop on your own?

3. Rank the five values in order, starting with the one you live by most faithfully and ending with the one that is most challenging to live by:

Sharing

Come together as a couple to compare your answers. Notice where you overlap and where you differ. Be careful not to judge your partner or try to show how your values are the "right" ones. Take time to describe what each value means to each of you. Which words have the same meaning for you both, and which do you see differently?

Below are a few sentence stems to help you get started with the sharing process. Take turns sharing, and remember, the listener's job is to listen to the other person without judging, redirecting, challenging, or interrupting.

- Reflecting on my values showed me that...
- Something that surprised me about my values was...
- My five key values come from...[List each one along with where you learned it]
- The values I feel I am true to are...
- To be more aligned with what I believe, I need to work on...
- Three ways I can begin to do this are...

After you each share what you discovered, continue discussing in the following ways:

1. Name a shared value that you experience in different ways. For example, you might each value self-care, but one understands this as making time for vigorous exercise each day and eating what one

wishes, while the other may see self-care as eating a gluten-free, vegan diet.

2. Which differing values do you hold that could (or do) cause conflict in your relationship? How can you use the values you have in common to relieve some of the stress caused by the values that differ? For example, one of you may value stability and predictability, while the other values adventure and change. One example of how to relieve the stress of that difference is to build times of adventure into your relationship in ways that don't threaten the stability of it.

3. Because each of us grew up in a unique family system, every relationship is a joining of two different cultures. When we come together, we create a new culture. How can the values you share help you create and strengthen your common culture? For example, if you each value service to the larger community, consider how you might work together to make the world a better place.

Marco and Peter were partners who thought they held similar values until they moved in together. Marco was from a large strong Italian family where people came to visit without notice, engaged in "friendly" yelling at the dinner table about every topic under the sun, and hugged as readily as they fought. Peter came from a German family that was formal and scrupulously polite; his parents never yelled, visitors came by formal invitation only, and any public argument was seen as uncivilized. The two almost split up over these different definitions of family.

Peter and Marco valued their relationship enough to find ways to manage the culture clash. They acknowledged they cared deeply about the families they came from, but were willing to change some of the ways they interacted with them. Marco asked his family to call first if they wanted to stop by, while Peter accepted Marco's discomfort at spending too much time with Peter's "fairly stiff" parents (as Marco called them) and began to visit them more often on his own. We begin where we're similar and demonstrate flexibility in bridging the places where we're different.

JOINT EXERCISE: Culture Clashes and Overlaps

Thinking about your relationship, do you have any "culture clashes" similar to those of Peter and Marco? Using the following model, look at where your values are different and where they overlap.

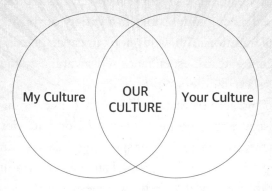

My Culture · OUR CULTURE · Your Culture

On a separate sheet of paper, make a list of traits, activities, or values that are yours, your "culture"; for example, you might value personal freedom, minimal spending, time for travel, running as exercise, and time spent alone. Have your partner do the same; for example, your partner might value financial security, designer clothes and the latest electronics, socializing, and biking as exercise.

Then together make a list of the things that already form your shared culture, for example, working together on your large vegetable garden, staying connected to your families through visits and emails, and going to plays and movies together.

Now look at the items that could be moved into the shared culture if they are important to you. Perhaps you could find a kind of exercise you both enjoyed and go to the gym together. Or perhaps exercising together is not a priority, and you are both fine with separate exercise activities on different schedules.

Now look at items that potentially cause conflict (for example, spending patterns), and see if compromises can be made that will allow you to move those items into the shared culture.

Self-Contemplation

In the modern world, we are encouraged to go after the next exciting thing out there instead of contemplating our inner lives. Our cultural emphasis on "doing" can take us away from the reflective gifts of "being." Contemplative practices return us to that sense of being, and they are cornerstones for living a mindful life. Contemplative practices like prayer, meditation, and pilgrimage have been used throughout history in a variety of spiritual, psychological, and philosophical traditions. They develop our capacity to explore our deepest inner truths, beliefs, and values; enhance self-awareness; and increase our authenticity as we relate to others.

Some people find active practices like yoga, dance, or tai chi work best for them. Others discover they go more deeply inside with devotional practices like mindfulness meditation, prayer, or spending time in nature. Group experiences of contemplation, rooted in spiritual and cultural traditions, are another great avenue for this type of deep self-awareness.

We're now going to explore two methods for looking deeply inside: journaling and the practice of inquiry. The more time you spend with these practices, the better you will become at knowing what feelings, responses, and reactions are coming from your true self rather than from the beliefs and dictates of others.

Journaling

Rita D. Jacobs, author of *The Way In: Journal Writing for Self-Discovery*, eloquently described the benefits of using a journal in an email to me: "Keeping a personal journal is an effective, scientifically proven way to sort out and get in touch with your feelings, daily experiences, and ideas. Not only will you get more in touch with yourself, but studies have shown people who keep journals maintain better mental, physical, and emotional health."

EXERCISE: Journaling for Self-Discovery

A prompt that Jacobs suggests to help get in touch with your inner self is making a long list headed by a declaration. For example: "I desire for my relationship to be..." or "Fifty things I'd like to hear someone say to me are..." Once you choose a focus, write quickly for ten minutes, jotting down as many items as possible on your list. After ten minutes have passed, review the list and see if you can find a theme running through it. There will probably be one, and you can use that theme to make a more conscious and extended journal entry next time.

Some other prompts to consider:

- What I want in a partner is...
- My six-year-old self believed that love was...
- What I wish my six-year-old self had known is...
- My twelve-year-old self wished for...
- What I wish my twelve-year-old self had known is...
- My eighteen-year-old self believed that relationships were...
- What I wish my eighteen-year-old self had known is...
- Something I feel confused about in my current relationship is...
- Something I feel upset about in my relationship is...
- Something I am grateful to my partner for is...

Sharing

If your partner has done the exercise, take turns telling each other what you wrote about. Remember the importance of listening to one another with curiosity instead of judgment, and make a point of learning something new about the other person. Make sure to discuss the following points:

- Something you learned from doing this exercise
- One thing that surprised you

- Something that made you sad
- Something that made you hopeful
- Any other feelings that came up as a result of doing the exercise

The Practice of Inquiry

In exploring the question of who you are, you will most likely find that many ways you define yourself come from old stories — from your family, peers, and cultural conditioning — and may never have actually been true. One way to peel back these layers is the practice of inquiry, an awareness-building technique meant to help us develop an interactive internal dialogue and talk to that part of ourselves that exists beyond our external identity, wants, and needs. This practice helps people engage with their thoughts and feelings by working past routine and conditioned responses to reach the core of who they are.

To understand how the practice works, consider a deceptively simple question: "Who are you?" Have another person ask you the question, and answer with the first thing that comes to mind. No editing allowed! After you respond, your questioner says "thank you" as a way of ending that thought and then repeats the question. Each time you respond, your questioner thanks you and then immediately asks the question again.

The first few answers often come quickly and tend to be determined by the most dominant roles we play in life. For example:

Questioner: Who are you?
Responder: I am a writer, a mother, a factory worker, and a skier.
Questioner: Thank you. Who are you?
Responder: I am a woman. I am forty-six. I am five feet, six inches tall.
Questioner: Thank you. Who are you?

The purpose of the inquiry is to gain deeper insight into yourself, and the most important answers generally lie beneath the first and second layers. The underlying layers become less concrete. Beneath the things we do on the surface are often signs and symbols that indicate deeper things we care about, things that touch our hearts and spirits:

Questioner: Who are you?
Responder: I am a nature lover, a dog kisser, and a sun worshipper.
Questioner: Thank you. Who are you?

After several rounds of the question, we may answer with even more surprising characteristics having to do with feelings, creative impulses, or our identification with aspects of the natural world:

Responder: I am sunlight. I am loneliness. I am resilience.

In the practice of inquiry, the question is a starting point, and it may take you to some surprising places if you allow it to. Don't become attached to any particular answer; instead, let the process continue until you feel there's nothing more to be learned — at least this time around.

When we use this tool, we need to allow whatever comes up to be acceptable. This will require you to manage your own discomfort and to silence the inner critic. For example, you might find yourself saying, "I am a raging tiger" or "I am a puddle of doubt." Try replacing judgment with curiosity. Instead of reprimanding yourself, try asking, "Isn't it interesting that I feel that way?"

EXERCISE: The Practice of Inquiry

If you're working with a partner, sit across from one another and decide who the questioner is and who the responder is. Begin by having the questioner ask the question you've chosen to explore (such as "Who am I?") and allowing the responder to answer. If you're playing the role of questioner, don't interrupt the responder. When the responder is finished, the questioner says thank you, pauses for a few moments, and then asks the same question again. Repeat until the responder feels done. Then change roles.

If you're working by yourself, use a journal to dialogue with the question. Write out the question, and then write your answer below it. Then write out the question again and give a new answer below. Repeat until you feel you're done.

When you are the one doing the self-exploration, go deeper and deeper into yourself each time you answer the question. Leave behind literal interpretations and watch for emotions, yearnings, desires, and metaphors. Continue for as long as the practice feels important and fruitful to you.

Once you've examined the "Who am I?" question, below are a few others to consider and to ask as a repeating question in the same way.

- What do I really want?
- What is my deepest fear regarding love?
- What is my heart's deepest wish?
- What's next for me?
- If I were true to my deepest self, what would my life be about?

Sharing

If you've done this exercise together, make sure you've each had an opportunity to play both roles. Then talk about what the whole experience was like, both as the one who questioned and as the one who shared. If you and your partner did this exercise individually, now's the time to reconnect and take turns sharing what you've learned. You can use the same discussion prompts you used to share after the journaling practice, or you can freestyle.

Eye Gazing

So far in this chapter we've explored two ways of looking inward — personal values and self-contemplation — each followed by the experience of sharing with your partner. This process of self-disclosure is invaluable for keeping closeness alive over time. Make a point to regularly engage in the practice of vulnerable self-disclosure and its rich byproducts, renewed closeness and trust. Likewise, as you move through this book, make sure you take time to reflect on the new information you're gaining about your partner.

In the next chapter, we'll further build on your ability to listen actively and empathetically. But before we move on, I have one more fun connection exercise I'd love for you to try, courtesy of Dr. Arthur Aron. It's called "eye gazing."

Why include an exercise on eye gazing in a chapter about discovery and disclosure? As the aphorism goes, the eyes are the windows to the soul. When we directly meet someone's gaze and hold it, we are acknowledging them in a raw, sometimes uncomfortably intimate way. Allowing someone to look at you, and only you, for an uninterrupted space of time — even just a few minutes — puts you in a vulnerable place. Your partner sees every twitch of the eye, every crease in your skin, and every emotion that crosses your face. We almost never look this closely at another person, nor do we ever really let someone look so closely at us. People who engage in eye gazing report seeing small things they've never noticed before in their partner's face, eyes, or energy — a tiny dimple, or a fleck of gold dust in their brown eyes — and many describe a greater sense of closeness from the activity.

JOINT EXERCISE: Eye Gazing

Sit across from your partner in bed, on the floor, or in two chairs facing each other. Set a timer for at least four minutes. Lock eyes, and don't look away until the timer goes off. You might be surprised what you learn. Afterward, don't forget to reconnect and talk about what the experience was like for each of you.

Talking deeply about things that matter, like your values, and playing in new ways through activities like eye gazing are just a few possibilities for bringing something new into your lives to bump up your connection and ignite your friendship. "We've found that the positives are more and more important," says Howard Markman, coauthor of *Fighting for Your Marriage*. "It turns out that the amount of fun couples have and the strength of their friendship are a strong predictor of their future." These are the ways we nourish and feed our relationship. We'll talk more about ways to bolster connection later on in Chapter 13.

Before we can further understand how to connect with each other, we first need to learn how to *talk* to each other — and talk well. In the next few chapters, we'll be exploring the five essential aspects of mindful communication, which I like to call the Big Five.

The Power of the Pause

9

Picture a pattern of upright dominoes that have been positioned just far enough away from one another to highlight the gap between them, but just close enough to hit each other if one of them tips over. Hit a single domino and it sets off a chain reaction. Oftentimes, our own actions, reactions and counter-reactions, criticisms and defensive responses function like dominoes. When we're not able to access our mindfulness, reactivity takes over.

— ALICIA MUÑOZ, psychotherapist and author, from *Mindful Loving*

Before Tim and I were married, he lived in New Zealand and I lived in the States. One way we coped with the distance was by making cassette tapes for each other, which we would send via snail mail. Sometimes we shared news of the day, personal information, and future dreams. Occasionally, in the middle of the night, the messages were passionate and deeply private — as only 3 AM messages in the grip of longing and limerence can be.

One day, I had a client who was interested in the teachings of a meditation instructor with whom I was acquainted, so I offered to make her a tape of a session from the instructor's workshop. I grabbed a blank tape from a nearby basket, used my recorder to dub one of the sessions, and passed the tape on to her. A few days later, she asked if she could come by my office for a moment. When she arrived, she was uncomfortable and flustered as she handed the tape back to me.

"Uh, I — I don't think you meant this for me," she stammered. Then she abruptly left my office.

My heart seized. I knew which tape it was before I even listened to it. It was a recording so steamy I hadn't even sent it to Tim. Somehow, instead of getting thoroughly erased or tossed in the garbage, the tape had found its way into the blank-tape basket.

I can't find the words to describe my feelings. Crushing embarrassment surged through my body. When I made it home, I flung myself onto the couch and lay there for ten minutes, paralyzed with shock. "How could you have been so careless?" I berated myself. It felt like the end of my career. As my shame and self-castigation mounted, my ability to discern my options plummeted. I began to consider moving to another town.

Suddenly I remembered a training session on stress management I'd recently attended. It had advocated pausing long enough to take a slow deep breath whenever we feel overwhelmed and then doing something different.

I forced my leaden legs to stand and set the goal of touching an oak tree in the backyard before heading back to the couch. With effort, I got up and walked outside. When I reached my goal and gently touched it, I noticed a heron perched in a nearby tree, eyeing my fishpond with sinister interest. I moved into action, scaring it away by yelling at it.

By the time I returned to the couch, I was breathing normally. Although I was still embarrassed, the magnitude of my emotions had moved from a ten to a three. I'd begun to see I would not die of embarrassment, and my client would also recover from her shock. Pausing long enough to do something different stopped the chain reaction of the domino effect.

This is the biology of what happened. We each have a nervous system that operates outside of our conscious awareness called the parasympathetic nervous system. It's activated when we are at rest and not in distress. Essentially, in our normal conscious life the lights are on at the front of our brain, where the frontal lobe resides, and we make decisions that are reasonable, responsible, and rational. Our heart beats normally, and we generally eat when we are hungry and rest when we are tired.

When we are distressed, as I was when my client returned the tape to me, our brain switches gears and mobilizes the sympathetic nervous system, which causes the "lights to go out" in the frontal lobe and the "lights to go on" in the back of our brain where the amygdala (the brain's 9-1-1 center) resides. So we react from another center, the system that tells us we are in danger, are embarrassed, or are under some other kind of threat. Our heart beats faster, our blood circulation slows down, and our body reacts as though we are under attack — even if the attack is coming from our own thoughts, as it was for me. Some of us don't eat, others eat more than they need, some people collapse into sleep, and others stay awake with tingling limbs and racing thoughts.

None of that is fun for anyone. The good news is, it's totally fixable if we can remember to take a moment to pause. Working with our breath and moving our body — touching a tree as I did, for example — reassures the body that the danger is gone, and the lights can come back on at the front of the brain.

My story is a reminder of how important it is to *manage our own internal reactions* before we can respond to a situation in a healthy, productive, reasonable way. Taking a moment, a breath, or a stretch helps us rebalance in the face of distressing interactions; we can think wisely about what to do next rather than act from panic and reactivity. I call this skill *the pause*.

"Practice the pause," Lori Deschene, founder and director of Tiny Buddha.com, reminds us. "Pause before judging. Pause before assuming. Pause before accusing. Pause whenever you're about to react harshly, and you'll avoid doing and saying things you'll later regret." We need the "lights on" in the thoughtful part of our brain when we interact with our partner, especially when we are under stress, and the pause is a reminder that we can be in charge when that happens.

Mindfulness: The Key to Pausing

At spiritual retreats, it's a common practice to ring a bell at unexpected times throughout the day. People are asked to stop what they are doing for a moment when the bell rings — they must stop folding clothes, put down their forks, or take a break from their conversations — and turn inward. This develops the practice of becoming still enough to take a breath and check in with our wise and centered selves rather than giving in to our first reaction.

Everywhere we go, noise distracts us from tuning in to this deeper part of ourselves: music plays in coffee shops, the TV drones in the background at home, and electronic notifications beep ceaselessly from our smartphones. I watch people walking in local nature reserves wearing earbuds and head-phones, unable to hear the music of the birds, the whisper of the trees, and other soft nature sounds that let us slow down enough to experience our own breath and the deeper music of our own thoughts.

Even when we stop the outer distractions, there is often inner noise. A committee of voices resides in our heads, constantly dictating what to worry about, judging what we are doing, and chattering about ideas and plans. Most of this is not bad or wrong (although we could do quite well without the judg-ing voice); it's the way our brain functions.

Sometimes these voices can enhance creativity, lead us to face challenges, and identify sources of interest, all of which are important parts of life. But sometimes we frighten ourselves, belittle ourselves, or convince ourselves we are in danger when we are not. In our relationship, those inner voices can build an entire case against our partner when he or she forgets to pick up the milk on the way home. That's why the pause is the first and most important part of positive couples' communication.

Seven Small Steps to Help You Pause and Rebalance

1. Notice when your body is tense and stressed.
2. Accept your reaction without judging it as wrong.
3. Take a few deep breaths to slow yourself down.
4. Tense and relax the muscles in your limbs.

5. Do something to get back to your body. Go for a walk, run, or do some other kind of exercise. Touch a tree and scare away a heron, as I did. Take a shower, chew on an ice cube, or smell some lavender.

6. Do something that quiets the mind. Listen to a soothing piece of music. Say a prayer, practice a mantra, or recite a poem.

7. Notice again what is going on in your body.

You might have picked up on this already, but practicing the pause is inextricably intertwined with practicing mindfulness. Pausing involves observing your emotions and noticing your mind's desire to react from its fear center, and it also involves redirecting the mind's attention to more soothing, physical rituals like breathing and moving.

Through the following exercises, we're going to build up our ability to pause — an invaluable skill needed for day-to-day interactions with a life partner — by first working on developing our mindfulness skills more broadly. You'll also practice connecting on a physical and spiritual level with your partner in a way that helps both of you make pausing a part of your common language and tool kit. When you practice mindfulness with your partner, you both become more intentional about choices, actions, and reactions.

Sound good? Let's begin!

EXERCISE: Practicing the Pause

Within you there is a stillness and sanctuary to which
you can retreat at any time and be yourself.

— HERMANN HESSE, *Siddhartha*

Let's begin by finding your inner stillness. You can complete this exercise individually or with your partner, though it should be primarily an internal experience. You might want to make an audio recording of yourself reading the following italicized instructions and play it as you practice letting go and experiencing the pause.

When you have some quiet time, find a comfortable place to sit, straighten your back, roll your shoulders and hips, and let your body relax. Then take a moment and deepen your breath. Breathe in and out slowly through your nose, letting your chest rise and fall slowly with each breath. Now expand the breath to your belly so that your abdomen expands. Then breathe out slowly through your mouth (or your nose, if that feels more natural), letting all of your nerves and muscles relax.

Notice your thoughts. Remember, you have thoughts, but you are not your thoughts. Imagine they are clouds passing above your head; notice them and allow them to move on.

Now be aware of your feelings, right in this moment. You have feelings, but you are not your feelings. Let your feelings simply move through you, changing form like passing clouds. Let each one move on and watch the next one float in.

Be aware of your body now. Remember that you have a body, but you are not your body. Feel the breath, and let it go. Observe where you are tight and where you are soft, and keep breathing consciously. Do this for five breaths. Then bring your attention back to where you are sitting, stretch for a moment, and take a deeper breath.

Next, close your eyes and repeat the exercise without reading these instructions.

Reflections

A minute or so after you finish the exercise, reflect on your experience by answering the following questions:

1. Notice your physical body, your emotional state, and your mental state. How do each of these aspects feel?

2. Do you notice any differences between how you feel now and how you felt before doing the exercise? Describe these differences.

EXERCISE: One Mindful Minute

Here is one more exercise that can help you practice the pause. This is an excellent exercise to return to in a heated moment when you need to get centered before responding.

Without trying to change anything, notice and observe:

- What do I smell?
- What do I see?
- What do I hear?
- What am I touching?
- What do I taste?

Notice a thought and let it go like a cloud passing.
Notice a feeling and let it go like a cloud passing.
We create mindfulness one breath at a time.

Pausing Together

Now that you've practiced pausing and rebalancing on your own, here are three more exercises to help you practice with your partner. If you are not a meditator, these exercises might make you feel self-conscious or even a bit uncomfortable at first. Try them anyway. The more you engage with them, the more natural they'll feel.

Besides sharing something new with your partner, practicing mindfulness skills together will give you a common understanding of how important it is to "keep the lights on" in the decision-making part of your brain. It can help you create a common understanding about what happens during the inevitable times of reactivity and give you a common language to talk through those times without blaming.

The following three exercises are specifically for couples. You may want to space these exercises out instead of trying to do them all in a row in one sitting.

After trying each of the exercises, use the sharing section at the end of the first one (Breath Matching) to reflect on the experience together.

If you're working through this book on your own, consider inviting your partner to join you for one or more of these exercises. If not, save them for another day and move on to reading about the Big Five mindful communication skills.

We've long known that new lovers often synchronize their breathing without knowing it, just as they tend to match their steps when walking. In a similar fashion, mothers and babies can match their heartbeats down to the millisecond through touching and smiling, and dolphins have been recorded breathing in sync. In one Australian study, researchers put heart monitors on dogs, separated them from their owners, and then reunited them. Although their heart rates differed, the breathing of the dogs and their owners synchronized when they were reunited. This is a phenomenon found in many mammals.

When our hearts and minds are in sync, our bodies become more connected. Intentionally finding a way to do this with your partner slows down reactivity, increases connection, and can even be fun!

JOINT EXERCISE: Breath Matching

Allow fifteen to thirty minutes for this exercise. Find a comfortable place to be together: a bed, a couch, or a comfortable position on the floor. Hold one another close enough that you can feel your partner's breath. Close your eyes for five to ten minutes, noticing your breathing and the position of your belly as it rises on the inhale and falls on the exhale. When your attention wanders, redirect it to your breathing. Now notice your partner's breathing as you carefully hold each other close. Consciously match one another's breathing for another five to ten minutes. If it is hard to match breathing, try humming or making some sort of vocalization (such as "ahhh" as you exhale), at least for the first few minutes.

Sharing

Use the following sentence stems to share your feelings. As you share your experience, remember to refrain from criticizing your partner. If you would like something to be different, say so in the third feedback guideline below. Rather than complain, give your partner a positively phrased alternate suggestion.

1. What I liked about this exercise was...
2. Some of the feelings I had when we were doing it were...
3. What would make it even better for me would be...
4. Thank you for...

We've long read about the benefits of maintaining a meditation practice, including reducing stress, enhancing self-awareness, and even increasing our patience and tolerance. We live in a culture where there is a busyness epidemic, and our "doing" tends to get in the way of our "being." A joint meditation practice helps you and your partner create a mutually calming effect for each other, enhancing intimacy and helping you feel more open and less reactive with one another.

JOINT EXERCISE: Meditation for Two

Begin by deciding what kind of meditation you want to practice. This can be a fun research project to do together. You can find a guided meditation on Google, YouTube, or a smartphone app, or you can get a CD from the library. Alternately, you can meditate by focusing on an object such as a candle as you breathe. You might even choose to find a teacher who will work with you and show you various techniques.

Once you have decided how to begin, agree on a comfortable place where you won't be interrupted and decide how long you will sit. When you first start the practice, I recommend doing it for about five to ten minutes and correct as needed. Make sure you both understand and agree to the instructions before you start. Once you are practicing, take care not to judge, correct, or try to manage your partner's technique. Allow yourselves to be together with the intention of exploring meditation as a way to connect and as a means to enhance your appreciation of each other.

I suggest you and your partner agree to test joint meditation at least seven to ten times before deciding whether to make it a regular practice in your lives.

Sharing

Use the sharing suggestions at the end of the Breath Matching exercise to reflect together on your experience.

If one or both of you are in a fragile space emotionally or sexually, come back to the next exercise at a later time. If not, this activity will allow you to try hugging in a new way. A melting hug provides a deep body-to-body connection. It is a way to experience yourself melting into the other person at the same time that you are connecting to yourself. I suggest both partners agree beforehand that this exercise is not going to be sexual; however, do let yourselves feel the deep sensuality of the experience.

JOINT EXERCISE: Melting-Hug Meditation

Allow at least ten minutes for this exercise, but allow it to go on as long as you like. To begin, stand facing one another or lie side by side in a "spooning" position, whichever feels more comfortable. Close your eyes for a moment, breathe in, and begin to connect with each other. Take five deep breaths, in and out, and on the fifth breath out, sink into your partner's arms. Imagine that you are connecting to yourself on each breath in and that you are melting into one another on each exhale. Feel the power of simultaneously holding on to yourself and melting into your partner.

Sharing

Use the sharing suggestions at the end of the Breath Matching exercise to reflect together on your experience.

Mindful Communication: The Big Five

Now that you've spent some time practicing the pause using mindfulness, it's time to apply your pausing skills to the relationship area they're most needed in: communication. There are five essential elements of mindful communication, which I call the "Big Five," all of which utilize the pause. Here's a convenient acronym to help you remember:

P is for *presence* through listening.
A is for *accepting* the "and."
U is for *undefended connection.*
S is for *speaking* with skill.
E is for *emotional intelligence.*

Over the next three chapters, we'll discuss each of these five qualities in detail. In addition to pausing, these skills all emphasize the importance of connecting even during conflict. Inevitably, intimate partners disagree about issues, but more important is the disconnection they feel when they react to the other's feelings and thoughts with defensiveness or anger. When we behave this way, we lose touch with the heart of our relationship, sacrificing it to our sense of righteous indignation. We barter curiosity and compassion for the fleeting high of *being right*. In the end, we find ourselves lonely in the presence of the one person who once seemed to understand and appreciate us better than anyone.

Mindful communication dissolves the isolation that comes when we feel unseen, unheard, and closed off from the person who once offered us unconditional acceptance. Incorporating the Big Five communication skills into our interactions can help us stay connected with our partner and reignite the safety, interest, and passion we experienced early on in our relationship.

Listening and the "And"

10

If we only listened with the same passion that we feel about being heard.

— HARRIET LERNER, author of *Why Won't You Apologize?*

I was walking with my husband, Tim, along our favorite trail with our three aging Jack Russell terriers, each of which had begun showing major signs of slowing down. We knew they would probably die around the same time, and we dreaded losing them. Neither of us had been without a dog since we were children. We referred to the situation as "a very hard year coming up soon." Suddenly, Tim turned to me and said, "You know, when we lose these three dogs, I don't want another one."

I was stunned. First I froze and just stared at him. Then "fight" hormones flooded my body, and I flipped into attack mode. "I wonder where you will be living," I said icily, "because I never intend to be without a dog."

"Fine," he shot back. "Where I live won't be your problem. I'm not going to have another dog."

Gridlock. Shutdown. We were frozen in opposing positions. We had traveled the country to learn communication skills and then gone on to teach these skills to hundreds of couples for almost twenty years. Yet there we were, standing on a country road talking about living apart, breaking every rule we knew about how to manage conflict and the importance of listening to one another.

We spent about fifteen minutes walking in frigid silence. Then Tim said, "I probably didn't deliver that message very well."

I thawed a bit and said, "I guess we need our pillows." That was our shortcut way of speaking about the old pillow-talk exercise, which I described a few chapters ago and which Tim and I often used to understand the other person's point of view, even when we didn't agree.

I'm telling you this story for two reasons. First, I want to emphasize how learning new skills, no matter how practiced you are, doesn't prevent you from falling into old habits under stress.

The second important thing is what we did next. We repaired things quickly and walked home together, calm and connected once again. We moved past the gridlock using some intentional steps that didn't feel easy or natural but that we both believed in. Before I introduce these steps, let's talk about the importance of listening to one another. Later in the chapter I will share the outcome of this gridlock!

Why Should I Listen to You?

When we think about what we're looking for in a partner, one of the most important criteria is someone who can love and value us as the unique beings we are, with all of our imperfections and strengths. Our partner's acceptance instills in us feelings of safety, openness, and passion. All of this comes easily in Stage One, when our differences seem charming or even exciting. As we journey deeper into love, however, the differences between us begin to challenge instead of charm, and we need to develop new skills to help us return to that place of mutual warmth and trust. One key skill is the capacity to genuinely listen.

Three Magic Words

We often equate the expression "three magic words" with "I love you." But there are three other magic words that can allow you to discover important things about your partner (and others) that you'd never have imagined. Just as important, these words will help your partner to feel deeply cared about and seen — and to want to respond to you in kind. The words are, "Tell me more."

"Tell me more" is a powerful phrase when backed by a genuine willingness to pay attention to the answers. Listening with true presence — that is, taking in what the other is saying without judging, suggesting, or trying to fix — is a gift that we can offer another person. As author and National Humanities Award recipient Krista Tippett has said, "Listening is about being present, not just about being quiet." Fundamentally, it's about recognizing that the conversation is about *the other*, not about you.

Too often, a conversation goes like this:

Shanice: I had a tough day today.
Evan: Oh, your job is always getting you down.

> or

I'm worried that you're not getting enough sleep.

> or

Well, the problem is that your boss is a jerk.

But if Evan used the three magic words, the conversation would go very differently:

Shanice: I had a tough day today.
Evan: Oh? Tell me more.
Shanice: My mind just isn't on my work.
Evan: What are you thinking about?
Shanice: I've been thinking about my grandfather a lot lately for some reason. He's on my mind so much that I can't seem to focus like I want to.

Evan: That's interesting. What is it about your grandfather that's gotten your attention?

Shanice: Well, he was so important to me when I was a kid, and I miss him a lot. Oh wow, I just realized the tenth anniversary of his death is this week.

Evan: How do you think that's affecting you?

Shanice: Well, until this moment, I hadn't realized it was the anniversary. Until we started talking, I had no idea why I've been so distracted. Huh. You know, I think I need to spend some time with my grandmother. Visiting Grandma is exactly what I need to do. I bet she's missing him too. We can miss him together.

In the second version of the exchange, Evan doesn't take the conversation in a predetermined direction — that is, where *he* wants it to go or where *he* thinks it might or should go. Instead, he decides to truly hear her. He is able to see Shanice as different from himself, and because of this, she is able to discover what's really bothering her and even find a way to help herself.

Try this with your partner, your neighbor, your cousin, or anyone else who calls just to catch up. When they tell you something about their life, say, "Tell me more." And keep listening. Let them dive deeper and deeper into their thoughts and feelings. Notice what happens.

Listening is one of the most powerful ways we let other people know they are important to us. How we respond when they are talking is critical, but another component is important as well: recalling later what they said. For example, in the story above, Evan might follow up a few days later and ask if Shanice had any more thoughts about her grandfather or visiting her grandmother.

And listening isn't just good for the person being heard — it's good for the listener as well. When we feel close to another person, our brains release oxytocin, the chemical that promotes bonding. Just think about those times you've felt a genuine sense of intimacy with someone else when you were laughing together, crying together, or feeling truly heard and understood. It's exciting to feel so connected, and at the same time it's deeply calming, like stroking a pet or sitting by the ocean.

Sometimes it is hard to really tune in. An example is when your partner wants to talk about a point of view that's directly opposed to yours and may feel like a criticism — or *is* one. It can also be tempting to tune out when you're distracted by your own concerns, feelings of defensiveness, or simple boredom when it comes to the particular topic. At such times, the last thing you may want to say is "Tell me more." Yet the rewards of increased trust, well-being, and connection are well worth a commitment to attuned listening.

There are four kinds of listening:

1. **Pretend listening:** Although you make listening gestures like nodding and murmuring "mmm-hmm," your mind is somewhere else. You might say nice words such as "I hear you," but your partner won't be fooled. Your thoughts, facial expressions, and body posture suggest that you're not hearing at all.

2. **Selective listening:** You "semi-listen," merely searching the other person's words for bullet points on how to respond when it's your turn. "Yeah, I know what you mean," you might say, or "Sounds like a tough day." But your reaction is more about you than the other person, and you're silently criticizing, judging, or deciding whether you agree.

3. **Careful listening:** You're paying more attention to the other person than to yourself, but you have your own conversation going on in your head at the same time. You are still agreeing, disagreeing, and sometimes judging, but not as much as with selective listening. You may mentally wander off mid-conversation, but you bring yourself back to the other person and try to formulate your responses with care.

4. **Deep listening:** You're acutely aware of the other person, as though you've crossed a bridge into his or her world and have temporarily left your own behind. You're not judging or distracted; instead, your goal is to make the other person feel connected to you and reassured of your total focus. You're also paying attention to nonverbal cues — the messages conveyed by the person's eyes, body language, and tone. Rather than behaving as though you're

present but remembering maybe 25 percent of the conversation, in deep listening you remember most of what the other person has said. Whether or not you agree, you seek to understand your conversation partner's perspective, and you show genuine empathy and respect for the thoughts and feelings being expressed.

Good listening is more than just a mechanical response. It's a skill that requires us to quiet the compelling distractions that compete for our attention when someone else is sharing with us, such as thinking about what we are going to say in response, evaluating the person speaking, and reflecting on our own lives. Of course, mindful listening doesn't mean we don't have any internal dialogue. It simply means we are aware of this "background noise" and are willing to work diligently to bring our focus back to the other person.

When you and your partner are in gridlock about a seemingly unresolvable issue, doing what you can to preserve the connection is vital. Making an effort to truly hear one another's point of view and acknowledging that neither of you is crazy or wrong can create an environment of empathy and help both partners to lower their defenses. This can make the problem seem much smaller, and although it may not resolve the issue, it sustains the connection between partners.

Of course, we can't listen deeply all the time. Sometimes we just like to spend time together while engaging in small talk. Other times we just want information and not much more. What's important is that we remain aware of the different kinds of listening and that we possess the emotional sensibility and skills to know when it's time to tune in to each style of relating. One way of doing this is to agree that when either of you needs deep listening, you will ask for it.

Listening Quiz

This questionnaire is meant to help you explore your "default" listening level. If you're working on this book with a partner, each of you should do this exercise separately and then come together to compare your results.

There are four eight-item sections. Rank each item based on the scale below:

1 = I never do this
2 = I rarely do this
3 = I sometimes do this
4 = I often do this
5 = I always do this

After completing each section, tally up your score by adding your responses for all the items in that section. The section that you have the highest score in is the listening level you operate in most frequently.

Level 1: Pretend Listening

Score

1. My mind tunes in and out during conversations. _____

2. I like to give the impression that I'm listening, even when I'm not. _____

3. I've mastered the "I hear you" line and when to nod or agree with what someone is saying, though I'm not always sure what I'm agreeing with. _____

4. I avoid looking at my phone or starting other tasks during conversations, but it takes a lot of self-control for me to do so. _____

5. To me, listening is more of a passive process (as opposed to an active process). _____

6. After someone is done speaking, I have a general idea about what they've just said rather than any specifics. _____

7. I usually don't encourage further discussion, because I'd prefer to be doing something else with my time. _____

8. Serious conversations don't last long with me. People eventually stop talking because there's no back-and-forth; the conversation just "sputters out." _____

TOTAL SCORE _____

Level 2: Selective Listening

Score

1. When someone is talking, I'm thinking about what I'm going to say when it's my turn. _____

2. I fixate on one specific thing someone says and tend to make the conversation all about that one issue, rather than focusing on the larger topic at hand. _____

3. If I'm not leading a conversation, I get bored. _____

4. I tend to relate anything in a conversation back to myself. ("Oh, I had that experience just yesterday! Let me tell you about it!") _____

5. While I'm "listening," I'm trying to analyze how the speaker is wrong about the issue or needs to look at it differently. _____

6. If someone mispronounces a word or I don't think they understand the word they've just used, I will interrupt to correct them. _____

7. I appear to be a very engaged listener, but I'm usually engaging in order to drive the conversation in a direction I want it to go or that I find more interesting. _____

8. I've been known to finish people's sentences for them or suggest a different way of saying something they're explaining. _____

TOTAL SCORE _____

Level 3: Careful Listening

Score

1. When I'm not sure about what someone has just said, I ask them to recap it for me, or I may rephrase what I think they just said back to them to see if I got it right. _____

2. I can become so focused on analyzing what someone is saying and how they are saying it that I can feel sort of like the person's personal therapist.

_____

3. When someone is speaking, I am conscious of making eye contact with them.

_____

4. Although I listen with care, sometimes I naturally make faces or gestures that reveal my "internal dialogue" (like a sigh of relief, a shocked face, rolled eyes, or a confused expression).

_____

5. I may have a background conversation going on in my head, but my primary focus is the person in front of me.

_____

6. My friends often come to me for advice, but less often for me to "just listen."

_____

7. I ask questions that will "lead" the speaker to a solution or a realization I think is needed.

_____

8. I have the speaker's best interests at heart, so I try to be a source of sage, thoughtful advice that's personalized to the current situation.

_____

TOTAL SCORE

Level 4: Deep Listening

Score

1. I use most of my speaking time to ask questions and encourage the other person to elaborate.

_____

2. I don't interrupt; I wait until the speaker is finished. Even then, I give my personal opinion only if the other person specifically asks me for that.

_____

3. I set aside any judgment and seek only to understand where the speaker is coming from. Even when I normally wouldn't agree with what's being said, I allow the speaker to say what he or she is thinking, and I try to see things from the speaker's point of view.

_____

4. I lose track of time when I'm listening to someone. Everything but our conversation seems to fade away.

_____

5. My goal is to validate the speaker and make sure the person never feels embarrassed or upset about telling me something.

_____

6. I don't allow my emotional reactions to consume me or become a new topic of conversation. I know how to empathize without absorbing the other person's emotional state and becoming upset myself.

_____

7. I notice nonverbal cues and the speaker's tone, but I try not to jump to conclusions about their meaning. I understand that some people don't show much emotion in their faces, voices, or bodies, and that trying to analyze subtle cues distracts from my ability to be present and listen.

_____

8. When I'm the listener, I'm aware that the conversation is not about me. It's about the speaker and what he or she is saying and feeling.

_____

TOTAL SCORE

_____

Reflections and Sharing

Finish the following sentence stems, and then share with your partner.

1. Taking this quiz made me realize that I...

2. The score that surprised me the most was...

3. One of the ways my partner has described me as a listener is…

4. How I responded when I heard that was…

5. I realize that, as a listener, I…

6. One way I could improve my listening would be to…

7. One way that improvement would benefit my relationship is…

More Than Puppy Love

So let me return for a moment to my conversation with my husband about dogs. Tim and I returned home and agreed we both felt so vulnerable at the thought of losing our three dogs that we were reactive to the other's point of view. We agreed not to broach the subject again for a few days. We were a little stiff with one another, but we cooked a delicious dinner in tandem and then watched a movie. We went to bed on friendly — if not the warmest — terms. We agreed before going to sleep to take time that weekend to simply hear and understand where the other was coming from and not to make any decisions until we could find a way through our logjam.

When we finally sat down together on Saturday morning, I was able to really hear my husband as he talked about being a vet for almost fifty years. He described many of the dogs he had cared for during that time, as well as his own nine dogs. Tim explained that he felt responsible for each of these animals and told me how, with his own pets, he could never set aside his concern for them. He'd always made certain that his dogs had daily walks, he'd worked hard to figure out how they could accompany him on outings and trips, and he'd planned most of his holidays around them.

He had carried each of his dogs through their lives and into their deaths, and with the impending passing of ours he wanted a break from that level of attachment, care, and loss. In the thirty-three years we'd been together, it had never occurred to me that Tim might feel this way. It didn't change my position, but it did fill me with empathy. I understood it wasn't a lack of caring causing him to want a break from dogs — it was from caring so deeply.

Tim listened to me in the same deep and present way. I told him about the German shepherd Ranger, who possibly saved my life when I was two years old. I wandered too close to a creek and fell in; Ranger barked frantically until my parents came and lifted me out. I described Skipper and Schmoo and Bonnie, two mutts and a collie, who formed one of the most important support systems in my young life. Yet my parents believed "dogs belong on farms," and I never had one of my own until I was an adult.

He said he understood why it was so important to me to have a dog now, and I told him it made sense to me why he needed a break. Together, we decided we would see the three dogs out, take some time off from having pets, and let the conversation come up again naturally. To my surprise, after two years without a dog Tim told me he wanted one. Meanwhile, I'd been feeling the relief of not having one, and we shared our differing feelings with each other. Another year passed. Then one day, to our astonishment, at the same moment in time we both admitted to wanting a puppy. Not long afterward, we welcomed Jackson into our lives.

By taking a pause immediately after our fight, Tim and I were able to tap into the first essential element of mindful communication: *presence through deep and active listening* (the *P* in our PAUSE acronym). Once we could truly hear one another and each felt really listened to by the other, we felt more empathy and understanding for our partner's viewpoint. Although our positions about what we wanted didn't change, we were still on the same team and didn't see the person with the different point of view as the problem.

Using "And" Instead of "But"

The next essential element of mindful communication involves a recognition and acceptance of more than one truth. One of the biggest obstacles people face when trying to establish effective communication is thinking that someone has to be wrong for someone to be right. This applies whether the topic is chores, child-rearing, love, politics, religion, or anything else. Psychologists often refer to this dualistic thinking as polarization.

On a larger scale, polarization can occur between ethnic groups, countries, or political factions and lead to disastrous events like war. In couples, polarization happens on a smaller scale, but it can still be intense. Two people may argue about how to spend money or what to do with leisure time, or one partner may want more connection and togetherness while the other seeks more distance and autonomy. When people try to change, convince, or overpower each other to get their way, they often do so at the cost of intimacy and goodwill.

To manage this, consider the difference between the word *but* and the word *and*. In a conversation that includes two truths, one gets canceled out when the word *but* is used:

"I know you feel strongly about taking a vacation, but I don't think
this is the right time."
"I love you, but I don't feel like making love tonight."

How do you feel when you hear such statements? The use of the word *but* invalidates the first part of the sentence, leaving the second part as the only truth, even when we're talking about ourselves.

Using *and* instead of *but* allows both parts of the statement to be true and valid. It's a reminder that we live in a world where many things are true simultaneously. Neither person needs to be wrong. For example, "I love you, and I don't feel like making love tonight" is a way of honoring both truths.

Observe how you feel when you use and hear the word *but* in everyday conversations. See what happens when you stop, remove the *but*, and replace it with *and* instead. How does this change the meaning of your statement? Does this change how you (and others) feel and react to the conversation? Oftentimes that seemingly small change can actually eliminate the most painful part of most disagreements — that is, the alienation people feel when their point of view is discarded. We can stay connected even when the people around us have different opinions and experiences.

In mindful communication, we don't minimize or brush aside another person's feelings or words. When you're practicing your pause, keep in mind the importance of *accepting the "and"* (the *A* in our PAUSE acronym).

EXERCISE: Replacing "But" with "And"

You can complete this activity alone or together with your partner. Think about conversations that you've had with each other, a close friend, or someone else over the last week where one or both of you felt defensive, unheard, or dismissed. Can you think of sentences where you or the other person could have replaced *but* with *and*, so things could have gone better? Write them down in the chart below and play with this idea. Replace *but* with *and* — and vice versa. See how this changes the meaning.

Using "But"	Replacing with "And"
I know you want to go biking with your friends, but I want to spend the day with you.	I know you want to go biking with your friends, and I want to spend the day with you too.
I know you are tired of vegan food, but I am really trying to clean up my eating and need to keep making it.	I know you're tired of vegan food, and I am really trying to clean up my eating and need to keep making it.

Reflections

Take this space to reflect on and write down some of what you've learned from this chapter.

Sharing

Now, sitting across from one another, share what you have learned from this exercise.

In the next chapter, we'll continue our exploration of mindful communication's Big Five skills and how they relate to the practice of pausing. Next up, we look at the importance of nondefensive connection and speaking smartly.

Managing Defensiveness and Speaking Smartly

11

The key is to understand the difference between a perceived attack and an actual one. Responsibility takes courage. It's safer to counterattack. It feels better to shoot back a snarky, indignant comment. It's easier to play the victim. But all of those responses are barriers to a healthy relationship.

— ZACH BRITTLE, author of *The Relationship Alphabet*

Since writing *Love Cycles: The Five Essential Stages of Lasting Love* in 2014, I've published over eighty shorter articles on relationships, four of which were on defensive behavior. Although I've received many responses overall, the calls and emails I've received about defensiveness outnumbered all other topics four to one. That suggests defensiveness might just be one of the biggest troublemakers in relationships.

We all have defense mechanisms that protect us, and we need them. When they are underdeveloped (i.e., when we have poor boundaries) or when they're overly developed (i.e., when we constantly try to shield ourselves), our ability to love wholeheartedly is undermined. This chapter explores how too much defensiveness hurts our relationships as well as how to speak in ways that allow you to stand up for yourself while preserving connection.

Defensiveness is a protective strategy that requires a lot of energy to maintain. Although it's meant to minimize our feelings of shame, defensive behavior actually deepens our experience of shame. Defensiveness on your part also leads your partner to shut down emotionally, and these emotions will emerge eventually, in either explosions of rage or acts of passive revenge, such as sharp-edged teasing, criticizing you behind your back, or withholding love, sex, or expressions of appreciation.

There are two sides to defensive communication: the initial communication that sparked it and the reaction. Later in the chapter, we will look at some of the ways that confronting our partner can lead to the erection of emotional barriers, and I will offer suggestions for how to bring up tough issues in ways that give you the best chance of being heard. First, let's consider *why* we react the way we do and the impact of knee-jerk defensiveness on our most important relationships.

Why We're Defensive

Your childhood history deeply informs how you respond to criticism. If your family members or other important adults shamed, belittled, or punished you harshly when you were a child, as an adult you still may feel the need to try to protect yourself whenever someone seems angry with you. This is an unconscious, automatic response to a perceived danger.

We are all wired to protect ourselves with a fight, flight, or freeze response. If we see a coiled snake, we flip into an automatic flight reaction. That's reasonable and smart. If in childhood an angry parent says to us, "You forgot to empty the garbage; you're hopeless," it may feel almost as distressful and dangerous to us as a coiled snake. As an adult we may react to even a teeny criticism by instinctively freezing — that is, we do whatever we can to keep the complainer from continuing to express negative comments.

When your partner says, "Hey, you forgot the spinach" or "I was upset you told your friends we had a fight," these statements aren't actually sources of danger. But to our emotional brain, they may *feel* like danger, and we instantly act to try to protect ourselves. We need to learn how to rewire our knee-jerk impulse for self-protection, remembering that a partner's complaint, protest, or even a mild criticism need not trigger a life-or-death reaction. We're adults now. We can protect ourselves appropriately.

Your childhood history isn't the only factor that determines the degree and go-to type of your reactivity. Inborn temperament is also involved. Some of us come into the world with a "thinner skin" than others. (If you review Enneagram types in Chapter 7, you may get another window through which to understand the characteristic defensive responses of your personality type.) Your defensive behaviors are not character flaws. They're simply human responses. And with the application of intention and skill, we have the power to change outdated, unhelpful behaviors.

Defensive Strategies

In Chapter 9 on pausing, we talked about the ways that stress turns out the lights in the rational and reasonable part of our brain and turns them on in its 9-1-1 center. We have three automatic protective strategies — to freeze, fight, or flee — and each of us has developed one of these as a characteristic response based on our childhood experiences and temperament. Freezers play the victim, agreeing with others no matter how unjust their comments and trying to placate them just to stop what feels like an attack. Fighters fiercely counterattack; they argue over details and dispute the perceptions of others. They justify themselves and blame the other in turn. Those who rely on fleeing will withdraw, stonewall, or walk away.

EXERCISE: Your Defensive Style

Answer the following questions about your defensive style.

1. Which defensive strategy shows up when you are feeling the need for self-protection from friends and family?

2. Which style do you typically use when interacting with your significant other? Is there also a secondary style you may use? (For example, first you freeze — and then you get angry.)

3. Think back on a recent situation in which you behaved defensively. Maybe your partner, parent, or a work colleague said something you interpreted as critical, so you immediately launched into self-protection mode. Describe the situation below.

4. Did you react by freezing, fighting, or fleeing? Describe your behavior.

5. Do you think you were in actual or perceived danger? Describe.

6. Now rewrite this scenario as one in which you behave in a non-defensive way. Maybe someone said something that sounded critical to you, but you were able to stay in the moment, avoid getting triggered, and respond by explaining how you felt rather than fighting, freezing, or fleeing.

7. Now repeat this exercise, but this time write down a time when someone else acted defensively about something *you* said or did. Write down what happened — both how you opened the conversation and how the other person responded.

8. How did it feel to have the person respond defensively? Think back to the emotions you felt when he or she responded that way.

9. Now rewrite this scenario as one in which the other person responds in a nondefensive way. What might you have said in response?

Sharing

If you're working with a partner, come together to share your results after answering the questions separately.

Learning to Pause

Even if you are a hyperreactive person, this process can teach you to manage your own inner instincts. Listening to another's complaint, accepting their truth (the *and*), and *practicing undefended connection* (the *U* in PAUSE) can together dramatically deescalate conflicts and promote healthy channels of communication that are safe and nourishing for both of you.

Here's how to pause when you're feeling the need to defend.

1. **Be aware when you start to feel defensive.** Here are some signs. Which are familiar to you?
   - Tightening of muscles
   - Taking offense
   - Feeling your IQ drop and losing words
   - Wanting to be right
   - Inner voice saying why what you are hearing isn't true

- Needing to explain
- Wanting the last word
- Justifying
- Talking quickly
- Withdrawing into silence
- Using cynicism
- Using sarcasm
- Attacking (the best defense is a good offense)
- Heart racing
- Crossing arms
- Personalizing everything
- Jumping to conclusions
- Trying to placate
- Feeling like a child

2. **Breathe.** To counteract the tension in your body, become aware of your breathing. Slow it down, soften your belly and shoulder muscles, and remind yourself that you are not truly in danger. Turn on the lights in the front of your brain.

3. **Acknowledge your reactivity.** It is important to tell others that you understand their criticisms and to encourage them to share their feelings. But if you feel yourself shutting down or wanting to fight or run away, acknowledge what is happening. You might say, "I want you to tell me more, but I can feel myself becoming defensive. I want to take a moment to calm myself so I can hear what you are saying." This provides time and space to calm yourself.

4. **Remember, it's not always about you!** Often, criticism is more about the giver than the recipient. Perhaps your partner is simply tired or has misunderstood something — or perhaps you've unwittingly triggered a response that is really about someone or something else. Acknowledge the other person's point of view. Ask, "Is there more?" or say, "Help me understand," which may help you both find the deeper reason for what is going on that might have nothing to do with you. Don't use the conversation to counter your partner's perspective or point out faults as you see them.

5. **If you want to really stretch yourself, thank your partner.** Express appreciation to your partner for bringing up the issue and acknowledge that it's important to talk about these things, even if they are hard to hear.

6. **If an apology seems in order, offer one.** If apologizing is generally hard for you, it might be helpful to read Harriet Lerner's book *Why Won't You Apologize?* or watch her TED Talk "Why Won't He Apologize?" One of her most useful pointers is not to use the "if" word. "I'm sorry *if* I hurt you" isn't an apology. It's a way to weasel out of responsibility. "I'm sorry *that* I hurt you" is a genuine apology!

If you want to express a reason, if you have an excuse, if you want to take time to talk about your side, that is all fine — but don't do it at the same time the other person is talking. First, hear the person out. *After* he or she feels heard, you can say something like, "I understand why you felt upset when I didn't come to the softball game, and I'm sorry you were worried. I wish I had remembered to text you, and I will be sure to if this happens again. Would you like to hear what happened on my end?"

Remember, behaving nondefensively is actually the best strategy to protect yourself in your relationship with your partner. (Important note: If you are in actual danger from an assault or the threat of one, immediately leave the scene and seek out support. Insist that the other person get help before you agree to be with that person again.)

Speaking Smartly and with Intention

We need people in our lives with whom we can be as open as possible.
To have real conversations with people may seem like such a simple,
obvious suggestion, but it involves courage and risk.

— THOMAS MOORE, *Care of the Soul*

If we don't learn how to address our grievances directly, they will inevitably make themselves known indirectly in more toxic forms. When we aren't willing to speak up (whether out of fear, self-doubt, or an impulse to please), it's impossible to heal issues in our relationships. At the same time, it's unhelpful to blurt out our grievances and accusations. Part of mindful communication is considering how to *speak skillfully* (the *S* in PAUSE).

The way we broach an issue with our partner has a lot to do with whether the conversation will go well — or poorly. Let's look at the two scenarios below to see how the way we begin discussions can play out in a relationship.

Scenario One: Pete comes home exhilarated. He has just received a fantastic promotion at work *and* beat his biggest opponent at squash. He dashes into the house, excited to share his news with his partner, Annie. He finds her unpacking from a business trip in the bedroom, and she barely smiles when she sees him.

Heaving a big sigh, she looks disconsolate. "Hi," she mumbles. She returns to unpacking.

Pete briefly notes that Annie is not her normally warm, buoyant self, but he is too excited about his day to find out what is wrong. "What an amazing day I've had!" Pete exclaims. He begins to recount all of his successes to Annie.

Imagine you're Annie. You're exhausted, and something upsetting has happened on your business trip. How do you think you would respond to Pete?

Scenario Two: Megan is starting to get annoyed. Jason, her husband, was due home at 5:30 PM, so they'd have time to get ready for a dinner party. Where *is* he? She has repeatedly texted and called him, but he doesn't answer. Her annoyance increases with each passing moment, and by 5:45 she's remembering all the other times he's been late. She realizes she has been carrying a grudge for years over Jason's lack of punctuality — and that the grudge is well-deserved. "I think I've spent most of the last eleven years waiting for him to get home!" she grouses to herself.

Megan is flooded by memories. She remembers that Jason was late the first time she brought him to meet her family. She recalls how, even when they start out at the same time to go somewhere, she is inevitably the one left waiting — car keys in hand — while he has to do "one last thing" before they can leave the house. It's outrageous!

At 6:15, Jason pulls into the driveway, parks the car, and walks in the door. He looks troubled. But by this time, Megan can't contain her fury. "I can't believe you're late again!" she rages at him. "I feel like I've spent my whole life waiting for you. The least you could've done is called me!"

Imagine you're Jason. You were late because you saw a car accident happen while you were driving home and stopped to assist the victim and call 9-1-1. How would you respond to Megan?

I imagine you've predicted that neither of these scenarios would end well. Most of us can recognize the problem in both of these stories: each partner began a conversation with a lot of intensity and feeling, and neither partner paused to recognize the emotional condition of the other person. In both cases, the speaker forgot the first rule of initiating a conversation: how you start it will affect what happens next. And you can't start it well without pausing to see and hear your partner.

A conversation is an interactive process. This means that if you want to share something big — whether expressing what a great day you've had or sharing your irritation with your partner — you need to take care to be "timely and kindly." If your partner feels either attacked or invisible right off the bat, the response will be to fight, flee, or freeze rather than being open to what you have to say. Assume the best intentions before diving into a list of grievances.

Below are six rules of "smart speaking" to help you initiate a conversation that will ensure the best outcome for both of you.

Rule #1: Manage yourself first. Before you speak, become aware of your emotions, because they'll speak loudly and clearly through your facial expressions, body language, and the look in your eyes. If you're not aware of your own emotions, you won't be aware of the nonverbal messages you are sending to your partner. Always take a moment to take in a mindful breath before speaking. Pause.

Rule #2: Check in with your partner. When you are going to talk about something that has a lot of "energy," whether sharing good news or feeling upset, you need to check in with where the other person is emotionally. Don't assume your partner is able to meet your need for a particular kind of conversation at any particular time. This begins by noticing the nonverbal cues, such as their facial expression, body language, and eye contact, and then actually checking in.

Rule #3: Invite your partner to any significant conversation. Give your partner a chance to accept or decline your invitation to a significant discussion. If your partner says no, then wait for an appropriate time over the next day or so for an invitation to such a discussion. When your partner isn't receptive, don't push.

Rule #4: Be respectful. Always begin a conversation with respect and a sense of goodwill, even if you're upset. If you begin with an interrogation, an angry expression, or a loud voice, the other person will automatically go into self-protection mode against whatever you go on to say. You might even say, "I'm feeling a lot of anger," but rather than add "because of *you*," you might follow up with a statement about yourself, such as, "I'm really angry right now, and I know some of it is more about me than you. Maybe I'll take a walk before we talk."

Rule #5: Understand the difference between a criticism and a complaint. A criticism is an attack on a person's *character*, while a complaint is a request for change in a person's *behavior*. An example of a criticism: "You *always* forget my birthday. You're the most inconsiderate person I've ever known." By contrast, a complaint is descriptive and specific, avoids words such as "always" or "never," and doesn't label the person's character. Ideally, it includes an invitation to brainstorm about alternatives. An example of a complaint: "This is the second year you have forgotten my birthday. Birthdays matter to me, and I wonder if we can talk about a way for you to remember it next year."

Rule #6: Wait for the right moment to speak — even if you want to express love. Those of us who use words as our language of love (which we'll get into more in Chapter 13, on connection rituals) can't get enough praise, affection, and appreciation. Others may find it annoying to hear how much their partner loves them when they're studying instructions on how to play a better game of pickleball, planting a tree, or watching a movie. Even when you're speaking sweet words, remember the number-one rule of wholehearted loving: your partner is *not* you. Your partner may have a different love language than you do. Spoken words of affection may be appreciated, but the preference may be for short and sweet. Offering that person a long mushy declaration of love may set you up to feel rebuked, even when that's not your partner's intention.

A conversation is the responsibility of both people. However, whoever starts the conversation bears the primary responsibility for setting the mood for how it proceeds.

For the person who is being asked to participate in the conversation, I suggest you both agree on the twenty-four-hour rule. This means a partner can always say "not now" if he or she doesn't want to have a particular conversation, but a time to have it must be found within twenty-four hours.

EXERCISE: Starting a Conversation

Complete the following worksheet.

1. Have you ever started a conversation without first checking in about your partner's emotional state? Briefly describe one of those conversations here.

2. Now imagine that you did check in first to understand your partner's emotional reality. How might the conversation have gone differently?

3. What are some phrases you could use to check in before having an important conversation?

4. If your partner wants to start a conversation, what are some ways you might respond if you are not feeling like it at the moment your partner asks?

Sharing

If your partner has done the exercise, share your answers with each other.

Mirroring

Mirroring, the process of accurately reflecting the content of a message from your partner, is a helpful "smart speaking" tool in the face of tension or conflict. To mirror, one person (the "sender") speaks about something meaningful, taking no more than two minutes. The other person (the "receiver") listens and restates what the sender said without editing, interpreting, or judging it. Then the receiver checks for accuracy and asks if there is anything more the sender would like to say. This process helps make sure you are hearing what your partner is saying without omitting anything or putting your spin on it. Here's an example:

Sender: I'm really worried about the project I am starting on at work.
Receiver: Let me mirror you. You are really worried about the project you are starting on at work. Did I get it right? Is there more?

Then the sender and receiver switch roles and repeat the process. Remember, this is *not* a conversation. It is a practice of sharing and listening. Because of this, it's important to directly say, "I'd like to mirror you to be sure I hear this correctly," so that it doesn't sound as though you are a parrot. You should both be consciously embarking on a process you both understand and agree with.

It's important for senders to do the following:

- Use short, "bite-size" sentences, staying on one topic.
- Speak about yourself rather than about your partner.
- Remain open, curious, kind, and aware of your nonverbal messages.

Because mirroring is a practice in listening and expressing empathy, receivers should remember to do the following while listening:

- Keep the focus on your partner, not on your own thoughts, judgments, or similar life experiences.
- Maintain eye contact, and look at your partner with "soft eyes," the kind you use to show caring and affection.
- Remain open, curious, kind, and aware of your nonverbal messages.

JOINT EXERCISE: Mirroring

Practice mirroring with your partner. If you're working on your own, invite your partner to join you for this exercise; otherwise, simply read through it to glean the knowledge and save the tool for the next time you need it in conversation.

Select one person to be the sender and one to be the receiver. Use mirroring while sharing the lessons you've each learned in this chapter about defensiveness and speaking with intention using the sentence stems below. The sender should complete the sentence stem while the receiver listens; then the receiver repeats the exact words the sender uses. Try to do this with interest and understanding. Here is an example:

Sender: What I learned from reading about defensiveness is that I often respond to your criticisms by acting as though you are wrong and then secretly beating myself up for what I think you are accusing me of.

Receiver: What you learned from reading about defensiveness is that you often respond to my criticisms by acting as though I am wrong and then secretly beating yourself up.

Go through all seven stems; then switch roles.

1. What I learned about myself from reading about defensiveness is...
2. One way my defensive strategy may cost us in our relationship is...
3. I realize that I...
4. I appreciate that I...
5. Something I can work on to help us be more open and whole-hearted is...
6. What I learned about myself from reading about speaking intentionally is...
7. I appreciate that you...

Reflections and Sharing

1. How did this method of communication differ from the way you might have communicated if you weren't engaging in mirroring? Discuss this with your partner.
2. What are the most important takeaways from each of these two PAUSE skills? Write them below.

Undefended connection:

Smart speaking:

You've now got four of the Big Five communication skills under your belt: presence through active listening, accepting the *and*, undefended connection, and speaking smartly. You're well on your way to being a mindful communicator. In the next chapter, we'll tackle the last and perhaps most important element of mindful communication: emotional intelligence.

The Five
Top Habits
of Emotional
Intelligence

12

The last of the Big Five skills of mindful communication represented by our PAUSE acronym is *emotional intelligence*, which is the ability to recognize, understand, and manage emotions, widely considered to be the most important quality of successful leaders, mindfulness practitioners, and intimate partners. It is what helps us feel compassion for our partner even in the face of stressful and threatening logjams. Strong emotional intelligence allows us to recognize the deeper issues at hand and helps us choose the most useful skills to work through the problem rather than resorting to the two most common companions of relationship stress: blame and defensiveness.

Many of the other skills we looked at in the last few chapters, including active listening, accepting the *and*, and undefended listening, actually require and contribute to our emotional intelligence. Now we will explore some other aspects of it and discuss how you can raise your emotional skill level in five simple ways.

Clarissa and Lainey: "I Can't *Believe* What You Did!"

Clarissa and Lainey arrived at my office for an emergency appointment. They had seen me several months before, and I'd assumed they were doing well. Then Lainey left me a phone message saying, "Things are dire." She was practically screaming into my voice mailbox. "We're in a fight that could end our relationship."

They arrived the next day, their faces pinched and eyes blazing with contempt for one another. Each sat on opposite sides of my long sofa, making sure there was a pillow between them.

"I can't believe what she did," began Lainey, her voice shrill and threatening. "She told my family about my financial trouble, and she actually shared details about my credit-card debt. I would *never* talk to anyone about her business. And believe me," she added quickly, "there's *plenty* to hide about her."

Clarissa countered, "Maybe I shouldn't say this, but I can't help it. Lainey tells everyone everything about our private life. And *you* told me" — she looked now at her partner with piercing eyes — "that you tell them everything about your financial problems yourself. I didn't know this was a secret, but of course you stretch the truth with me most of the time."

Clarissa rolled her eyes, turned away from her partner, and took a long, loud drink from her water bottle. Then she blurted out, "She stole money from our vacation savings to pay the last credit-card bill!"

I remembered when the two women had taken my Love Skills class a year before this meeting. We had spent a whole morning on the lesson that the opening sentence of any confrontation determines how successfully — or unsuccessfully — it will go. We had gone over the five essential habits of emotionally intelligent people, and they seemed to get it clearly. Yet in their current confrontation, Clarissa and Lainey had broken most of the rules of emotional intelligence.

So I worked with them to help them genuinely listen to each other, feel and express empathy, and see the story from the other's point of view. This process helped both of them to calm down enough to begin to repair the original trouble and resolve the mess they'd made with their inability to use their emotional intelligence, which I knew they both had within them.

A Case Study in Emotional Intelligence

Make sure you're caught up on Clarissa and Lainey's situation above. As we look at each of the five habits of emotionally intelligent people below, see if you can identify the mistakes Clarissa and Lainey made that escalated their disagreement into an all-out war. Feel free to complete the accompanying exercises together with your partner, taking time to reflect on questions separately and then sharing your responses with each other before moving on.

Habit #1: Self-Regulation

Do these statements sound familiar?

"I just *had* to say it."
"I sent that email before I'd thought it through."

These statements indicate someone whose behavior is ruled by impulsivity. If one doesn't pause for a moment before responding, such emotion-driven behavior can lead to disastrous outcomes.

EXERCISE: Regulating Emotions

Answer the following questions, first the ones about Lainey and Clarissa and then the ones about yourself.

1. On a scale of 1 to 5, with 1 being "no ability to regulate emotions" and 5 being "exceptional ability to regulate emotions," how do you think Lainey and Clarissa scored? For each person, give three reasons why you gave her this score.

   Lainey _____

   a.

   b.

   c.

   Clarissa _____

   a.

   b.

   c.

2. Using the same scale, how would you rate yourself on your overall interactions with your partner when you're feeling upset, angry, or vulnerable? _____

3. Think back to a time when you felt emotionally upset with your partner and didn't do a very good job of regulating your emotions. What happened? How did you feel afterward? How did you and your partner behave toward each other afterward?

4. Now think back to a time when you felt upset but were able to regulate your reactions. What happened? How did you feel afterward? How did you behave toward each other afterward?

Habit #2: Awareness of and Empathy for Others

When we talk about conflicts with our partner, we usually focus on our feelings, concentrating on how we felt about our partner's actions: "*I* felt this way when *you* did *that*." Emotional intelligence allows us to reverse that process, to leave the zone of "I" and enter the zone of "you."

Part of this process is simply about being aware of what others are going through. Emotionally intelligent people are able to detect both verbal and nonverbal cues about others in order to recognize their moods, emotions, and sensitivities. This helps them know what to say and when to say it.

Empathy takes that awareness a step farther. It's a core component of emotional intelligence and perhaps the most important communication skill of all. Empathy helps us personally tap into the emotional reality of another person: when your partner is sad, you can not only recognize that sadness, but also understand what it would feel like to be in your partner's shoes. It's like crossing a bridge: you're able to leave your vantage point, go to the other side of the bridge, and see the world from someone else's point of view.

Signs of empathy include:

- Making eye contact
- Nodding your head appropriately
- Refraining from interrupting
- Mirroring the other person's feelings
- Acknowledging the other person's perspective
- Showing curiosity, compassion, and interest

You know you are being empathetic when the conversation deepens and when others feel safer and more supported instead of feeling the need to defend their perspective or emotional responses. Importantly, you do *not* have to agree with the others' point of view to empathize and understand what they're going through.

When we can intimately feel and understand the emotions of people around us, it's a lot easier to work out differences. If Lainey had responded with awareness and empathy for Clarissa, she would not have said, "I can't believe what she did." Instead, she might have tried to imagine what had driven Clarissa to talk to Lainey's family, and she might have discovered that Clarissa's fear over the debt Lainey had accumulated prompted Clarissa to act out of desperation to try to get help. If she had dug even deeper, she would have heard about the time when Clarissa's parents were out of work and had no savings, and five members of her family lived cramped in her uncle's small trailer for two years.

This does not mean it was okay for Clarissa to speak to Lainey's family about Lainey's debt. But if Lainey could stretch to understand the underlying fears that provoked Clarissa's behavior, she'd be more likely to confront the problem more calmly, without slinging blame.

An empathetic approach from Lainey might sound something like this: "Clarissa, I know I have a real problem with spending. I get that it was really a betrayal when I took the money from our vacation account and didn't tell you. I'm going to get some help to work on this, and I am really sorry about the pain I've caused you."

Once Lainey has taken responsibility for her part and apologizes for it, she can then tell Clarissa how she felt when Clarissa discussed the issue with her family. She can ask her partner not to do it again. But this needs to take place in a different conversation, or at least once Lainey has owned her part of the turmoil and asked Clarissa how she feels in response.

Of course, there is no guarantee that a more empathetic approach will result in less anger on her partner's side. (A good and vital point.) This is a good time to remember that all we can do is respond in a way that seems fair and compassionate. We can't control how our partner reacts.

As for Clarissa, she might have approached the conversation with more empathy by saying, "Lainey, I am so sorry I betrayed your trust and talked behind your back to your family. I realize how horrible that must have been for you, and I promise I won't do that again."

A note about justifications: In these approaches, we see no excuses or self-justifications. There is simply a sincere effort to understand and validate the other person's point of view and make a genuine apology. Clarissa can convey how upset she is about the money at a later point when emotions have calmed. Once we've owned our own side and apologized for it, it's important not to backtrack and justify our own bad behavior by referring to our partner's "crimes." Avoid saying something like, "I'm sorry, but let's not forget that I only did that because you gave me no choice." Instead, an apology needs to take full ownership for what you did, regardless of what the other person did. "I am sorry I did that to you; I can see why it hurt you, and I regret saying it."

As each woman comes to understand how she contributed to the trouble between them, the couple are creating a much softer opening to talk about the deeper issues at hand: that Lainey is a big spender and took the couple's joint vacation money to pay her debts, and that Clarissa revealed these facts to Lainey's family without her partner's permission.

Habit #3: A Healthy Inner Dialogue

Think about your own "inner dialogue" — the repetitive conversations you have in your head about yourself. Are you generally kind to yourself? Or are you largely critical?

Emotionally intelligent people recognize the textures of their own inner dialogue and manage self-criticism by countering it with more positive messages. Some of our negative self-talk comes from our younger selves, who remain very active within our psyche, telling us we are stupid, a klutz, or not as important as other people. When we develop a healthy inner dialogue, we recognize those critical voices and counter them with words from our wise and nurturing adult selves.

EXERCISE: Inner Self-Descriptions

Here you will investigate the language you use to describe yourself.

1. List ten words that you regularly use in your head to describe yourself, especially when you haven't done things perfectly:

2. When you review these ten words, how many are negative or critical?

3. List some words you'd rather use to describe yourself:

Sometimes it helps to name the voices that are criticizing, shaming, and doubting you. I have three different "shamers" in my head who bear the names of the people who originally caused me to doubt my worth. When I hear those inner messages now, I am generally able to say, "Oops, there goes Aunt Anita," or "Sounds like Sister Winifred is after me again," or "Whoops, I'm not in the fourth grade again — that's an *old* story."

I also silently identify the people in my young life who gave me positive messages, and I call up images of those people whenever I catch myself putting myself down. I remember an older girl at boarding school, Barbara, who always told me I had a "big spirit" in response to the nun who berated me for being "too much to handle"; my friend Del Nan, who told me I was capable of anything even if I didn't know it myself; and Nellie Frances Lutzi, my nanny, who made me laugh when it seemed the world was falling apart and, if that didn't help, pulled out a poem that always soothed my soul.

EXERCISE: Naming Your Inner Voices

Answer the following questions to begin identifying your inner voices.

1. Can you identify at least three of the voices that trigger self-doubt, other negative reactions, or a fear of hearing someone's feedback? Name them.

2. Who were three cheerleaders for you? These can include a parent, grandparent, older sibling, teacher, friend, or even a furry companion who let you know you were good enough.

When you observe yourself listening to your negative inner dialogue, call on your cheerleaders to help you feel balanced again.

Habit #4: Understanding and Managing Triggers

If your emotional abilities aren't in hand, if you don't have self-awareness, if you are not able to manage your distressing emotions, if you can't have empathy and have effective relationships, then no matter how smart you are, you are not going to get very far.

— DANIEL GOLEMAN, psychologist and author of *Emotional Intelligence*

Each of us has triggers stemming from earlier stress or trauma that continue to set off stress reactions in us. Imagine you were bitten by a raccoon when you were a child. Now, even as an adult, just seeing a raccoon (or even a photo of one) can activate fear chemicals that make your heart race and your muscles contract, throwing you into fight-or-flight mode. Emotional triggers set off the same kinds of stress reactions. An emotional trigger could be an angry face, someone who treats you with disrespect, or finding out that you've been left out of a gathering. In the case of Lainey and Clarissa, one of the triggers that prompted Clarissa to go to Lainey's family was the childhood memory of not having enough money and the years of hardship it created.

Here are some common emotional triggers:

- Feeling misunderstood
- Having plans switched on you
- Having promises broken
- Feeling ignored or left out
- Encountering someone's anger toward you
- Being questioned
- Hearing criticism and/or complaints about yourself
- Being gossiped about
- Being left out of the loop by people you care about
- Being compared to another

EXERCISE: Your Triggers

To explore what triggers you, answer the following questions.

1. List three moments when you got very upset about an issue that others felt was "no big deal." What do you think might have triggered your upset?

   a.

   b.

   c.

2. What might you have done differently to deescalate the situation? Think of three things you could have told yourself or the person(s) who triggered you? (Hint: Empathy is key.)

a.

b.

c.

Habit #5: Recognizing Feelings

When I told a neighbor I was writing a section of my book about communication and feelings, she laughed nervously. "My husband better read that!" she said, rolling her eyes. "He's a great guy in many ways. But feelings? No way! He doesn't seem to have them or want to hear mine. It's good to have girlfriends who understand me."

Indeed, such gender stereotypes are the fodder of numerous jokes, songs, and clichés that suggest women are much more emotionally attuned than men. Women connect face-to-face while men stand side by side; men want sex while women want emotional connection; men are rational while women are sentimental. The stereotypes are endless.

But the truth is, no research suggests one gender feels more than the other — we all long for relationship, authenticity, and emotional connection. Men experience as much depth of feeling and longing for connection as women do. They are as limited as women are by a culture that defines, determines, and restricts them according to their physiology.

What Are Feelings?

Feelings are interpretations of our body's reactions to stimuli. For example, a dog's growl prompts an automatic physical response that we interpret as fear, while snuggling into a puppy's furry softness prompts the physical sensation of pleasure. We label these and other reactions with words like *joy, sadness, fear, rage,* and *happiness.*

Some feelings are automatic interpretations that have likely evolved from our ancient ancestors' survival instincts, such as fear when we see a coiled snake. It is also true that people have different temperaments that cause them to react; some people are considered more "highly strung," while others are naturally more comfortable and easier "in their own skin." However, some of our go-to feelings are rooted in childhood experiences. These may feel natural and logical to the person experiencing the emotion, but they are based on experiences that create their own automatic responses. This is why people can interpret the same event in different ways.

For example, Bob was referred to me for anger-management issues at work. He would raise his voice when subordinates didn't finish a task, and he once left a meeting abruptly, slamming the door behind him. He was an ideal client, though, who was determined to change. Therapy, medication, and hard work helped turn this around, and as a result he regained both self-respect and the respect of his coworkers.

Several years later, Bob's daughter Marilyn came to me with marriage troubles. I suspected her issues were related to her father's angry outbursts, but I was wrong. In fact, she expressed empathy for her father's struggle. When I asked how the family had been affected by his chronic anger, Marilyn said, "We weren't. If Dad had a bad day, he would head to the wood pile and chop wood. We knew he was getting his anger out before coming into the house." Bob had taught his family that they didn't need to fear his anger.

Another client, Jean, couldn't be with someone who was expressing anger of any kind. This affected her job as a nurse, because she frequently had to deal with angry patients. Whenever one of them got upset, she felt physically ill. Jean had also grown up with an angry parent, her mother. But unlike Bob, her mother took her frustrations out on Jean by slapping her and yelling at her. Unlike Marilyn, Jean perceived anger as dangerous.

Basic Human Feelings

Let's examine the four primary human emotions: anger, sadness, fear, and happiness. *Anger* is the feeling that occurs when we are blocked from attaining what we want or need. We feel *sad* when we have lost something or are disappointed or lonely. *Fear* is the feeling that comes up when we are faced with losing something we value or are not able to attain something we believe we need, such as safety, health, money, or a relationship. *Happiness* occurs when we feel we have what we want or need.

Although these are the four basic feelings, they are each subject to many emotional variations, nuances, and labels. Below is a cheat sheet I give my clients to provide some labels for feelings, because some of us have trouble finding the right word.

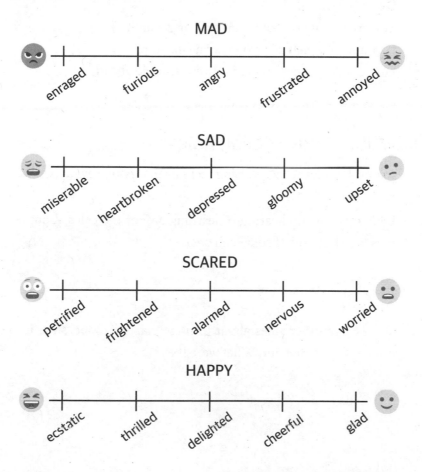

MAD

enraged — furious — angry — frustrated — annoyed

SAD

miserable — heartbroken — depressed — gloomy — upset

SCARED

petrified — frightened — alarmed — nervous — worried

HAPPY

ecstatic — thrilled — delighted — cheerful — glad

"Rules" about Feelings

The cultures and families we were raised in conveyed rules about feelings, giving permission to express them or imperatives to deny them — rules that still affect us today. Common rules about anger, sadness, fear, and joy include:

- Don't be negative.
- Don't upset your mother (or father) with that talk.
- Boys don't cry.
- Girls need to be helpful.
- You shouldn't be sad when you have so much to be grateful for.
- Keep your problems to yourself.
- Don't be irrational.
- You are out of control if you cry (or get angry).
- If you let yourself cry, you may never stop.
- Don't be too happy; there is always trouble ahead.

EXERCISE: Your Feeling Rules

Write about the rules for expressing feelings that you grew up with.

1. Did you grow up hearing or learning any of the rules about feelings listed above? If so, which ones?

2. Were there other rules about feelings that were operative in the home you grew up in? What were they?

Essential Truths about Feelings

Here are some things to remember about feelings:

1. Feelings are not under your conscious control. They are not right or wrong, good or bad. They just are.
2. You can deny that you have certain feelings if you find them unacceptable when you feel them, but they will show up in some form.
3. Though you can't choose feelings, you are responsible for expressing them appropriately. So it makes sense to know what they are.
4. Successfully managing a feeling requires letting yourself feel it, so that you can choose what to do with it.
5. Your feelings are important messages about yourself. Recognizing them will empower you.
6. The way your parents managed their own feelings or responded to yours as they raised you is probably the way you treat your feelings now.

Recognizing Feelings

One way to work with our feelings is through the mindfulness practice of RAIN, developed by Vipassana meditation teacher Michele McDonald. It has four easy-to-remember steps following the acronym RAIN.

R is for recognizing and acknowledging our feeling.
A is for allowing it to be there without judgment, which means giving ourselves permission to feel it.
I is for investigating its source with curiosity.
N is for not identifying with it, which means not defining ourselves through it. (Feeling angry, for example, doesn't make one an angry person.)

We can use feelings as internal barometers to know ourselves more deeply and to experience fuller lives. Whether feelings are based in biology, family history, or social influences such as culture (or all three), they contain important information about us, and they will affect our relationships if we suppress them or let them take charge. Regulating feelings effectively begins with recognizing them, acknowledging them, and choosing how best to manage them.

JOINT EXERCISE: Emptying the Jug

The following is one of the most popular exercises we do in the Love Skills class. It was originally introduced by PAIRS founder Dr. Lori Gordon and her son Seth Eisenberg. (For more fabulous tools and suggestions, visit the PAIRS website, or find a PAIRS teacher at participant.pairs.com/about.)

This couples' exercise will give partners the opportunity to express all the things they're mad, sad, scared, and glad about at the present moment. Sit facing your partner and decide who will be the first listener ("receiver") and who will be the first speaker ("sender"). The receiver's job is to listen to the sender's sharing without judging, interrupting, or commenting, except to say "thank you" at the end of each sentence. The sender's job is to speak in short sentences that are easily followed by the receiver and to avoid attacking or blaming. If you are the sender, focus on your own feelings and behaviors, not on those of the other person.

Here's how it works:

Receiver: What are you mad about?
Sender: [Answers, naming one issue.]
Receiver: Thank you. What are you mad about?
Sender: [Answers again with one issue.]
Receiver: Thank you. What are you mad about?

Repeat until the speaker feels satisfied or finished. Then:

Receiver: If there were one more thing you were mad about, what would it be?

Sender: [Responds.]

Receiver: Thank you.

Now repeat the process with each of the next three emotions:

- What are you sad about?
- What are you scared about?
- What are you glad about?

Then switch roles and do all four questions for the other partner.

At the end of the session, both people thank each other for participating in the experience.

It is important to complete the entire exercise, going through all four of the emotions for each person. Typically, it takes fifteen to thirty minutes altogether, and it's important that the time allotted to each speaker is equal. You might want to set a timer for this purpose.

Reflections and Sharing

Sit facing one another and talk about what you thought and felt while "emptying the jug." What worked? Was there anything you didn't like or ways you could make it better for yourselves? This is not a time to comment on your partner's sharing but to reflect on your own experience as a speaker and a listener.

Remember the PAUSE

In the past three chapters, we've explored the five essential components of mindful communication using the acronym PAUSE.

P is for *presence* through deep and active listening.

A is for *accepting* the "and," which allows many truths to be present at once.

U is for *undefended connection*, which allows for vulnerability and receptivity.

S is for *speaking* with skill and intention.

E is for *emotional intelligence*.

The great news about all five elements of PAUSE is that with steady practice, we can greatly improve our skills. We just need to be patient with ourselves, as the process of communicating more effectively can be quite difficult for many of us because it involves a lot of self-awareness, self-control, and patience.

Discussion with Your Partner

Take time to talk with your partner about the most important takeaways from this section. Are both of you willing to commit to learning new habits to raise your emotional intelligence? If so, I suggest finding a book on emotional intelligence that appeals to both of you, watching a TED Talk, or listening to a podcast about it. I especially recommend anything by Daniel Goleman, Dan Siegel, and Brandon Cooper.

We're about to move on to a fun, sometimes thrilling, and sometimes frightening part of the Love Skills program: getting more intimately connected with our partner. We will explore specific ways to preserve and deepen our connection, so that when the inevitable troubles occur, we'll have more tools to help us make necessary repairs — and to build a bridge to greater intimacy, compassion, and pleasure.

Establishing Connection before Conflict

13

Love doesn't just sit there, like a stone; it has to be made, like bread, remade all the time, made new.

— URSULA K. LE GUIN, *The Lathe of Heaven*

During the early days of our marriage, Tim and I spent a lot of time taking self-help classes, reading relationship books, and passing on what we learned to other couples in the classes we taught. Often, we were tired before we even left home to attend a workshop. Each of us was working long hours and putting too little time into our relationship. It already felt solid enough, and other responsibilities called to us.

On one particular occasion, we had been on the road for an hour — heading to yet another relationship workshop, this time going as students and not teachers — when Tim suddenly said, "This is the third weekend in a row we'll have spent indoors. When will we be done with this?" He sounded annoyed.

A bit self-righteously, I answered, "I can't imagine we'll *ever* be done with learning how to have a better relationship."

He looked out the window. "I'm so sick of spending weekends indoors and being in groups, endlessly talking about feelings and connections," he groused. "Sometimes I feel like I'm going crazy in those rooms. I just want to ride my bike, walk in a forest, and feel the wind on my face."

When we fell in love during the early years of The Merge, I fell for Tim's outdoorsy, nature-loving side. He took me camping and hiking, and we ran rapids in rafts. He also happily accompanied me to the activities I loved — plays, restaurants, and classes on the meaning of life. I was enraptured by his New Zealand boyhood stories of climbing trees, building forts, and saving baby birds who had fallen from their nests. He couldn't hear enough about my San Francisco girlhood and the hours I spent in bookstores, attending outdoor concerts, and going to the theater. We called ourselves "the Kiwi and the American" — the country boy and the city girl. Our harmonious blend of nature and culture was dreamy and delicious: opposites had come together to make a whole.

Fast-forward a few years, and things weren't so perfect anymore. We were beginning to enter the second stage of love, Doubt and Denial. That day in the car, he grumbled, "I'm tired of talking about my childhood. I just need to feel some country air."

A heavy silence followed his outburst. Then I said something exceptionally unhelpful: "What does that really matter if we're doing this for our relationship? Isn't *that* important to you?"

More silence — the loud, unhappy kind.

Each of us began to feel resentful and misunderstood. Although the cramped car made movement difficult, we began to physically shift away from each other. I turned and looked out the window, while Tim leaned into the steering wheel. We began playing out our narratives in our heads, justifying our own positions and blaming each other for what had just taken place. I could feel our respective anger and tension rising.

When we arrived at the workshop and introduced ourselves, we presented ourselves as a polite, confident, responsible couple who were there to improve their relationship. I imagine people were impressed with us.

But as we began to practice the first exercise, telling one another about a frustration we were feeling, the tension between us continued to build. We held it together for about fifteen minutes, at which point a helper came over and sat down with us. She asked us how we were doing with the exercise. Within a minute, we regressed into our four-year-old selves, whining to a parental figure about how the other just *wasn't being fair.* Our voices and gestures escalated, and the helper, who was brand-new, looked increasingly overwhelmed until finally she got up and brought over a "senior" teacher.

When I reflect on this incident now, I'm amazed at how easily Tim and I became unhinged and how difficult it was for us to regulate our emotions. Fortunately, the senior teacher had seen it all; she invited us to go into another room with her.

There, she asked us to try an experiment. Despite our irritation, we agreed. Taking an orange out of her bag, she instructed us to stand facing each other, place the orange between our foreheads, and move around the room while keeping the fruit in place. I complained that this was the silliest task I'd ever been given, but Tim said, "Hey, we blew the whole weekend to be here. Let's do what she says."

So I set aside my indignation to play this utterly preposterous game. After about ten seconds of feeling stupid and self-conscious, we began giggling at the absurdity of our task. The game became playfully serious as we moved back and forth, gently trying new positions together to see if we could keep the orange in place. Within minutes, we were full-out laughing and playing together.

The instructor congratulated us on our teamwork and asked how we were feeling. To my surprise, I felt our deep friendship and affection bubbling back up. We had always laughed easily together, and that silly nonthreatening game had soothed our frustrations and softened our hearts. We hadn't really played together for months now, and this seemingly small reconnection had made us ready to talk and listen again. Although our opinions on how we should spend our free time didn't change, we felt connected again.

That's how I learned the most important lesson about communication, one that I'd like to pass on to you. Without genuine connection, talking about a stressful topic or one you disagree about can quickly break down communication between people who are already tired and irritable.

We had begun that car trip with a deficit in our connection, having lost touch with the heart of our relationship. Once we reconnected with the fun, affection, and friendship that are at the core of our relationship, we could better appreciate each other's perspectives and the ways our needs might not always be identical.

The research of clinical psychologist and world-renowned relationship expert Dr. John Gottman shows that stable and happy couples have a five-to-one ratio of positive to negative interactions. That means for every complaint or troubled exchange, we need five positive interactions to preserve the balance. The five positives are like a bank account into which you make regular deposits to maintain a reservoir of savings, which cushions the relationship when you make an unexpected "withdrawal" from the account, like an argument, time apart, or being distracted due to other stresses.

Here are some suggestions for creating those times of connection with your partner.

Sliding-Door Moments

In any interaction, there is a possibility of connecting with your partner or turning away from your partner. One such moment is not important, but if you're always choosing to turn away, then trust erodes in a relationship — very gradually, very slowly.

— DR. JOHN GOTTMAN, psychologist and relationship expert

Before I ever heard about sliding-door moments, I had an experience that forever changed how I interact with the people I love.

I love chickens. I love their enthusiastic pecking and clucking, and for years we have kept a few in our backyard. One of my best friends, Deb, finds them annoying, and we used to laugh at this difference between us. One day, she visited while I was happily watching my special hens dig for worms. She sat beside me and asked me to tell her about my "girls."

"But you don't like chickens," I said.

"No," she answered, "but I love you, and you love them. So tell me about them."

So I did. I told her their language includes up to thirty trills, peeps, clucks, and squawks and that they express anger, sadness, relief, and happiness with their cackles and growls. She started laughing, and I laughed with her, and we launched into a very funny analysis of what Enneagram types my three chickens represented.

Later that day, my husband began to talk about the "triple-chainring setup" of the gears on a mountain bike. I started to zone out, but then I remembered what Deb had said. Instead of nodding dutifully, I asked him to "tell me more." His enthusiastic response amply rewarded my effort, and I felt more connected to him for the rest of the day — and learned some interesting new things about bikes.

I don't think Deb will ever pet my chickens, nor will I become a gear expert, but we both had the unexpected pleasure of learning something new and connecting more deeply with someone we loved, because we walked through that open sliding-glass door and paid attention.

In a relationship, the "sliding-door moment" describes our response when a partner offers us some kind of connection, and we either step through the open door toward them or turn away. If you are what I call a Wave (see Chapter 6), turning toward your partner will come naturally. If you are an Island, turning toward the other person will be harder. Nonetheless, you can learn to increase your "yes" responses.

EXERCISE: Looking for a Door to Step Through

Once a day for the next week, look for a small bid for connection from your partner. It may be when she shares something about work, when he reports a conversation he had with a friend, or a show of enthusiasm about a basketball game or gluten-free restaurant. It may be something you don't care about, have heard many times before, or feel is insignificant. (This is what makes it a practice; you can't count on your own spontaneous interest to cause you to respond positively.) Instead of brushing your partner off, make a conscious decision to engage; ask her to tell you more or thank him for telling you.

Remember, it's not the big things that build trust. It's the collection of small moments when partners step through sliding doors, when they affirm they care about what matters to their partner enough to truly listen. Connection works.

Rituals of Connection: The Lifeblood of Relationships

A ritual is a meaningful behavior we practice regularly. We seldom think about whether we feel like doing a particular ritual; we simply get up, brush our teeth, start the coffee, and walk the dog.

Besides morning rituals, we have routines for bedtime, celebrations, funerals, holidays, observances for certain days of the week, and perhaps a celebration of the full moon. Some people have wordless rituals for letting their partner know they want to make love, such as lighting a special candle. Many parents use a portion of a wall to mark their children's height on each birthday or take a photo on the first day of each school year. Native Hawaiians practice a sunset ceremony every night: as the sun goes down, participants stand facing the ocean and silently reflect on the day. Did they keep their promises, do good work, and take that ocean swim they'd said they would? Which moments were touching, happy, or sad during the day? As the sun meets the ocean, that day, with its disappointments and its victories, is released, as they await the dawn and the chance to begin again.

Rituals comfort and nurture us. They become something we can count on no matter what is going on in our lives. Making regular time to connect with ourselves and others is not only the soul food of love, but it maintains us through the stormy and frosty seasons of our relationships. Meaningful gifts, memorable trips, or a single profound act of giving from a partner — such as agreeing to let your partner's sister live with you for three months while she gets her life together — are touching, standout moments in a relationship. However, research shows it's the steady sprinkle of smaller moments of kindness and care that create a trusting and healthy relationship. Consider my husband Tim's gesture of making me a latte every morning, a ritual he's maintained for some thirty-five years now.

Ritualizing our connection helps keep our relationship account in the black. Rituals ensure we stay linked to each other even when we are tired, annoyed, or feeling distressed at work. They are regular reminders of the friendship we share.

Daily Temperature Reading

The Daily Temperature Reading (DTR) was developed by family therapist Virginia Satir and later taught by the PAIRS Foundation. It offers a step-by-step process for communicating with your partner and requires that each person share an item that falls in one of five distinct categories. Although the exercise is ideally done face-to-face, people have done it through emails, phone calls, texts, and video conferences.

Practicing the DTR — even if it feels stilted and corny at first — will become a habit and will ease your communication. Almost everything you need to share regularly with your partner will fit into one of its five categories:

1. **Appreciations:** These are things you appreciate about each other. These statements can range from the simple ("I like what you're wearing today") to the sublime ("I love the way I can talk about anything with you and you seem to get it") and may address either characteristics or behaviors ("I like how caring you were with my mother yesterday").

2. **News:** This is information, which ranges from the incidental to the vital. One person in a relationship is often better at passing along information than the other. We often forget to update our partner about a change in plans ("I forgot to tell you that the neighborhood party was changed to next month on the third Sunday, so we are free to do something else next weekend") or about news ("I had this weird dream last night" or "I read in the paper that..."). Sharing news reminds us of our shared lives and helps us to stay connected.

3. **Puzzles:** These are worries or confusions. Clear up big or little mysteries before they grow and before concocting a story to explain them (without consulting your partner). Most puzzles have simple explanations. Try saying, "I am confused about..." or "I wonder..." ("whether you still have a toothache," "whether you

were upset this morning," "how the article you talked about a few weeks ago ended").

4. **Small complaints and requests for change:** This is information about small changes you'd like your partner to make. This is not a problem-solving tool but rather a practice of constructively voicing a complaint and giving the other person the information needed to change things if he or she chooses to do so. Addressing complaints and irritations when they occur stops anger from building up and erupting and prevents the Lumpy-Carpet Syndrome (which we'll talk about in Chapter 15). Here's an example of an effective complaint with a request for change: "When I see you've called and not left a message, I worry. Can you remember to leave a message and say why you called, even (or especially) if it's only 'I just wanted to say hi'?"

5. **Future dreams:** These are things you are looking forward to doing together, whether in the short or long term. These could be already-made plans ("I am so excited we are going to..."), plans you'd like to make ("I would love it if we could..."), or simply dreams you hope can happen eventually ("One day, I hope we can...").

JOINT EXERCISE: Daily Temperature Reading

Here's how couples can practice the Daily Temperature Reading:

- Find a time that works for both of you. Sit comfortably, and face each other when you speak.
- Speak in short sentences to prevent information overload.
- Have each person share one of the five temperature readings while the other listens without interrupting.
- During "Puzzles," the listener may respond to the speaking partner's question if it can be answered in a single sentence.

I suggest using this exercise three times a week for a month and then deciding if you want to continue with it.

The DTR is one of the most popular connection tools I have used in over two decades of teaching communication classes. I have met people who, years later, tell me they continue to practice DTR and that it continues to work its magic.

Eight Minutes a Day

One of the most common complaints couples have is not having enough time to work on — and enjoy — their relationship. We don't need to take long vacations or have extravagant nights out to stay connected. Regular walks, simple date nights, and setting aside short moments during each day when we come together and move apart are even more important than the more dramatic things like climbing Machu Picchu or taking a Mediterranean cruise.

Can you commit to eight minutes a day that will guarantee a huge return on your investment? If so, consider spending two minutes connecting with your partner at each of the four transition times described below.

> **Moment One: Waking up and reconnecting.** Thanks to Tim's lattes, I always start my day feeling grateful to him. If you can find a minute (or two) to meet, say hello, ask about each other's dreams, or silently spoon before rising, you can start the day with a sense of mutual openheartedness.
>
> I know one couple who take a walk on a beach near their house every morning, no matter how busy their day is or how rainy and uninviting the weather. Over their forty years of marriage, they have walked holding hands, sometimes talking nonstop and other times quietly looking in different directions. During some tough relationship seasons, they were so upset they didn't speak to one another during their walks — but they walked anyway. They have often said this morning ritual has kept them together through the rocky periods in their relationship. Having time for a walk is great, but two minutes of intentional focus can also make a big impact on how you feel toward one another the rest of the day.
>
> Beginning the day with connection also provides our bodies and hearts with a healthy dose of oxytocin, one of the "love

potion" chemicals that floods us in The Merge stage of our relationship — and is always available to us.

Moment Two: Leaving and separating for the day. The idea of the goodbye kiss makes me laugh (and slightly cringe). I think of those old TV programs and movies from the 1960s in which the man rushes out to work and his wife (already dressed in pearls and an apron) kisses him goodbye as she starts to vacuum. I find those scenes annoying, but science has demonstrated the power of that kiss. Even a quick kiss releases a burst of adrenaline and oxytocin. Taking a pause to say goodbye, looking at each other even for a moment, and wishing each other a good day sends you both off with a feeling of being cared for and connected and eager to reunite.

Moment Three: Coming home and reconnecting. Whatever distractions you may be dealing with, when you walk in the door set aside two minutes — at least — to say hello. Before you check email, return texts, or head for your workout room, stop and look at one another, ask how each other's day went, and give each other a welcoming hug. Two minutes — you can do that! (Maybe even three!)

Some couples share a ritual of a drink together each night: a kombucha drink, a sparkling Pellegrino, or a glass of wine. For others, mealtimes are a sacred ritual in which each person shares the highs, lows, and small moments of their day. Whatever you choose to do, make your daily reunion a time of welcome, genuine interest, and appreciation.

Moment Four: Going to sleep and separating. Going to bed is *not* the time to work out hassles or talk about problems. It *is* a time to keep technology to a minimum, release some of those great touch chemicals by kissing, holding, or making love, and appreciate that you each made it through the day. If you go to sleep at the same time, take just a moment to connect. If you go to bed at different times, tuck each other in with care and kindness.

Another thing you can do anytime is hug. Research shows couples who hug each other on the same day they have a fight tend to be less upset about the fight. Think of it as an insurance policy. If you hug and don't fight, it will feel great. If you hug and do fight, you will get over it much more quickly!

JOINT EXERCISE: Eight Minutes a Day

During a quiet time together, conduct a short "interview" with each other to find out how each of you would most like to feel nurtured during the two-minute connections. Fill in the worksheet below, and then start to practice. After three weeks, revisit the worksheet and change it however you need to, including adding an extra three minutes to spread out where you can among the four moments.

	Nonverbal	Touch	Words	Actions
Waking up and reconnecting				
Leaving and separating for the day				
Coming home and reconnecting				
Going to sleep and separating				

Discovering Each Other's Love Languages

My conclusion after thirty years of marriage counseling is that there are basically five emotional love languages — five ways that people speak and understand emotional love. In the field of linguistics, a language may have numerous dialects or variations. Similarly, within the five basic emotional love languages, there are many dialects.... The important thing is to speak the love language of your spouse.

— Dr. Gary Chapman, *The 5 Love Languages*

As Dr. Gary Chapman explains, we each have our own way of expressing and enjoying affection. One of the simplest ways to improve your relationship is to understand your partner's primary "love language," recognizing that you and your partner are two separate, different people who may prefer different means of conveying love. Otherwise, you're likely to give your partner what *you* want to get and then wonder why it is not appreciated. Similarly, if you don't share your own preferred love language with your partner, you may also not get what helps you feel connected.

Here are the five love languages according to Dr. Chapman:

Words: Affection is conveyed by freely offering positive affirmations — praise, affection, empathy — both verbally and through texts, emails, and notes. If this is your partner's language, focus on using direct communication to show how you feel. Remember an upcoming event and wish your partner luck. Whisper something sexy. Verbally appreciate your partner's body, hair color, sense of humor, or some other quality you love.

Touch: Physical touch is what shows affection. If this is your partner's language, connect via hand-holding or a quick foot rub while watching the news. If your sexual relationship is good, play with light erotic touch. However, if you're in a vulnerable place sexually — for example, if one person wants more sex than the other — let this go until we get to this topic in the next chapter. For now, snuggle, and if that's too much, a good neck rub or foot massage goes a long way.

Quality time: Spending time together in meaningful ways is what demonstrates affection. If this is your partner's language, accompany each other on a chore or errand day, do things you both love together, or watch the other play a sport. Go bird-watching, attend a lecture on astronomy, or take a class on wine-making. Express your affection with undistracted time together.

Acts of service: Affection is conveyed through attending to each other, doing each other favors, and generally going out of your way to make each other's lives better. If this is your partner's language, do a chore your partner doesn't like doing — filling the car with gas, going to the grocery store, or buying a gift for a parent. Make a date to do something together that your partner is particularly interested in, even if it's not something you would choose to do.

Gifts: Gifts are concrete representations of affection. If this is your partner's language, make a habit of picking up small presents for your partner every now and then. They don't need to be expensive — a brownie from the local bakeshop on the way home, a goofy mug you saw online that reminded you of your partner, or surprise tickets to a concert you know he or she would love. Every now and then, go big. If you don't know what to get, ask what your partner would like or go pick something out together.

Remember, what is important is knowing your own language and recognizing the language *your partner* speaks as different from your own. Let's say your partner is working in the yard all day. Let's look at how you would use *your partner's* language of love to show your appreciation and affection:

Words: Tell her how much you appreciate her efforts, and be specific. "I love where you put the peonies. You are making a beautiful park for us to live in."

Touch: Approach her when she is working and ask to hug her. Offer to give her a quick neck massage.

Quality time: Ask her if you can keep her company for a few minutes, helping her with tasks or just walking around, talking about different aspects of the yard.

Acts of service: Offer to put away the tools.

Gifts: Give her a gift certificate to her favorite garden store, or ask if she would like you to hire someone to help her for a few hours.

EXERCISE: Your Love Languages

There are numerous online tests as well as places in Gary Chapman's book to help you and your partner recognize your love languages. In the space below write down your love languages in order of importance and then your partner's.

My love languages:

1.

2.

3.

4.

5.

My partner's love languages:

1.

2.

3.

4.

5.

Working with Differences

Your partner is another person. Get it!

— Harville Hendrix, cofounder of Imago

When Jimmy gets sick, he feels vulnerable and afraid and wants a lot of attention, touch, and reassurance. When his partner, Sebastian, doesn't feel well, he responds very pragmatically. He wants the bare necessities and to be left alone. For years they tormented each other, each thinking the other responded to feeling ill in the same way. Whenever Sebastian got sick, Jimmy would fluff his pillows endlessly, hover by his bed, bring six kinds of juice, and profess his love. Sebastian felt annoyed and smothered. Whenever Jimmy got sick, Sebastian set a bowl of soup on the bedside table and asked if he needed anything else. That was it. Jimmy felt abandoned.

After ten years of doing this to each other, they had a conversation and realized each was giving the other what he would want for himself — not what his partner actually needed.

EXERCISE: Your Love Language Differences

Individually, write a brief response to each of these questions.

1. What makes you feel supported when you are sick?

2. How do you like to celebrate — big, small, or something in between?

3. What feels caring when you've had a hard day? Do you prefer connection or space? A little of both?

Sharing

If you're working with your partner, now exchange lists and discuss what you've written down using the following prompts. The takeaway: "You are not me. You are an individual with your own needs. I should ask, not assume, what you want." Ask the other person; don't assume you know.

1. When I look at your list, I am surprised by…
2. A way we are different is…
3. A way we are the same is…
4. One thing I appreciate about what you already do is…
5. What I will work on is…
6. **Stretch**: Something that I would be willing to commit to doing for the next two weeks is…[Hint: Ask your partner what would be most meaningful.]

Mirroring for Connection

Another very powerful tool to help us look at our partner's world is the process of mirroring, which we practiced in Chapter 11 while learning how to manage defensiveness. Mirroring isn't only a practice for conflict — it can also be a playful way to connect, learn about each other, and have fun together.

As a refresher, mirroring is the process of accurately reflecting the content of a message from your partner. When you mirror your partner, you attempt to use the *exact* words your partner has spoken, without changing, adding, or subtracting anything.

JOINT EXERCISE: Using Mirroring to Connect

For the following exercises, choose small nonthreatening responses about each topic. Then follow these instructions:

1. The sender finishes the sentence stems about each topic.
2. In response, the receiver echoes the sender's message word for word (to the extent possible) without paraphrasing.
3. When the sender has finished speaking, it's time for the receiver to

say the three magic words: "Tell me more." This may encourage the sender to go deeper, share more, or identify some surprising feelings, thoughts, or connections.

A Mirroring Exercise about Us:

What I remember about when we first met is...
What I found most attractive about you was...
What I remember about our first conversation is that...
I loved how you...
I knew it was getting serious when...
One of the best parts of those early days was the way you...
One of the most fun times we had was when...
A time I will always treasure was when...

A Mirroring Exercise about Childhood:

Something I loved doing as a child was...
One of my favorite gifts was...
A vacation I remember is...
A teacher who made a difference was...
A pet that meant a lot to me was...
A friend whom I liked a lot was...
A special book I read as a child was...
A song I remember singing was...[Extra points if you sing it now!]

A Mirroring Exercise about Life and Death:

I think life is mostly...
One of the wisest things I've ever heard is...
I think death is...

I feel death is...

If I could spend time with any person, living or dead, it would be...

What I feel about my own death is...

I want my legacy to be...

One thing about my life that I am grateful for is...

Other Ways to Connect

Some other ways to connect include:

- Make a date night and hold it as sacred, meaning *nothing* gets in the way.
- Use Alicia Muñoz's book *A Year of Us* to spend time each week answering questions about yourselves and your relationship together.
- Leave a loving note somewhere where your partner will find it.
- Send your partner a story via email about something he or she cares about.
- Read a book out loud together.
- Take a shower together.
- Give one another a massage.
- Work out together.
- Make a place on a dresser or bookshelf for special framed photos.
- Listen to a TED Talk together.
- Learn to play pickleball.
- Take up the tango.
- Initiate foreplay in the kitchen, garden shed, or somewhere new.
- Light candles in your bedroom.

EXERCISE: Ways of Connecting

Create your own list of ways you and your partner can connect as a couple.

1.

2.

3.

4.

5.

6.

7.

8.

9.

Sharing

After your partner completes the list above, share your lists and agree to do one item on each person's list per week. If that feels like too much, take turns. Whatever you agree on, do it whether you feel like it or not, even when you are busy or not feeling close to your partner.

Just as the "dance of the orange" brought Tim and me together — even making us laugh during a fight and helping me accommodate him for more outside time — making time to feed your relationship regularly will help prevent trouble, soften it when it comes, and nurture the heart of the relationship with companionship and love. Keep practicing these most important connection rituals as we move on to explore the arena of conflict. And just so you don't forget the essence of the connection that first brought you together, perhaps keep an orange handy.

A Few Things
about Sex
I Know
for Sure

14

Erotic images, sensual pleasures, and words from love poems speak to something deep within each of us, regardless of our age, health, or relationship status. We're almost never beyond the point where we can start again.

— *Love Cycles*

When setting out to write this book, I gave a lot of thought to how to address the topic of sex. I could not come up with anything that seemed entirely right, because *all* the options seemed right. Or possibly wrong. Maybe useful. Or maybe troublesome. And therein lies the crux of the whole sexual *mishegoss* (the Yiddish word for "craziness"). Sex belongs everywhere, yet wherever it goes, it can potentially be a source of difficulty.

Our sexuality is one of the most complicated aspects of our humanness. It is woven into who we are, along with its attendant qualities of love, anger, spirit, passion, power struggles, hope, connection, family values, past stories, respect, abuse, shame, and pleasure. Whether we are "in love" or in a long and committed relationship, and the sex isn't so great, we may listen to music, watch films, talk to our friends, and feel everyone in the world has a fabulous sex life except us. But this is not true. Of course, some people do have great sex lives, but only a few do so for their *entire* lives. Sex is too complex to be that simple.

Fern was the most prim and proper woman I had ever known. She didn't have a naughty bone in her body or an experimental idea or impulse that wasn't controlled by her strict religious background. When she was diagnosed with dementia, she went to live in a care unit in her hometown in the Midwest. At ninety-four years old, she couldn't remember the name of her beloved first-born child, Marci. Yet one day Marci received a phone call from the director of the home, who was stammering and apologetic. Fern had been found in her bathroom performing oral sex on another patient who also had dementia.

Marci asked if her mother had seemed upset.

The director hesitated before answering. "Well, it was a bit awkward, because when the aides tried to interrupt them, your mother became more upset than we have ever seen her before. She spoke more clearly than she has since she got here. 'Let us alone,' she said. 'Go away! We are having a wonderful time.'" (Yes, she used the exact phrase "wonderful time"!)

"Different people might interpret Fern's actions in different ways," said Alicia Muñoz, author of a fabulous book for couples called *No More Fighting*, when I told her the story of Fern. "Was she acting out? Was it her dementia? Or was her sexuality seeking new ways of expressing itself that defied social expectations? Human sexuality truly is a force of nature, like gravity, water, wind, or light, that's difficult to contain. Remove inhibitions and constraints, and it often finds a way to emerge."

The point of this story is to emphasize that we *are* sexual beings, all of us, from conception until we die. Our sexuality, skin, brain, thoughts, feelings, and spirit are all linked to the mysterious, troubling, and amazing experience of being a human being. It opens us up to some of the worst abuse and the deepest connections and pleasure imaginable. We deny it, become addicted to it, live for it, and somehow live without it. It shows up in our deepest dreams and longings. For some of us, it has very little to do with how we see ourselves. For others, it becomes a large part of our identity.

We live in a culture with tremendous ambivalence about sexuality. On the one hand, the Puritan ethic taught that sex was purely for the purpose of procreation and that to engage in it for any other reason was sinful, as was experiencing pleasure. Our current culture, on the other hand, thrives on sexual images in advertising, media, and music.

Fifty Shades of Grey, the erotic trilogy that weaves together a sexual relationship with bondage, sadism, and forbidden fantasies and ends with true love, picket fences, and babies, has sold more than twenty million copies! What do you suppose people are so desperately searching for in that book? We relentlessly sell sex in marketing and the media, and yet, according to a 2016 study at the University of Chicago, millennials report fewer sexual encounters than the two generations before them, and the same study showed a decline in sex among middle-aged married couples.

Meanwhile, history teaches us that sexual variety — from homosexual to bisexual to heterosexual and beyond — has been a fact of life since the beginning of time. The scientific view that sees this as a natural variation is supported by several recent studies indicating that genetics play an essential role in sexual preference. Yet some religions still insist we are all born heterosexual and choose to fall in love with same-sex partners, which is seen as a punishable crime in some countries and a sentence to fire and brimstone in some belief systems. I think our cultural debate about sexual orientation reflects our profound ambivalence about sex.

There is so much to say about sex. To narrow down our scope to the most practical and applicable advice, I chose four topics we've already covered in this book — namely, the cycles of relationships, the Enneagram, personal values, and mindful communication (the PAUSE skills) — and will show how sexuality relates to each. Then you'll find additional exercises to complete with your partner.

If you're working as a couple and one of you is feeling vulnerable about the topic of sexuality in general, consider this wisdom from bestselling Indian author Manoj Arora: "Coming out of your comfort zone is tough in the beginning, chaotic in the middle, and awesome in the end...because in the end, it shows you a whole new world." If this topic feels uncomfortable, give it a try anyway with an agreement you can stop at any time. If it feels like the wrong time to take it on, then skip it and come back to it at a later time.

Top Truths about Sex

Let's begin with the things I know for sure. These are the key truths I've discovered about sex. Reflect on them and, if appropriate, discuss them with your partner.

> Truth #1: We can't distill or dilute sex into a "where, when, with whom, how, and how often" formula that works for everyone, because our sexuality is as unique as our thumbprint.
>
> Truth #2: Sex has been a part of us from the time we were in the womb and will remain a part of us until the moment we die. There are ultrasounds of baby boys with erections in utero and of both boy and girl babies masturbating. On the other end of the age spectrum, consider Fern.
>
> Truth #3: Be kind to yourself — and to your partner — as you explore your sexuality. This is not the time to judge, criticize, or make the other person's experience solely about yourself.
>
> Truth #4: Nothing is true for all people all the time when it comes to life, love, and sexuality.
>
> Truth #5: Education is essential for a healthy and happy sex life and begins with learning about yourself. This includes knowing how your own body works, touching it, looking at it, caring for it, and knowing what you like and don't like. (This is true even though it may be in direct contrast to the messages we get about our bodies.)
>
> Truth #6: Hugging, touching, kissing, and rubbing one another's shoulders are all part of intimacy. Indeed, the largest sexual organ of our body is our skin, and we know touch reduces stress, improves pain management, and enhances well-being in our relationships. Sometimes, when a couple's sex life takes a dive, they also stop touching. Yet we can have a rich and full intimate life just caressing one another's skin.

Love Cycles, Sex Cycles

Let's begin by revisiting the five stages of a relationship, this time zeroing in on what's going on sexually in each stage.

Stage One: The Merge

Biological anthropologist and human-behavior researcher Dr. Helen Fisher and her team at Binghamton University split the topic of romantic love into three categories: lust, attraction, and attachment. Some people may only feel one at a time, while others may feel all three simultaneously. Each state creates a hormonal change that affects the brain, and the unique mixture we each have produces a different chemical cocktail that I refer to in *Love Cycles* as the "love potion." These chemical ingredients are partially responsible for how we react to another person sexually.

- Lust: High in romance, this state increases testosterone and estrogen, which are both sexual motivators.
- Attraction: This state reduces serotonin, which affects appetite and mood. When we are low on serotonin, we may not feel the need to eat or sleep. We experience something very similar to obsessive-compulsive disorder (also affected by low serotonin), which contributes to the overpowering infatuation we tend to feel in the early stages of love.
- Attachment: This is the essential piece in a long-term relationship. Oxytocin levels are high. Oxytocin is often called the "cuddle chemical," because it largely appears during sex, childbirth, and breastfeeding. It's what makes us want to touch, smell, taste, and hold on to the person we love.

This potpourri of chemicals reduces inhibitions and old taboos, so we are willing to explore new sexual adventures and initiate sex — even if it isn't in our nature to do so — and opens us to the wealth of possibilities of eroticism.

Stage Two: Post-Rapture Blues

Attraction can look a lot like addiction. Dr. Fisher examined brain scans and found the regions of the brain that light up when people are addicted to alcohol, cocaine, or other drugs also light up during our initial ecstatic attraction to our partner. In Stage Two, however, old taboos reappear as the love chemicals decrease, and we long for the easy euphoria of the first stage and the passionate sex that comes with it. Desire discrepancy, a natural difference in the amount of sexual craving and passion between two people, now takes the form of a power struggle, as the person who wants more sex feels pushed away and deprived and the one who wants less feels overwhelmed and then guilty. The goodwill and ease that could easily manage this decreases as the fight for control increases.

Stage Three: Disconnection and Disenchantment

Now the happy chemicals are really gone, and our old prohibitions enter, often in the areas of oral sex, nudity, sex toys, sensual exploration, and spontaneous lovemaking. This can lead us to become angry, disconnected, and sexually shut down. At this stage, we may have perfunctory sex or none at all. Sexual energy may be redirected into work or exercise, and our erotic fantasies may be directed elsewhere.

Stage Four: The Decision

In The Decision stage, there's something about the possibility of losing one another that can actually enhance the sex life of some couples. For most couples, though, it is the last thing they think about when they are emotionally shut down, at least with one another.

Stage Five: Wholehearted Sex

Do NOT do unto others as you would have them do unto you.

— PEPPER SCHWARTZ, sociologist, sexologist, and coauthor of *The Normal Bar*

Once we understand that each of us is a whole person within ourselves, we can embark on a joint adventure to recapture passion. This requires motivation, skills, honest conversation, and the willingness to go beyond our comfort zone. We can explore sexuality in new ways, which may include our evolving erotic preferences, discomforts, fears, and hopes. Wholehearted sex allows for a shared adventure and emphasizes Pepper Schwartz's Rule (above), reminding us of how important it is to remember our partner is not us. We cannot read our partner's mind or assume our partner will like what we like in each part of lovemaking, from foreplay to afterplay. We need careful, openhearted conversations to make room for the needs of two people.

EXERCISE: Where You Are Sexually

Complete the following sentence stems.

1. When I think about the topic of sex, the thoughts, words, images, or feelings that come to mind are...

2. The most exciting and inviting parts of exploring this topic are...

3. What I feel the most concern or fear about is...

4. If my current sex life could be expressed with a song, book, or poem title, it would be called...

5. The way I would like to describe my sex life is...

Sharing

Now share your answers to the above questions with your partner. Instead of sharing by having a discussion, use the mirroring technique described in Chapter 11.

Then if you *both* feel comfortable enough to continue the conversation, do so using the mirroring technique with the following sentence stems. If one of you wants to stop, come back to it at a later time you both agree on.

1. The way I first learned I was a sexual being was…
2. From my childhood, I learned that sex was…
3. The healthiest message I got about sex was…
4. The unhealthiest message I got about sex was…
5. How those early messages have changed for me is…
6. Something I like about my sexuality is…
7. Something I want to change about my sexuality is…
8. Some of the feelings I have about my body are…
9. What I'd like you to know about my desire level is…
10. One of the first things I found sexy about you was…
11. A real turn-on for me is…
12. I really love the way you…
13. A sexual memory with you I love thinking about is…
14. What I would like us to work on together most of all is…
15. What I appreciate about you right now is…

Sex and the Enneagram

Our personalities can certainly influence our approach to sex. The Enneagram types can be an interesting and insightful lens through which to understand our sexual personality. In her book *Sex and the Enneagram: A Guide to Passionate Relationships for the 9 Personality Types*, Ann Gadd details some sexual characteristics that lovers of each Enneagram type might be more likely to have. Here are a few notes she shared with me:

Type One: The Idealist

- Seeing themselves as morally "good" people, Ones might feel they earn sex by doing the right thing and attending to the practicalities of life (tidying the house, mowing the lawn, paying the bills, etc.).

- Disciplined Ones might strive to be better at sex, believe they know the correct way to engage sexually, and attempt to "improve" a partner's sexual performance.
- Generally, they believe limitation is better than overindulgence.

Type Two: The Giver

- Twos tend to be seductive and caring lovers who make things all about you, while secretly hoping you'll reciprocate.
- They devotedly cater to their partner's sexual needs, showering affection on them and flattering them with lines like "You're the best lover I've ever had."
- They pride themselves on believing they alone know their partner's intimate desires.

Type Three: The Performer

- Threes often believe if they're successful and shine their lights brightly enough, they will draw the partner of choice and the sex they desire, like moths to the flame.
- Performance tends to be important — how many orgasms, the length of time an erection is maintained, and so on.
- Sex can become about goals and performance rather than intimacy.

Type Four: The Romantic

- Passionate and emotional, Fours often long for a lover who "gets" them and with whom they can be deeply and authentically intimate.
- Fours tend to draw lovers to them by being mysterious, special, different, and intense and appearing unobtainable.
- Less integrated Fours can become self-absorbed and lost in sexual fantasies.

Type Five: The Observer

- Fives may generally find being on their own to be less of a hassle than engaging in relationships, so they may be likely to opt for quick intense sexual activity with no lasting obligations.
- Cerebral Fives may try to master sex through the study of it, rather than emotionally experiencing it.

Type Six: The Loyal Skeptic

- Cautious Six lovers may be less inclined to explore the new sexually, preferring to stick to a safe and familiar routine. "The condom could break!"
- They are generally very loyal, faithful lovers.

Type Seven: The Epicure

- Free-spirited Sevens believe that if they present an upbeat exciting, interesting, enthusiastic persona, people will be drawn to them, and they can then start making sexual demands.
- Hedonistic Sevens usually want excitement and enjoy risk-taking. "Quickies" with strangers can be wildly enticing; boring vanilla sex is not.
- They may enjoy anticipating conjugal action, often as much or more than the actual experience.

Type Eight: The Protector

- Eights generally need to be in control when having sex — they want to be the dominant person, with things done according to their needs (though they may occasionally agree to explore their vulnerability in a more submissive role when they're with someone they trust).
- Sex is passionate and plentiful, but gentle foreplay could be missing.

Type Nine: The Mediator

- Sensual, adaptive Nines can merge their needs with their partner's to maintain harmony and can thus appear to be ideal lovers. Yet not having their own sexual needs recognized results in suppressed anger, which inhibits sex.
- Nines can find it hard to prioritize sex.
- Nines have good imaginations, which bodes well for spicy sex.

Sexual Values

Your sexual value system includes your beliefs, attitudes, and feelings about your own sexuality and sex in general. As we read in Chapter 8, our values reflect the core beliefs that really matter to us. They help guide us when we don't know which way to go. We also looked at how complicated a value can be, because any particular value may have a different or even opposite meaning for two people. For example, each partner in a couple may value a close and meaningful sex life, but one may view that as having caring and predictable sex, while the other may view a good sex life as experimenting with behaviors and constantly seeking new erotic thrills.

When Values Collide

Maggie had a lifelong history of anxiety, and her physician suggested counseling to help her manage it better. At one of our sessions, we talked about sex. Maggie told me she grew up in a deeply religious family in St. Louis. She graduated from high school in 1964 and planned to marry her then high-school boyfriend, who attended her church, soon after. They weren't allowed to have any friends outside the church, she told me, and women were not encouraged to go to college. A few weeks before the wedding, her mother entered her room to give her "the talk."

"My mother said, 'Soon you will have to perform a wife's duty and let him have his way with you,'" she explained. Maggie was overcome by a sense of paralysis and struggled to breathe as she continued with her story. "Then my mother put her small hands together and said, 'Dear, when it happens, you must close your eyes and remember Our Lord on the cross.'"

"And that," Maggie said, "was the end of my sex education."

The day after that conversation with her mother, Maggie ran away to San Francisco. She rented a room in a huge Victorian house in Haight-Ashbury with several other young people. She was soon swept up into their culture and got a job selling Grateful Dead T-shirts. She believed she was beginning to free herself from a childhood in which she had lived in fear.

Someone invited Maggie to a "Dance-In" at the Fillmore Auditorium, and she eagerly went, hoping to find another way of "becoming free." She described people clothed in velvet, leather, and top hats. Dazzling strobe lights threw brilliant colors all around as Jefferson Airplane blasted from the loudspeakers. The smell of incense was nearly overpowering. Huge rubber balls — each several feet high — began to roll into the auditorium for them to dance with, around, and over. The lights were flashing, Maggie recalled, and people were laughing and singing and flopping all over one another. She fell against a green rubber ball and rounded her body against it.

At this point in the story, Maggie stopped talking for a moment as if to gather the strength to continue. Then she described a man coming up behind her and rubbing himself against her, faster and faster as the beat of the music quickened.

"Something felt wrong, but I pushed the thought away," she told me. "Then I realized that he was dry-humping me. My older brothers used to laugh about our dogs doing that, so I knew what it was. I couldn't believe that it was happening to me."

Maggie described hearing two voices, one yelling, "Get the hell out of here! Push him off! This is sick!" and the other one screaming, "That's just the kind of thing your mother would say. Do you want to stay an uptight farm girl forever?" She started shaking and was sick to her stomach. She ran out the door and all the way home.

Our sexual value system tells us when (and if) sexual encounters are acceptable, but sometimes we have two conflicting values that scream loudly at us, one in each ear. We don't seem to be able to hear our own voice or find our own intuition about what's true, which may be neither voice. Maggie's inner voices, one representing her upbringing and the other rebellion against that upbringing, were at war inside her, causing her understandable and devastating anxiety. Her job would be to find her own voice and values — those that came from deep within — rather than either automatically absorbing the ones she was taught or reacting against them.

EXERCISE: Your Feelings about Sex

Circle (or write down on a separate sheet of paper) the words that stand out for you. Next to the selected words, write *C* for "curious," *U* for "upset," or *T* for "turned on."

Affair	Gentle	Naughty	Self-pleasure
Attracted	Gross	Passionate	Sensual
Beautiful	Hot	Phone sex	Sex toys
Boring	Immoral	Playful	Sex with a stranger
Celebration	In love	Pleasurable	Silk scarves
Comfortable	Intimate	Pleasure	Sinful
Connection	Kissing	Polyamorous	Smelling
Dangerous	Lesbian	Porn	Spank
Depraved	Licking	Procreation	Spiritual
Disgusting	Loud	Relaxing	Straight sex
Enjoyable	Lusty	Relieving	Taboo

Erotica	Man	Repulsive	Tantra
Exciting	Married	Rough	Taste
Exploitative	Masturbate	Sacred	Temptation
Forbidden	Moan	Same sex	Transgender
Fun	Naked	Satisfying	Virtual
Gay	Natural	Scary	Woman

Reflections

1. My first reaction to doing this exercise was…

2. What I find interesting about this exercise is…

3. What I want to explore further about this exercise is…

4. What worries me about this exercise is…

5. What reassures me about this exercise is…

EXERCISE: Your Sexual Values

The following questions will help you explore your own sexual value system.

1. Write down six statements about sex without thinking about them. Include any clichés, wishes, or warnings that come to mind. Begin with the sentence stem "Sex is..."
2. Next to each, write down your reaction to each statement you wrote.
3. Next to those, mark the statements based on what influenced your reaction. Mark those that are inherited from your "history" with an *H*. Mark those that are a "reaction" to what you learned with an *R*. If the statement really comes from deep inside you, representing what you believe is your "true feeling" about it, write *T*.

Statement	Reaction	Origin
1. Sex is		
2. Sex is		
3. Sex is		
4. Sex is		
5. Sex is		
6. Sex is		

Ask for help if you need it. If you are unclear or concerned or have a history of any kind of sexual abuse, get help from a trusted professional who can help you better understand your history and its impact on you.

Like Maggie, when we don't get support, we need to trust our own voices. We often spend our lives fighting conflicting voices in our head and never hear the one we need.

Sexual Conversations

Couples collude in silence. They decide it is easier to have no sex at all than to deal with the hurt feelings and unpredictable emotions, such as guilt or anger.

— KIMBERLY RESNICK ANDERSON, LCSW and certified sex therapist

Open communication is the key to a satisfying sexual relationship, whether you are brand-new as a couple or have been together for decades. For many of us, it doesn't come naturally; in fact, researchers agree one of the most common and problematic sexual issues is not talking about sex, including issues of frequency, style, and the need for negotiation. We each have a separate history, unique fantasies, and physical realities (including limitations, strengths, and differences in desire). Because of these inevitable differences, it's often easier to ignore the topic of sex altogether. At best, we make vague hints or mumbled suggestions that fly under the radar or are misunderstood. Or because they stir up our partner's anxiety, they are ignored or pushed away, which only further fuels our fears and frustrations.

So why do it? Because talking about sex can also:

- Be sexy.
- Enliven our relationship.
- Result in changes that benefit both people.
- Stop our sex life from shutting down as we experience inevitable changes in our bodies over time.
- Create more safety to connect more deeply than we thought possible.
- Be exciting.
- Result in more sex, which is better for our physical, mental, and relationship health.

We can use our PAUSE skills to more mindfully communicate about sex. The more we practice how to observe and describe what we feel inside and the more easily we can hear each other without judging the information (or the other person) as good or bad, the deeper the relationship and the better the sex can be.

Listening

Because it's often so hard for people to talk about sex, they tend to approach it with hesitation and embarrassment. As a listener, it's your job to be gentle, noncritical, and as nondefensive as possible.

Remembering the And

Two things can be true at the same time, and this includes your own thoughts and feelings about sex. Nobody addresses this as well as the psychotherapist and author Esther Perel when she says:

> So what sustains desire, and why is it so difficult? And at the heart of sustaining desire in a committed relationship, I think, is the reconciliation of two fundamental human needs. On the one hand, our need for security, for predictability, for safety, for dependability, for reliability, for permanence — all these anchoring, grounding experiences of our lives that we call home. But we also have an equally strong need — men and women — for adventure, for novelty, for mystery, for risk, for danger, for the unknown, for the unexpected, surprise — you get the gist.

Nondefensive Sex Talk

Conversationally, it can be harder to stay nondefensive while talking about sex than it is with other topics. Many of us are particularly vulnerable around the issue of sex due to all the double messages we have been given throughout our lives. One way to manage this vulnerability is to begin your conversation by owning how hard it is for you to talk about this subject. Ask your partner to respect your wishes when you need to take a break from the conversation. Just be sure you return to it after taking a breather.

Speaking with Skill about Sex

Here are three suggestions for sexual conversations:

1. No surprises. Start softly, with an agreement to talk about talking about it. For example: "I've been thinking about some things I'd like to share with you. They have to do with my own sexuality. Can we go for a walk this afternoon and talk about sex?"
2. Make requests rather than complaints. Beneath every complaint is a longing, so begin with the longing. Take care to keep your tone gentle and respectful. You might say, "I loved how we used to laugh and talk in the mornings together after we'd made love. I'd love to bring that back into our lives again." Or, "I love your touch so much. I'd love to feel more of it before we make love, because I don't get aroused as easily as you do."
3. Start the discussion somewhere other than your bedroom and not after sex.

Sexual Intelligence

Emotional intelligence also includes sexual intelligence. As the seasons of our lives change, we all need ongoing sex education. The most important component of all is knowing ourselves. There are many fabulous books, podcasts, talks, classes, and online courses to learn more about this ever-evolving topic, and I have listed a few in the Resources section at the end of the book.

Understanding Our Libido

We are each responsible for our own sexuality: understanding it, talking about it, and making it happen. We are also responsible for managing our own sex drive, which begins by acknowledging that it's a normal and healthy part of our humanness.

One of the most popular theories about libido, or sex drive, is that the hormone testosterone is the chief determinant of a person's level of sexual desire. Because most men have more testosterone than most women do, men are thought to have a greater and more constant libido than women. However, this is a generalization. Marriage therapist and writer Michelle Weiner Davis observes: "As someone who is in the front lines with couples, I have grown increasingly aware that women have no corner on the low libido market. In fact, based on my clinical observations and casual conversations with colleagues, I'd say that low desire in men is America's best kept secret." (This, of course, brings us back to the fact that nothing is true for everyone, especially generalizations about the genders.)

Although conventional theories say sexual desire is governed by hormones and biochemicals, sexuality expert Emily Nagoski, the author of *Come as You Are: The Surprising New Science That Will Transform Your Sex Life*, believes our minds are more in charge of our sex drive than our biology. She says we have a series of accelerators and brakes in our nervous system that send signals to the brain to "stop" or "go" sexually. If we want to increase our desire levels, we have to learn what our internal "driving system" is telling us.

EXERCISE: Sexual Accelerators and Brakes

On this worksheet, list what you believe are your sexual accelerators (turn-ons) and brakes (turn-offs). I offer some suggestions, but try to identify your own as well. Complete this exercise individually; then there are sharing instructions below.

Your Sexual Accelerators

Complete this sentence: I'm turned on by...

Examples: Words, gifts, eye contact, snuggling, wrestling, tickling, sharing steamy fantasies, dressing up, sex toys, certain clothes, being naked, erotic images, kissing.

Your Sexual Brakes

Complete this sentence: I'm turned off by…"

Examples: Too much aggression, too much passivity, hygiene issues (bad breath, dirty hair), going too fast, going too slow, dogs on the bed, kids at the door, sex toys.

Sharing

Exchange lists, and then use the prompts below to discuss them as a couple. You can use the mirroring technique again if it helps. Be sure to use your PAUSE skills for this exercise: listen, accept the *and*, practice undefended connection, speak with skill, and draw from the best of your emotional intelligence to manage your own triggers. Ask for a break if you start to feel overwhelmed and be gracious about accepting your partner's request for one. Finally, remember to always end these discussions by expressing your appreciation for one another.

1. Doing this list reminds me of…
2. What I liked about it was…
3. What I didn't like was…
4. What I need to work on is…
5. You could help me accelerate my sexual driving system by…
6. I don't know how to talk to you about…
7. What I appreciate about you is…

Conversation, Sharing, and Research

Sex as an act isn't terribly complicated, but mindful sex, sex with awareness, often takes tremendous courage, patience, and a willingness to hang out in our vulnerability. Mindful sex is about showing up as our whole selves, allowing ourselves to be seen, and being willing to truly see the other person or other people.

— YAEL SHY, founder and director of MindfulNYU

Talk with your partner about the prospect of a newer and better sexual relationship. Use the suggestions below as possible ways to make that happen. If one of you is reluctant to continue, let it go for a while and come back to it at a later time. If both agree, continue with this list.

1. Increase your sexual intelligence by learning about yourself in new ways and sharing with your partner. An example of this is to think about what kind of touch turns you on. Some people like soft, slow touch, while others like a firmer, more assertive touch.

2. Increase your sexual intelligence by finding new books, podcasts, TED Talks, and teachers and learning from them together. Some suggestions are in the Resources section at the end of the book.

3. Commit to setting a regular time for exploring your erotic relationship as well as your sexuality. Decide on the frequency of such meetings (once a week usually works well) and the length of uninterrupted time you'll set aside for them (from thirty minutes to two hours). Take turns being the one to request ways of enhancing sexual accelerators while the other partner reciprocates or accommodates the request (at one meeting you will say what you would like to explore, and at the next meeting your partner chooses).

    This could be a nonerotic massage, or maybe a full-on erotic massage. Or maybe you would just like to find out more about which senses are the most exciting for you — tasting, smelling, seeing? What kind of setting turns you on sexually — music, candles, soft lights? Give one another a lot of room to ask for what you want.

    Decide ahead of time whether these conversations can lead to lovemaking or if they're only to explore without any specific goal. No matter what you choose, make sure the decision is mutual.

4. Practice mindfulness. Mindfulness helps us to enhance both our physical and our emotional well-being, so imagine all the ways it can strengthen our sex lives. Practicing the pause reminds us to take a breath first and enhance our awareness of what we feel and think. I've heard mindfulness described as aligning your mind and body in the same space. Think about skiing downhill, paddling over a river rapid, or learning a new yoga pose. It can be so intense that your mind and body become entirely in sync.

   Practice keeping your body and mind in the same place. Let go of distractions and return to what is happening in the moment. You and your partner are on an adventure of exploration together. Just as you would on a sailing or climbing venture, you need to stay in the present moment.

EXERCISE: Fast Facts

Below are a few fast facts that have great possibilities for discussion. After talking about them with your partner, start a game in which each person finds three more facts over the next week to talk about. Remember, this is an experience of discovery and sharing, not judging, criticizing, or trying to make a point to your partner.

It is also a way to become more comfortable talking about sexual topics, which leads to greater ease between you and your partner in talking about your own sexual relationship. Begin with topics that seem easiest for each of you and then work your way into learning together about the topics that may be more tender, such as porn, oral or anal sex, sex toys, or sexual shame.

Fast Fact: Graham crackers were invented and marketed as part of a diet that would quell sexual urges, especially masturbation.
Fast Fact: Men fake orgasms too. According to one 2014 article in *Time Out New York*, more than 30 percent of men have faked an orgasm.

Fast Fact: A study in the *Archives of Gynecology and Obstetrics* suggests a new twist to the old adage, "An apple a day keeps the doctor away." In a study of 731 Italian women who were sexually active, the apple eaters reported increased lubrication and overall improvement of sexual function!

Fast Fact: The orgasm gap, which holds that men climax 95 percent of the time while women only get there about 65 percent of the time, is basically nonexistent in same-gender sexual relationships. Gay men get off 89 percent of the time, and lesbians get off 86 percent of time. Clearly biology isn't really the issue!

Fast Fact: One study from Brown University found that women who are longtime meditators have more intense orgasms. (I'm sure it's true for other genders as well!) Maybe it's because it helps them be less judgmental about their sexual preferences and more honest about sharing their fantasies.

Fast Fact: Research shows that people who talk more during sex (both verbally and nonverbally) have more satisfying sex lives. Some 57 percent of survey respondents told a condom company they feel more confident when their partner is making noise in bed.

Add the new facts you and your partner discover to this collection.

Fast Fact:

Fast Fact:

Fast Fact:

Fast Fact:

Discovering new ways to appreciate and celebrate your sexuality is possible at every age and stage of our lives. Like all of the cycles of love, it is a never-ending journey.

By now we've spent a lot of time looking at ways to enhance our relationships by creating more moments of connection and enriching our mutual sexual satisfaction. Now it's time to look at navigating the stormier times of relationship and learn new ways to manage the inevitable seasons of winter — or at least the seasonal storms.

Conflict

Everyday Squabbles, Big Troubles, and Intractable Differences

15

Between stimulus and response there is a space. In that space is our power to choose our response. In our response lies our growth and our freedom.

— Stephen R. Covey

Sitting at a restaurant table at my favorite place on earth, the destination health spa Rancho La Puerta, in Tecate, Mexico, I was eating dinner with a couple who had just attended my lecture "Conflict Is Inevitable, Repair Is Optional." The husband, Saul, said he was relieved to hear he and his wife, Joni, were normal because they argued over "stupid things."

"But there's something I don't understand," Saul said. "I work with this guy Jake, who tells me that, in over fifty years of marriage, he has never had a fight or even exchanged one angry word with his wife."

In one of those rare and amazing moments of perfect harmony, Joni and I responded in unison, "I wonder what his wife would say!"

Fights and conflicts do not cause breakups. In fact, an absence of conflict is often a red flag to therapists. Most of us have known that seemingly perfect couple who suddenly ended their relationship, shocking everyone around them. And often the couple themselves didn't know it was coming.

Conflict is not a sign that a relationship is in trouble. Any two human beings with different histories, values, and personalities will always disagree. Beliefs and feelings about kids, stepkids, in-laws, fitness, food choices, money, sex, pets, housework, how to spend time off, and many other issues can trigger intense reactions in people and cause conflict. Personality traits (such as introversion, extroversion, and different levels of self-disclosure) and emotional sensitivities (such as jealousy and social anxiety) can also cause conflict. Not wanting your partner to wear that checked shirt you can't stand doesn't mean something is wrong. It means you are human.

What *does* lead to breakups is when one or both partners lack the skill to manage conflicts or personal sensitivities (like that upsettingly ugly shirt). When we hide our feelings, blame our partner, or try to defend ourselves, we lose our connection with the most important person in our life. This feels like heartbreak, and so we react by becoming sad and angry and by closing ourselves off emotionally. In other words, the actual disagreement often accounts for only 20 percent of the trouble; the other 80 percent results from the protective strategies of reactivity, withdrawal, and defensiveness — the true enemies of love.

For that reason, let's start by talking about *how* we fight. Then we'll move on to talk about what we fight about and how to best approach each type of conflict, from small to big to impossible.

Three "Don'ts" and a "Do"

People typically manage conflict in four ways:

1. One person goes along with everything in order to get along. If this becomes a habit rather than a choice, that can create resentment. Jake, the man who believes he has the perfect marriage,

might be married to a woman who uses this strategy. Holding your tongue in the face of conflict is not the same as having tolerance for your partner, a necessary quality we will discuss later in the chapter.

2. Instead of spending a lot of time smoothing over conflict or pretending it doesn't exist, the couple avoid anything contentious. This is an approach that goes back to that unrealistic ideal that every person is just one half of a whole and that love means total agreement. This creates Lumpy-Carpet Syndrome, which we'll address later in this chapter.

3. The couple have the same heart-wearying fights over the same issues day after day, month after month, year after year until they give up, give in, or space out.

4. The couple learn to manage conflict intelligently. Smart-conflict management includes the Big Five PAUSE communication skills, which help couples slow down troublesome discussions and really listen to one another, preventing small disagreements from becoming big messes. These skills can help repair the relationship after the couple have reacted to stress collisions or ongoing trouble loops, two concepts we'll talk about in this chapter.

I think you know which one of these is the healthiest path forward. The good — even *great* — news is that anyone can learn how to manage differences without harming love. Even in the face of intractable differences, it is possible to approach distressing relationship issues with mindfulness rather than reactivity.

Stress Styles:
Implosions, Explosions, and Disappearing

One day about forty years ago, I went to pick up a friend for lunch. When I arrived at her house, she opened the door and whispered, "Wait in the living room. Paul and I are having a fight."

As I sat on the couch feeling acutely uncomfortable, I could hear the two of them yelling at one another in their bedroom. I was glad their door was shut. Suddenly, I heard a loud crash and screams. Later I would learn Paul had thrown the telephone against the wall.

The next thing I knew, I was sitting on a bench in a nearby park. My limbs were shaking, my heart was pounding, and I had no memory of how I had gotten from the living-room couch to the park bench across the street. (Paul was eventually able to manage his dramatic and frightening reactivity to distress through several years of therapy and apologized to both of us more than once over the years!)

Chapter 9 describes what happens to our brains when we are stressed. The light dims in the brain's frontal lobe — the center of mindful response and rational thought — and comes on in the back part of the brain, where the 9-1-1 emergency center is located. This center, often called the reptilian part of the brain, only addresses two questions: Will I eat it? Or will it eat me? Sometimes, when we react to something, we barely know we are in that mode until we find ourselves sitting on a park bench, not knowing how we got there. This is an automatic response. We don't have a choice about how our body reacts.

But we do have a choice about how we *manage* that knee-jerk reaction. Management begins with identifying our primary stress styles and learning the clues that tell us our brains have gone into automatic protection mode. (You might recognize these three stress styles from Chapter 11; they're synonymous with our three defensive strategies.)

Freezers typically remove themselves from trouble by denying that it's happening. They may try to placate the other person, or they may intellectualize the situation and close off their emotions. Freezers may feel numb or detached under stress or may have a sense that their body is collapsing.

Fighters become oppositional or aggressive. They insist on their point, loudly, and try to quash the other person's point of view. Under stress, fighters may feel their body is getting bigger and harder, as though preparing for battle.

Flee-ers withdraw or stonewall; in other words, they may find themselves sitting on a park bench. Under stress, a flee-er may feel a growing sense of panic — and a desperate need to get away.

None of these reactions are bad or wrong; we are set up to survive, and we need both parts of our brains to do so. But when our brains are on alert and clash with our partner's brain, which is also on alert, the result is trouble — with a capital *T*.

When Stress Styles Clash

Carlos and Angie were on their way to meet their friends for dinner and a concert. Carlos was driving. They were calmly discussing how much they were looking forward to the evening when a loud car — filled with teenagers, spewing loud music over the growl of a broken muffler — zipped across two lanes and cut them off.

Carlos managed to pull into another lane and avoid a collision, but he became furious, screaming and swearing. Angie, holding her breath in fear, asked him in an anxious tone not to shout. Carlos shouted back that he had managed to keep them safe, demanding why she had to be so critical. Then she retorted that he had "a real anger problem." Each turned away from the other, concluding they were in a relationship with an impossible person.

This conflict arose because Carlos's response to stress was to fight, while Angie's was to freeze. Rather than recognizing these responses and finding a way to help each other calm down, both acted in a way that further distressed the other. Because they had no language to help them understand that this was a collision of stress styles, each thought the other was the problem. The original issue — a second car behaving dangerously — had nothing to do with their relationship, but because their stress styles collided, it created a new problem between them.

EXERCISE: Identifying Stress Styles

Answer the following questions.

1. How do you think you would have responded in Carlos and Angie's situation?

2. How would your partner have responded?

3. What could Carlos and Angie have done differently if they had practiced PAUSE skills once they realized they were triggered?

4. What can you do differently when you are in a similar situation?

5. How will that impact your relationship?

Sharing

If working as a couple, share your responses with each other.

Loops: More Stressful Collisions

Loops often begin when one person, perhaps unwittingly, does something that activates a partner's vulnerability. This causes a surge of cortisol — the stress hormone — that signals danger to the partner, and the partner then reacts in one of three ways: fighting, freezing, or fleeing. This reaction, in turn, is the very behavior that triggers vulnerability in the original person, who then reacts in his or her own primary stress style. That reaction further triggers the other partner's reactivity, and around and around they go.

This vulnerability is often an emotional overreaction to a situation that resembles a past trauma or unhappiness. Our emotions can't distinguish the past from the present. For example, imagine being four years old, sitting happily on a park bench, when suddenly a feral cat jumps up and scratches you so badly you need stitches. Thirty years later, in another park, you hear a cat hissing. It's not the same time or the same cat, but the alert center in your brain warns you of trouble.

As mentioned earlier, this is called a trigger. Childhood events that made us feel insecure, shamed, blamed, or afraid can cause the same emotional responses later in life.

When your partner triggers such memories, perhaps with a remark, nonverbal gesture, facial expression, or all of the above, you react with all the intensity evoked by the original situation — an emotional allergic reaction, if you will.

Let's say that Sofia fears disconnection, while Owen's biggest vulnerability is receiving criticism. Without discussing the matter with Sofia, Owen makes plans to hang out and go biking with his friends on Saturday, while Sofia secretly imagines spending the weekend alone with Owen — also without discussion. When Owen tells her his plans, she feels abandoned, which activates her fight response. She says something critical, which activates Owen's default instinct — flight. He withdraws and becomes distant, which only intensifies Sofia's fear of disconnection. She leans harder into her criticisms. The loop progresses and builds momentum, as illustrated in the following vulnerability loop.

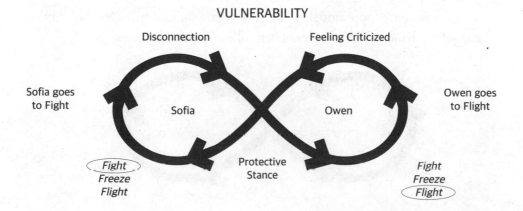

VULNERABILITY

EXERCISE: Working on Loops

Complete this worksheet on your own. If you're working through this book as a couple, you'll find instructions for sharing at the end of the worksheet. If you're working on this alone, I recommend talking with your partner to think through these exercises after you've finished them — loops are a two-person dance, after all.

Here are some examples of emotional triggers. Circle (or write on a separate sheet of paper) the ones that make you feel especially vulnerable.

Feeling inadequate	Feeling angry	Feeling unsafe
Being told what to do	Needing to be right	Not being valued
Feeling out of control	Experiencing unpredictability	Being treated unfairly
Not being liked	Feeling misunderstood	Feeling left out
Feeling abandoned	Being seen as incompetent	Being teased
Not feeling respected	Feeling judged	Being the target of another's anger

In this blank loop model, write your name on one side (left or right) and your partner's on the other. Then follow the instructions.

1. List your top three emotional triggers from the items you selected in the chart.

2. Choose one emotional trigger you'd like to explore. Write it here.

3. Now work with this emotional trigger by finishing the following sentences addressed to your partner:

   ◆ The trigger I am going to explore is...

   ◆ When this happens, I respond by...

   ◆ When I react this way, I feel...

   ◆ What I tell myself about you is...

   ◆ What I tell myself about me is...

   ◆ I usually protect myself by fighting, fleeing, or freezing (circle one).

   ◆ The price we pay for this in our relationship is...

   ◆ I would like to respond (rather than react) by...

   ◆ I can soothe myself when I am distressed by telling myself...

   ◆ You could help to soothe me by...

Sharing

Share your trigger explorations with each other. As you discuss your triggers and stress responses, see if you can identify one (or more) loops that you might be falling into. Fill out the loop model on the previous page together. Place each person's vulnerability on the top of his or her side of the loop and each person's stress response on the bottom. Draw arrows indicating which action leads to which response, following all the way around the loop.

Then talk about ways to help each other when you get into a loop. Go back to the Imago exercise we did in Chapter 6 ("Your Unfinished Business") to see whether, in that exercise, you wrote about any of the vulnerabilities that come up in your loops with your partner.

Even if you don't identify a specific loop you two get into together, note each other's triggers and primary stress responses — this knowledge alone can help you deescalate conflicts before they take off.

The Loops Wheel

If you want to further explore your loops with your partner, the Loops Wheel is another inquiry that you can do together. Adapted from the PAIRS Dialogue Wheel, this process will help you slow down enough to respond mindfully and understand what lies behind the trigger and the blame. You and your partner can then see the deeper issue and replace blame with empathy. Each spoke of the wheel explores a different aspect of the same situation, including what happened, your "story" and judgment about what happened, your feelings about it, how it relates to your history, and what you would like to be done differently. The next page shows what a Loops Wheel looks like.

If Sofia were using the Loops Wheel with Owen, it might go something like this:

1. When you told me you were going biking with your friends, *I felt abandoned*.
2. The story I tell myself about you when this happens is that *you care more about your friends than about me*.
3. The story I tell myself about me is that *I am less interesting than your friends and not very lovable*.

The Loops Wheel

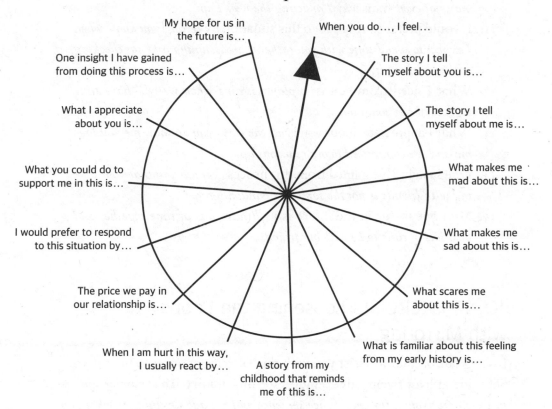

4. What makes me mad about this is *that we barely see each other during the week, and I think of weekends as time for just us.*

5. What makes me sad about this is that *I miss our time together.*

6. What scares me about this is *suspecting you don't love me enough to make this last.*

7. What's familiar from my early history about this feeling is *when my Dad left our family and found less and less time to be with me on weekends and finally stopped coming to see me.*

8. A story from my childhood that reminds me of this is *my mother telling us he didn't care about any of us, which is why he stopped coming.*

9. When I am hurt in this way, I usually react by *being sarcastic and saying something mean.*

10. The price we pay in our relationship is that *this hurts you, and you may not even know why I'm acting the way I do.*

11. I would prefer to respond to this situation by *letting you know when I expect to spend time with you rather than assuming and not checking with you about it.*

12. What I need from you is *to plan with me when we will have time together I can count on.*

13. What I appreciate about you is *all the ways you do show me you love me and are committed to our relationship.*

14. One insight I've gained from this process is *realizing that your biking with friends is not the same as abandoning me.*

15. My hope for us in the future is *we'll have lots of time together and also lots of time to be with our friends.*

JOINT EXERCISE: Loosening the Loops with Mirroring

Invite your partner to assist you with this exercise in order to mirror you. Set aside at least twenty-five minutes for this inquiry. *Your partner's job is just to mirror you at the end of each sentence and not add anything to what you say.* Your partner will have a chance to respond when he or she does the exercise later; this is your time to do a deeper dive into what's going on. Every few minutes, thank your partner for listening, and then continue.

1. When you do…, I feel…
2. The story I tell myself about you when this happens is…
3. The story I tell myself about me is…
4. What makes me mad about this is…
5. What makes me sad about this is…
6. What scares me about this is…
7. What's familiar from my early history about this feeling is…
8. A story from my childhood or early life that reminds me of this is…

9. When I am hurt in this way, I usually react by fighting, freezing, or fleeing (circle one), which I do by...
10. The price we pay in our relationship is...
11. I would prefer to respond to this situation by...
12. What you could do to support me in this is...
13. What I appreciate about you is...
14. One insight I've gained from this process is...
15. My hope for us in the future is...

Reflections

Use the following space to write about what you learned from this exercise.

Sharing

If your partner has also done this exercise, you can fill in that information on the page above in the loop model and talk about ways to help each other when you fall into a loop. You also might want to recall the Imago exercise we did in Chapter 6 ("Your Unfinished Business") and see if some of the vulnerabilities you observe in your loops with your partner are the ones you wrote about in that exercise.

About Conflicts

Some conflicts matter much more than others. The specific tools you need to handle a given conflict often depend on its severity. Minor annoyances may require nothing more than tolerance, whereas major issues need to be brought to the table to be dealt with collaboratively using specific communication and problem-solving skills. Some conflicts that matter are very manageable and solvable; others are intractable differences that can't be solved but can be lovingly approached and softened.

Increasing Tolerance

No matter how hard you try, you can't make your partner your clone. There's a deep irony here. Most of us fall in love with someone because of the ways the two of us differ. Then we spend the rest of the relationship trying to make that person more like us by blaming, criticizing, bribing, advising, or trying to correct his or her behavior. None of this will go well!

An important skill in conflict management is distinguishing the issues that really matter from less important problems and then increasing our tolerance for the "small stuff." There are many ways our partner may perpetually annoy us, and vice versa. Often our partner represents another way of doing things, but when we forget that, what we are left with are annoying habits. Some examples:

- Buying too much of everything versus not buying enough
- Disorganization versus organization
- Being on time versus taking one's time
- Throwing out food that is still perfectly good versus letting it go bad in the fridge
- Talking quietly in the same room versus yelling from another room
- Worrying if the gas goes below a quarter tank versus letting it get too low
- Throat clearing, sniffing, swallowing, chewing, or using a toothpick in an irritating way
- Constantly texting and/or checking social media
- Committing Netflix adultery (starting a series with your partner and later watching episodes alone)

The list is endless. Pay attention to the issues that make you want to judge and criticize your partner. When you roll your eyes and say nastily to yourself, "Not *that* again," ask yourself if this is an issue worth fighting over or trying to change. Is it among the top five, which may need to be on the table, or is it something you can let go of?

It is a good idea to choose your battles carefully. We can all afford to be more tolerant of our partner in certain areas. Here are some ways to do that:

- List five things you do regularly that might be annoying and think about how your partner accommodates them.
- Now list five things your partner does that you find annoying.
- Think about how you currently manage yourselves in relationship to each other's behavior.
- Question your assumption that the annoying behavior is "wrong." Is someone who angrily throws the phone across the room in the same category as a constant sniffer? Is your partner's behavior a symptom of a character flaw or behavioral management problem, or is the real problem your own intolerance?
- Distinguish between deal breakers — the unacceptable differences that need negotiation — and those that require some acceptance on your part. For example, for misophonics chronic sniffing might be a deal breaker, but for others it's an annoying problem that might pale in comparison to all their partner offers.
- List some ways your partner accepts things you do that might be deal breakers for someone else.
- Ask yourself which of your partner's "annoying" habits you noticed frequently during the beginning stages of love. Most of them probably didn't matter to you then, because you were so enchanted by your partner's good qualities. Make it an ongoing practice to regularly appreciate your partner, noticing and saying what you admire about your partner.

If you follow the suggestions provided here, your list of intolerable annoyances will probably get significantly shorter.

It's important to note that what counts as "small stuff" for some people might be more serious issues for others. Take the misophonia example mentioned above. If you have this condition, certain sounds like chewing and yawning might cause you to flip into a genuine flight-or-fight response, including increased heart rate, sweating, and other biological alarm signals. Then your partner's annoying habit of eating caramel corn in bed may move very quickly from a two on the Richter scale of trouble to a ten. Likewise, some conflicts involving two opposite ways of doing something are small enough to shrug off (like how to do the dishes), while others are not compatible and need to be worked out (one thinks all of a couple's free time needs to be spent together, while the other deeply values individual alone time in a relationship).

Even among the conflicts that matter, most of them can be managed, if not solved, with a little empathy and collaboration.

A Common Tale of Manageable Trouble

Let's look at a couple in trouble. Zane and Kelly both had ten days off from work. Zane decided to celebrate by making a smorgasbord of their favorite foods: a selection of fresh, plant-based tacos generously loaded with mango and gourmet guacamole, grilled salmon, roasted sweet potato fries, and handmade gelato. He used his skills as a professional landscaper to arrange the food beautifully, just to delight Kelly.

When Kelly returned home from running errands, delicious smells washed over her as she stepped inside. Then she saw the kitchen: pots, pans, spatulas, garlic, half an onion, a variety of spices, and open half-empty cans of black beans scattered around the counter. Everywhere she looked, there was a mess.

"Why can't you ever put things away?" she demanded angrily. "What a way to start our holiday together!" Self-righteously, she pointed at a piece of mango skin on the floor. "I can't believe you didn't even bother to pick this up!"

"Nothing pleases you, Kelly," Zane replied. Deflated and dejected, he thought to himself, "Soon, I'll stop even trying."

What happened here? How could Zane have handled this situation better? How could Kelly have handled it better? What do you think is next for Zane and Kelly? Which of them do you think was wrong?

Here is a hint. Entomologists have found that insects have different thresholds of tolerance for uncompleted tasks. If bees with different thresholds are paired together, the bee that is most disturbed by a low honey level works harder, sometimes working itself to death. One study has found that similar thresholds exist in humans. For example, roommates with different thresholds for order have much less relationship satisfaction and a lot more conflict than those with similar thresholds. In other words, creatures, including partners like Zane and Kelly, may be hardwired for difference.

This, of course, means neither is wrong and this "threshold difference" is something that needs mindful management by the couple rather than coercive means to change one person or the other.

Since conflict is inevitable, we need to learn four skills in order to manage conflict in ways that don't kill love:

1. How to react constructively when we are blindsided, confronted, or fail to get our way
2. How to identify our part in the problem
3. How to repair the relationship quickly, so the connection is not broken
4. How to manage differences with generosity

You'll notice these are skills deeply related to the lessons we've already learned about pausing, self-awareness, defensiveness, and prioritizing connection in the face of conflict.

Let's see what Zane and Kelly's story looks like when managed with these skills and a little intention. Zane and Kelly know they have differences relating to order. Zane, who describes himself as "laid back," realized early on in their relationship that he didn't notice things that Kelly called messy. To him, a clean kitchen means the food is in recognizable piles and the dirty dishes and pots are neatly stacked near the sink, ready to be washed another day. However, Zane realizes he needs to make more of an effort to pick up after himself, and so he challenges the part of him that thinks, "That's just the way I am."

Kelly, meanwhile, knows her standards of neatness are not the only way to live. She understands that Zane puts up with things about her that he finds deeply annoying, such as forgetting where she puts the keys and preferring to stay home with a book rather than hang out with their friends. Rather than vilify one another, they both begin to make an effort to make life easier for one another. It helps to remember what they love most about each other too. (Here's a hint: It isn't how they clean the kitchen.)

So Zane made an effort to keep the kitchen relatively clean while he cooked, and Kelly noticed the mess the moment she walked in the door but made herself focus on and appreciate the kindness and thoughtfulness behind Zane's elaborate, beautifully prepared meal.

Relationship Repair:
An Essential Part of Staying Connected

Even the most eminently self-aware and attentive partners will at times slip and hurt each other. No matter how much you love one another, one of you will do something to create a rupture in the relationship bond. You might:

- Say something that hurts your partner.
- Start a nasty fight.
- Snap at your partner because something is stressing you out that has nothing to do with your partner.
- Say something critical.
- Forget something important.
- Insist on being remote when your partner wants connection.
- Miss or ignore a cue to respond with empathy when your partner is hurting.

There is an endless list of the thoughtless or reactive things we each might do out of carelessness, tiredness, or just plain humanness. The real issue in these ruptures is not that they happen, but rather that we don't repair them quickly.

Here's what to do in the midst of a relationship rupture:

- For the person who feels the rupture: Let your partner know how you feel if he or she is not already aware of it. Use all your PAUSE skills to state your hurt without further attacking your partner. Do not do this when you are in the middle of reactivity, but when you are able to talk about it without causing further harm.
- For the person who created the rupture: This is not the time to excuse, blame, or justify. Hearing your partner's experience and responding in an appropriate and empathetic way can change this from a major ongoing power struggle about who is right into a smaller blip that is resolved easily.

Here is a chart of how this occurs. The example below may sound somewhat robotic in the same way mirroring can sound unnatural when you first learn how to do it. Stay with it because, like most skills, with practice it will become easier and more natural.

Connection
↓

Rupture (can be minor or major)
↓

Protest (speaking with skill and intention rather than blame and criticism)
↓

Response to protest (speaking nondefensively, with empathy and apology, if appropriate)
↓

Repair (appreciation for being heard and acceptance of apology, if applicable)
↓

Reconnection

For example:

Connection: Things are going well in Will and Liz's relationship.
↓

Rupture: Will offhandedly shares something with his brother that Liz had told him in confidence; he didn't feel it was significant.
↓

Protest: Liz finds out and confronts Will without attacking him.
Liz: "Will, I am upset you told your brother I'm worried about my job being outsourced. I asked you not to tell anyone, and I feel betrayed that you did that."
↓

Response to protest: Will responds nondefensively, with empathy, and apologizes.
Will: "Liz, I'm so sorry I said that. I wasn't being careful with what you told me. I would be upset if you did that. I need to pay more attention to your requests about privacy."
↓

Repair: Liz tells Will she appreciates being heard, and Will attempts additional repair.

Liz: "Thanks for hearing me, Will. I could have been clearer about asking you to keep it private too. I know I said it in passing."

Will: "Is there anything I can do to clean this up?"

↓

Reconnection.

Liz: "Not really, but I appreciate your listening. Thanks. Let's go for our walk."

This is not useful for big betrayals, repeated ruptures (such as if Will were to constantly tell other people Liz's secrets), or when one person is finding fault with the other because of a deeper and ongoing problem that isn't being dealt with and instead comes out as a steady stream of complaints about minor problems. For these deeper issues, consider using Imago Dialogue.

Imago Dialogue: Seeing the Other Side

Do you want to be right, or do you want to be in relationship? Because you can't always have both. You can't cuddle up and relax with "being right" after a long day.

— Harville Hendrix and Helen LaKelly Hunt, *Making Marriage Simple*

The two of you have a problem. Maybe one of you is neater than the other, maybe your partner wants a pet and you do not, or maybe you have very different ways of managing money. Or perhaps you have different levels of sexual desire, and it is pulling you apart.

When these kinds of issues arise, one person often points at the other as if to say, "It's you. You are the problem. What you need, feel, and want, or how you manage money, friends, or the yard...*that* is the problem."

Instead of pointing fingers at each other, consider a different scenario. You and your partner are standing side by side, on the same team. You are touching each other gently, perhaps holding hands, and you feel connected. You are both pointing at the problem, which is in front of you. The problem may be annoying or difficult to work through, but now you're not making it more difficult by pushing away your best friend. Instead, you and your partner have become caring collaborators.

Managing an impasse in a relationship requires a certain level of vulnerability and a departure from your comfort zone. Communication fitness — like physical fitness — requires time, practice, persistence, and compassion for yourself and your team (in this case, your partner).

The Couples Dialogue (or Imago Dialogue) is another tool created by Imago therapy founders Dr. Harville Hendrix and Dr. Helen Hunt for managing conflict. This is not a discussion, and the desired end result is not always agreement. It requires understanding and the removal of destructive energy from the issue to find a collaborative path forward. For example, imagine you and your partner are standing on the Golden Gate Bridge looking at the ocean below. You are on one side, and your partner is on the other, so you have different views. Which view is correct? Often, you are both right, and you need your partner to hear and acknowledge your view before you are willing to make concessions.

JOINT EXERCISE: Imago Dialogue

Once couples have become adept at mirroring each other, I encourage them to go on to the next step of the Imago Dialogue: validation. In this part of the exercise, they learn how to affirm the internal logic of each other's remarks. In essence, they are telling each other, "What you're saying makes sense to me. I can see how you are thinking, and why you would think that way."

— HARVILLE HENDRIX, *Getting the Love You Want: A Guide for Couples*

In this couples' exercise, one person will be the sender and the other the receiver. After going through the entire process, you'll switch roles and do it again, so both people have the opportunity to be in both roles. There are three steps in the process: mirroring, validation, and then empathy.

Step One: Mirroring

1. The sender begins by describing her point of view using "I" statements and focusing on her own feelings.

2. The receiver mirrors the sender's message, repeating back what she said without judging, questioning, or adding his own point of view. At the end he asks, "Did I get it?" The sender clarifies if necessary.

3. The receiver then asks, "Is there more?" The sender then adds anything else she wants to add. The receiver repeats the question until the sender feels finished.

Step Two: Validation

1. Now the receiver goes a step beyond just hearing the sender — he also lets her know that what she said makes sense to him. If not all of it made sense to the receiver, he should start with the parts that did. He can use phrases like "I can see what you're saying…" or "That makes sense to me because…" (Remember, you don't need to agree with someone to acknowledge that their perspective or feelings are valid and reasonable.)

2. Now if there are parts the receiver didn't understand, he may ask. He should try something like, "Although that part made sense to me, can you say more about…?" or "Can you help me understand the part where you said…?"

3. The sender says more about the parts the receiver asked about. The receiver should mirror all the new information and then validate it using the same steps above.

4. Once the sender feels the entire message has been fully validated, both move on to the next step.

Step Three: Empathy

1. Finally, the receiver tries to imagine how the sender feels based on the information he now has. He should try statements like "I imagine you might be feeling…" and then add simple feeling

words like *happy*, *angry*, *sad*, *lonely*, *frustrated*, or *hurt*. Then he should ask for accuracy: "Is that what you're feeling?"

2. The sender confirms the receiver's guess. If the receiver is wrong, the sender clarifies her feelings and offers any additional messages necessary for the receiver to understand. The receiver should again mirror and validate these messages.

3. Once the sender confirms her feelings, the receiver should mirror them once more. "Yes, you're feeling scared and alone."

After the process is complete, switch roles. Now the person who received the message will become the sender and can address anything that came up for him while his partner had been speaking.

Lumpy-Carpet Syndrome

One common issue many couples face is the denial of conflict, or what I like to call Lumpy-Carpet Syndrome. Couples who don't realize that conflicts are normal may try to pretend their differences don't exist by sweeping their anger, hurt, and conflicts under the rug. The result is a very lumpy carpet, leaving much to trip over. And over time, those lumps begin to feel like landmines. This pattern is only sustainable for so long; eventually the grievances erupt all at once, resulting in an epic fight or painful distance.

The remedy is learning to talk about our own and our partner's grievances in a timely manner, *whether or not they seem fair or even correct to us*. Healthy relationships avoid lumps in the carpet, and healthy partners don't keep a black book of their resentments. Instead, their relationship includes a safe structure for dealing with problems as soon as they come up.

Intractable Differences

Sometimes you are dealing with an issue on which you won't compromise or collaborate. Maybe your partner wants an open relationship, and you aren't willing to go along with it. Perhaps you feel a pet is essential to your well-being (or a child, a move from the city to the country, or a four-month journey to walk the Camino de Santiago alone), and your partner opposes it.

The first step is to explore deeply what this issue means to you. Using some of the inquiry skills learned in Chapter 8, go more deeply into your initial feeling that the issue is "important because it is." Look for what's under it. For example, people sometimes want a child because it's an instinct and a deep dream they can't imagine being without; other times, people feel panic because they haven't found deep meaning in anything else. Perhaps you wish for an open relationship because you feel bored and sexually constricted with your partner. A move from the city to the country might come from your yearning to get your hands in the dirt and grow tomatoes. In these instances, an intractable issue can become manageable.

After doing your exploration, the next step isn't to give in to the knee-jerk reaction that you are right because you "want it." Instead, approach the issue with your partner. Here are a few important things to consider when sitting down to talk about a deep conflict like this:

1. **Remember that under every complaint is a wish.** Instead of complaining, start by describing the wish you have just explored. Your partner will be more open to hearing you than if you start with what he or she is doing wrong.

2. **Beware of building a case.** When you repeatedly get upset over an unresolved issue, it's easy to start building a case against your partner and collecting evidence to prove you're right. The psychological term for this is *confirmation bias*, defined by British psychologist Peter Wason as "our tendency to pursue and believe facts that 'prove' what we already suspect or believe to be true." Case building takes us down the lost highway of self-righteousness and certainty. We steer away from the real questions: What is at the core of my anger or my need? What is my responsibility and my vulnerability in this?

3. **Pause and center yourself before you begin a conversation.** Make sure you're not in a reactive mode. The research is clear: how we

address an issue significantly affects how well our partner can hear us. A soft start-up is an invitation to the other person without a threat. A soft start-up addresses only one issue at a time. When we are upset or invested in proving a point, we tend to bring in supporting evidence that might also raise other loaded issues. Rather than winning agreement, this approach only makes our partner defensive.

4. **Give up on winning.** The urge to win is natural; it makes us feel powerful and strong. However, if you win, your partner loses, and if that happens, the relationship loses. Think of the issue as a "we" problem, not a "you need to change your mind" problem. Remember that your partner is not your enemy, but simply has a different opinion.

5. **Slow down the outcome.** Using the Imago Dialogue technique above can help you understand the deeper issues under the immediate problem, which, even if you and your partner never agree, may help you empathize with each other's position. That goes a long way toward creating willingness to negotiate.

6. **Brainstorm ways to solve the problem.** Talk about your reactions to the issue. Don't start by insisting that you are right; instead, describe how your stress style and your Enneagram style may help explain why you experience certain emotions. Think of some solutions you can try, and set a time in the future, maybe in a few weeks, to talk about how the new plan is going.

7. **Bring in a third person.** If you cannot find a resolution together, agree to find another person to help you resolve it in a way that you can both live with.

8. **Express affection and care for one another.** Throughout the dialogue, remember that you are on the same team solving a problem together. The problem is not the other person.

9. **Finally, end with gratitude.** Just like players on the soccer field and the tennis court, always thank one another for the conversation when you are done.

When we can dialogue about tense subjects skillfully and also understand the art of apologizing and forgiving, we can move forward to reconnection. Couples who don't understand this art tend to sweep issues under the rug. Those issues later resurface as grudges, damaging blowups, or quiet resentments that eat away at love.

Continuing to Learn How to Fight Better

There are many articles, books, classes, podcasts, and online courses on how to talk through conflict. I have listed some of my favorites in the Resources section at the end of the book. The two programs I most often recommend are the Imago program and PAIRS relationship classes; this book includes many of the teachings and wisdom I gained from these programs.

Created by Dr. Hendrix and Dr. Hunt in the 1980s, Imago relationship therapy and courses (imagorelationships.org) focus on the connection between early childhood experiences and frustrations in adult relationships. The techniques and tools they teach help you move from blame and reactivity to understanding and empathy to create a deeper, more conscious connection with your partner. This is where the above Imago Dialogue exercise stems from.

The Practical Application of Intimate Relationship Skills (PAIRS) programs (www.pairs.com/toolkits) provide a comprehensive system to enhance self-knowledge and to help participants develop the ability to sustain pleasurable intimate relationships. The program was first developed by pioneer therapist Virginia Satir in the 1950s and then expanded into a well-respected international program for couples by Dr. Lori Gordon and her husband, Morris Gordon. It offers a tool kit of practical innovative methods for managing trouble and enhancing connection.

Local counseling centers; community colleges; churches, temples, and synagogues; and many therapists also offer classes and coaching in the art of fighting fair.

Depression and Other "Shadow Syndromes"

Although it can be painful and uncomfortable for most couples to admit, biology and brain structure can increase conflict in a relationship. In fact, some of those "annoying habits" we talked about earlier in the chapter may result from what John J. Ratey and Catherine Johnson describe as subtle but undiagnosed "shadow" disorders in their book *Shadow Syndromes: The Mild Forms of Major Mental Disorders That Sabotage Us*.

In a talk I had with Dr. Ratey at Rancho La Puerta in 2019, he described how some people who are great partners in many ways may also have a "difficult disposition" characterized by annoying habits, such as interrupting people, being chronically late, not remembering important things their partner has told them, or always resisting going to parties or large family gatherings. This may be the case not because they are willful or had a traumatic childhood, but because they have a mild form of a common condition, such as ADHD, social anxiety, or depression.

Rather than representing a pathology, these behaviors are sometimes the flip side of great qualities, such as being innovative, creative, and energetic. What is important in addressing "shadow syndromes," as emphasized in the rest of *Love Skills*, is having the courage and willingness to understand our unique personal biology and its impact on our life and that of our partner. Dr. Ratey discusses the importance of mindfulness and exercise in managing the more insidious forms of these issues. In fact, one of his most common remedies for milder symptoms is to "lace up your running shoes."

Sometimes, however, these milder expressions can become more serious, of which depression is an example. We all experience the blues — feelings of melancholy or sadness — but for some people, especially those who are biologically predisposed, the blues can descend into clinical depression. Depression is a devious beast. A cloud forms over everything that matters and distorts the sufferer's view of the world. Feelings of worthlessness, a lack of pleasure, and an inability to look forward to anything or believe that things will ever improve are the hallmarks of this painful illness, along with a diminished or nonexistent libido. When people are depressed, their relationship can feel like one more thing that isn't working, and they may even see their relationship as the problem.

If you're the depressed partner, you need treatment from a therapist or psychiatrist. It's important to recognize the ways in which your depression may be affecting your relationship and your partner, and it's more vital than ever to prioritize and protect your mental health.

If you are the partner of a depressed person, do *not* try to fix your partner's depression and do not take it personally. Instead, listen as compassionately as you can. Remember that a key symptom of depression is a skewed sense of reality. You didn't make your partner depressed, and you can't fix it with love any more than you can fix a broken leg with love. Some people express depression as sadness; in others, it comes out as anger. Still others withdraw into themselves, sometimes finding it difficult to get out of bed or even speak in more than monosyllables. However depression shows itself, outside help is essential, and it may fall to the nondepressed partner to find the professional help needed to support both people through the crisis.

If your partner is getting treatment but you still feel the illness's effects on the relationship — or if you simply want to learn better ways to support your partner — reach out to a professional or find a good book or other resources on supporting loved ones with depression.

Big Troubles

Big troubles involve profound, ongoing disconnection, hurt, violations of trust — and even safety. These include:

- Major betrayals, such as an affair or financial infidelity (when one person makes a financial choice without telling the other, putting the partner's well-being at risk)
- Addiction such that one partner's relationship with drugs, alcohol, or gambling has become more important than the relationship and the person's own well-being
- Lying or abuse of any kind — physical, emotional, or sexual
- Ongoing personal problems, such as the inability to hold a job or take care of health issues or repeated conflicts with the law, colleagues, or other people

Most couples can't get through such big troubles by themselves with their relationship intact. This doesn't mean that couples cannot recover from big troubles if both partners are committed to doing so. But for these kinds of issues, professional help is a necessity.

Leaving a Relationship

Another kind of big trouble is when one person has withdrawn from the relationship and is psychologically done. People who are "done" may go through the motions of counseling or other attempts at reconnection, but their heart isn't in it. They don't really engage. They are marking time with a made-up mind and a heart that is closed to the possibility of reconciling the marriage. In *Uncoupling: Turning Points in Intimate Relationships*, Diane Vaughan describes it in this way:

> Uncoupling is primarily a tale of two transitions: one that begins before the other. Most often, one person wants out while the other person wants the relationship to continue. Although both partners must go through all the same stages of the transition in order to uncouple, the transition begins and ends at different times for each. By the time the still-loving partner realizes the relationship is in serious trouble, the other person is already gone in a number of ways. The rejected partner then embarks on a transition that the other person began long before.

Some books insist couples should always try to save their relationship, regardless of the circumstances. This is not one of those books. Because of my own tough beginnings in life, as a young adult my ability to select an appropriate partner was deeply skewed. My earlier relationships had issues that could not have been fixed with any kind of counseling or Love Skills practice. It was only after I had worked on healing my own deeply distressful childhood patterns that I became self-aware enough to choose a different partner for the right reasons, one I could go the distance with.

It's impossible to make general statements about anyone's relationship based on how it looks from the outside, including who should be together and who should not. No outsider really knows what goes on between the two people in a relationship, the bonds that hold them together, or the ties that break loose. I do know that some relationships end, and in spite of the disappointment and often excruciating pain, the end of a relationship offers as many possibilities for individuals to become more wholehearted as a relationship does that goes the distance.

Moving On

To live in this world, / you must be able / to do three things: /
to love what is mortal; / to hold it / against your bones knowing /
your own life depends on it; / and, when the time comes to let it go, / to let it go.

— MARY OLIVER, "In Blackwater Woods"

For the fifty years that I knew them, I called two of my parents' close friends "Aunt Betty" and "Uncle Henry." I grew up listening to horror stories about the hatred that Uncle Henry's first wife — whom they called Betty 1 — had for Uncle Henry and Aunt Betty. After a brief marriage to Betty 1, Uncle Henry met Aunt Betty, left Betty 1, and was ordered to pay $100 a month in spousal support to Betty 1 for the rest of his life, which meant that Betty 1's unrelenting anger would haunt Uncle Henry's and Aunt Betty's lives forever. Betty 1 told their two children that if they chose to love their father and his new wife, she would not forgive them. After many years of rejecting Uncle Henry, his children finally made peace with him. Betty 1 cut them off and remained estranged from her children until her death.

Uncle Henry wanted to pay Betty 1 off in one check, but she refused. She wanted him to write her a check every month to constantly remind him that she was still alive and angry. When Betty 1 finally died, she was alone, having alienated her children and friends.

Although this story is extreme, it was one of the most formative stories of my childhood. Later, I heard the following anonymous quote in a college psychology class: "Resentment is like a poison you swallow hoping the other person will die." I remember thinking it was a perfect description of Betty 1.

Sometimes, even when you've done all you can, you can't work out what is unworkable, and a relationship ends. Other times, one partner would do just about anything to save the relationship, but, like Uncle Henry, the other one is out the door. This is painful for both people, but especially for the one who gets left behind. Heartbreak brings us to our knees, and in our despair we can feel our whole life has been — and will always be — a disaster. Expressions such as "a broken heart" and "a kick in the stomach" are consistent with new research that shows rejection triggers regions of the brain associated with physical pain. So heartache hurts terribly, not just emotionally but also physically.

Although it's hard to believe, even the most painful of partings can leave us more intact than we were before if we work with the two key love skills: mindfulness and wholeheartedness. Mindfulness helps us accept all that follows a breakup, including the overwhelming pain; however, it prevents us from clinging to that pain. Wholeheartedness invites us, even in the most painful times, to wish well for ourselves and others — even those who hurt us — and to allow a new story to emerge from the ashes of the old one through the power of forgiveness.

What I'm suggesting is not easy and is sometimes impossible during times of shock and grief. Often blame and resentment provide temporary comfort, because these emotions protect us from the hurt. Although it may feel better to rage against someone than to experience the grief of parting, staying in the rage long after the event holds us prisoner to an old story and thus prevents us from moving on to another.

I'm not suggesting you bypass angry and painful responses; avoiding these emotions is as unhealthy as fanning their flames. I am suggesting you allow the feelings to move through you and out. The worst thing you can do (other than deny them at the initial loss) is to reenergize them over and over again, so that you become a prisoner of your grudge, your longing, and someone else's decision. Bestselling memoirist Laura Munson says it best in her book *This Is Not the Story You Think It Is: A Season of Unlikely Happiness*: "Probably the wisest words that were ever uttered to me came from a therapist. I was sitting in her office, crying my eyes out...and she said, 'So let me get this straight. You base your personal happiness on things entirely outside of your control.'"

Here are four suggestions for getting through a breakup intact and possibly finding a new relationship that will be even better for you in the long run — and a healthy relationship with yourself.

1. **Pay attention to the story you are telling yourself about what happened.** Expressions such as "If I had only...," "I'm a loser at love," and "Women can't be trusted" are not only untrue, but they also perpetuate the feeling of being a victim.

2. **Allow all your feelings to come, and then allow them to go.** Rage, despair, and hopelessness are normal feelings, so don't try to push them away — but don't fan their flames either. You might say to yourself, "I'm feeling deep rage." Take a few breaths, and imagine your rage coming in and moving out through your breaths. Then visualize breathing it out and inhaling things that nourish you, such as your garden, your pet, or a violin concerto. Remember your PAUSE skills, and go for a run.

3. **Remember, the real gift of forgiveness goes to the one doing the forgiving.** Forgiveness isn't forgetting; it isn't saying that what someone did was okay; and it isn't a thing we do all at once. It is the choice to step gently and slowly into its possibilities. Forgiveness isn't for the other person; it's for us. It's what allows us to move forward.

4. **Get support.** A spiritual adviser, therapist, or coach can often help us through this journey more quickly than we can go ourselves.

"When there's a big disappointment, we don't know if that's the end of the story," Pema Chödrön reminds us in her book *When Things Fall Apart: Heart Advice for Difficult Times.* "It may be just the beginning of a great adventure." Wholeheartedness, which incorporates acceptance, vulnerability, and compassion, creates win-win solutions to conflicts and disappointments of all kinds, even those as painful as the end of a relationship.

The End of the Road — or a New Beginning?

All this said, I've read a lot of articles about knowing when it's time to leave a relationship. Many of them identify some of the normal challenging stages of a relationship as deal breakers; in fact, several of the challenges can actually be worked through. Things like feeling bored, missing your friends, and finding your partner annoying are normal parts of love. I've also seen some of the strongest marriages I know grow out of the worst messes imaginable, because when trust has dissolved and the container that you know as your marriage is broken, the only thing you can do is rebuild something new from the ground up.

In a long-term relationship there are many seasons and transitions, some requiring us to start again. Many people are able to do this with the same partner they started with.

The conflict management skills you've learned in this chapter — in addition to our lessons on self-discovery, mindful communication, and connection rituals — can be powerful, transformative tools even for couples years into their relationship who may feel set in their ways. Change and renewal *can* happen when paired with a good-faith effort and a genuine commitment to wholeheartedness.

So what exactly is wholeheartedness? Our next and final chapter will break down this essential quality at the heart of each and every love skill.

Wholehearted Love

16

Wholeness does not mean perfection: it means embracing brokenness as an integral part of life.

— PARKER J. PALMER, activist and author, in
A Hidden Wholeness: The Journey toward an Undivided Life

"Wholehearted loving" has such a lovely sound to it. It conjures up heart-ful images of unconditional support, acceptance, and caring between two people who are themselves whole. Having left disconnection, misunder-standing, and reactivity behind, together they create a sphere of perfect love for one another.

Here is the trouble with that image. The concept of wholeheartedness is a lot like love; it's a feeling that comes and goes. We may work hard to be wholehearted, and, as with any other kind of fitness, the more one works at it, the better one gets. Still, it isn't a cure for the human condition, which includes ambivalence about most things (including our relationships) and days when we're more aware of feeling broken than whole. Or to use a quote I recently saw in a cartoon of a woman in a yoga position: "I meditate, I do yoga, I garden and drink green tea, and still I want to smack some people."

To explore the meaning of loving with a whole heart, we have to start by looking at the heart troubles that can get in the way.

Heart Troubles

In the words of Wordsworth, we come into the world "trailing clouds of glory,"
but the fire is soon extinguished, and we lose sight of the fact that we are whole,
spiritual beings. We live impoverished, repetitious, unrewarding lives
and blame our partners for our unhappiness.

— HARVILLE HENDRIX, *Getting the Love You Want: A Guide for Couples*

A Merged Heart

We know the themes present in The Merge, the first stage in the Love Cycles model. Longing, torment, and ecstasy cause us to act at our most foolish, destructive, or heroic. Driven by our altered state in this first stage of "falling" in love, we are certain we have found our missing half in this other enchanting being. Slowly — and usually painfully — we separate from that state and remember we are not anyone else's other half. With this realization, we begin the necessary, brave solo march to reclaim ourselves.

Like a grown child unwilling to leave home and strike out alone, some people are not willing or able to leave the soulmate dream behind. They stay in The Merge, monitoring each other's activities, calling their partner "my other half," and posting endless photos on social media of their perfect life together. People who get stuck in this stage tend to steer clear of any conflict or disagreement and to resent it when their partner takes time alone. The couple stays frozen in Stage One, which can easily result in the second heart trouble — an addicted heart.

An Addicted Heart

In the 1980s, the term "codependency" was introduced in the field of addiction, describing an unhealthy relationship between addicts and their partners. As an unknown source once keenly said, "Being codependent means that when you die, someone else's life passes before your eyes." These chilling words aptly describe the codependent state, in which the meaning of one's own life is tangled up in that of another person.

Romantic codependency often shows up as a dynamic in which one prioritizes keeping a partner happy, minimizing conflict, and avoiding the sometimes lonely burden of finding one's own authentic, joyful way, all to stay within the fantasy of a merge. Such a person might sacrifice friends, family, dreams, and his or her own identity for the sake of the relationship or the idea of an "us." In this way, relationship addiction is another way in which a merged heart can get stuck.

When you're addicted to love, you believe you need the other person to be whole — and sometimes even to live. These relationships are usually toxic and can even be dangerous. "Love addiction is just as real as any other addiction, in terms of its behavior patterns and brain mechanisms," says biological anthropologist Helen Fisher in an essay for *Discover* magazine. "Besotted lovers express all four of the basic traits of addiction: craving, tolerance, withdrawal, and relapse."

A Closed Heart

We can develop a closed heart as a result of childhood trauma or from a time when loving brought such anguish that we closed ourselves off to new possibilities rather than risk being hurt again. We deflect the pain by building walls around ourselves, replacing the human instinct to connect and trust with cynicism about love and life. The numbness and barriers that a closed heart create do not keep us safe; instead, they cause more isolation and pain than the risk of opening up again.

Half a Heart

When we are half-hearted, we have little to give in the way of enthusiasm, willingness, and appreciation. Oftentimes, this means we're not really in our relationship, but rather we feel obliged, stuck, or that getting out would just be too difficult. Because love is not a steady state of being, it needs a wholehearted commitment to the work, especially when we feel discouraged. Half-heartedness means we are settling for a relationship that is just "okay" and doesn't have a chance to improve, whether because it's dysfunctional beyond repair or because we just don't care enough to invest in it. We may be there physically, but our heart is not fully in it.

Recognizing Wholeheartedness

Before we can talk about what wholehearted love is, we need to understand what wholeheartedness itself is. While I was writing this chapter and pondering the meaning of this term, a government shutdown threw the country into chaos, perhaps most obviously at the airports. I had just checked out of my hotel in Washington, DC, to take a plane to Detroit. The man standing in line next to me was also going to the airport, and I remember his comment: "This is going to be a nightmare. Hundreds of people, and no one to check them in."

He was partially right. There was one huge check-in line for the entire airport with very few staff to move people through. Mixed together were families from India with overflowing carry-ons and backpacks, three brothers from Nigeria, and an elegant woman from Thailand who didn't speak English. There were women with headscarves, men with Afros, and businessmen in suits. It was a melting pot for sure, but instead of the expected angry faces and loud protests, something else happened that morning. The spirit of helpfulness was palpable, and no one complained even though some flights were being missed or canceled.

During the ninety minutes I stood in line, I saw several things unfold. A Muslim woman handed out apricot halal candy to a family from Guatemala with four kids. People chatted with one another, sharing their anxiety about missing flights and telling stories from their lives — about where they had come from and where they were going — more deeply and honestly than I'd ever heard strangers share. The Nigerian brothers insisted an older couple go in front of them and helped them with their large carry-ons as the line slowly moved forward. Many people thanked the few TSA staff for coming in to work that day without pay. Oxytocin — the "love hormone" — was in the air, and the spirit of goodwill was everywhere.

That is wholeheartedness. Out of life's brokenness, its troubles, and impossibility, we come together to care for and support one another in authenticity and intention. We connected that day through our shared struggle about the disruption to our lives, the vulnerability we were feeling, and the kindness we showed to each other in the midst of a fiasco.

Self-Love: A Misunderstood Phrase

A cliché has been circulating in the self-help world for years: "You can only love someone as much as you love yourself." I don't believe this.

Self-love is a complicated concept, and there is no easy way to understand what it means. Here's what we do know: self-love must involve self-respect, and showing love to others helps us *grow* our self-respect. When we're able to impact others in a positive way, as the people at the airport did, our self-esteem blossoms.

Countless studies show the relationship between helping others and our view of ourselves: we know that those who help strangers and neighbors more often tend to have higher self-esteem, and the benefits don't stop there. Dr. Suzanne Richards, at the University of Exeter Medical School, reviewed forty studies from the past twenty years and discovered that volunteering is even associated with direct health benefits like lower vulnerability to depression, increased well-being, and a 22 percent reduction in the risk of dying early. Certainly in the DC airport, it was clear to me that caring for others was making individuals less anxious and preoccupied with their own stories.

Think of wholeheartedness as a positive feedback loop. That feeling of strength and satisfaction from being able to make a difference for somebody else stays with us for a while, helping us smile more and softening our hearts.

Self-care is not a preoccupation with self. It is finding a balance in your body, mind, and spirit, so you can be present in the world and in relationship. It doesn't matter if you're in a crowded airport or just sitting with your partner having a cup of tea. We always have choices about how we treat one another, and that goodwill is contagious. It spreads among others and then it comes back to us. If there is one ingredient in loving ourselves that we can be sure of, it is the love we give to others.

Why Doesn't It Last?

As moving as the generous spirit at the airport was, inevitably even those wholehearted folks who stopped to thank the unpaid security staff would soon return to their separate little worlds and be back to forgetting to thank people and complaining about slow service, wherever they might be. As mentioned, wholeheartedness is not a steady state of being.

Why do we experience moments of wholehearted care, where we show our best selves in airports or during snowstorms or after hurricanes, but so predictably retreat into our own self-serving worlds filled with grudges and reactivity? It's because wholeheartedness is a practice. We must choose it consciously and consistently. Otherwise, we'll reach for what's easier: snap reactions rooted in fear and old patterns of behavior.

The more we practice wholeheartedness, the more we'll be able to act in it. Just remember that at times, it can — and will — disappear. That's a part of our human experience.

Tools of the Wholehearted

Like anything we hope to improve, be it the mind, body, or prowess at golf, there are practices we can use to support us as we work toward being more wholehearted. Here are five of the most valuable tools for you to use on your journey.

Tool #1: Owning Our Whole Story: The Best and the Hardest

Imagine two people are born on the same day, one in the countryside and one in the city. They are born to wonderful parents and live childhoods rich in love, fun, and safety. They meet each other as adults, fall in love, and become committed for life. They never exchange a cross word between them; they anticipate one another's needs and freely give their time, energy, and affection. They make love passionately, feel fulfilled at work and in their community, and share a deep, abiding love for the planet. The day they turn one hundred, they wake up for a moment, embrace, and then go back to sleep and die peacefully in each other's arms.

Who would buy that book or watch that movie? Nobody. We want to read about real people, people we can identify with. We want stories of loss and misfortune and brokenness and, eventually, recovery and resilience. Without hurting each other, there would be no forgiveness; without loss, there would be no appreciation of bounty. In all realms of life, issues of threat versus survival, fear versus courage, and hate versus love make great stories because they make up real life. We learn resilience by overcoming misfortune, compassion by working with our own struggles, and humility by accepting our defeats.

In her book *The Gifts of Imperfection: Let Go of Who You Think You're Supposed to Be and Embrace Who You Are*, Dr. Brené Brown says:

> Owning our story can be hard but not nearly as difficult as spending our lives running from it. Embracing our vulnerabilities is risky but not nearly as dangerous as giving up on love and belonging and joy — the experiences that make us the most vulnerable. Only when we are brave enough to explore the darkness will we discover the infinite power of our light.

It is the courage to accept and to share our whole human journey, with all its imperfections, disappointments, troubles, and triumphs, that creates wholeheartedness.

Tool #2: Staying Vertical in a Horizontal World

Your entire life only happens in this moment. The present moment is life itself.
Yet people live as if the opposite were true and treat the present moment as
a stepping-stone to the next moment — a means to an end.

— ECKHART TOLLE, spiritual teacher and author of *The Power of Now*

Nelson Mandela, South Africa's president from 1994 to 1999, spent twenty-seven years in prison, and much of this time was spent in solitary confinement. Despite these painful living conditions, his deep losses of freedom and family, and the uncertainty of his future, he inspired millions of people by managing to survive and even thrive in this state. He credited much of this strength to a fifteen-minute daily meditation practice that helped him stay in the moment.

As Eckhart Tolle reminds us, our lives happen in a given moment, not in the past or the future. I call the ability to stay in the present "being vertical in a horizontal world."

In order to better understand this, imagine two lines: one horizontal and one vertical. The horizontal line represents your entire life: the beginning of the line is your birth; the end, your death. In between are all the events that occur in your life as well as the feelings and thoughts you have about them. These feelings and thoughts are based on your interpretations (stories you tell yourself) of what has happened or will happen. The stories, however, are not real; they are just your versions of events, which are based on how you feel at any given moment — they are how you interpret your history.

The vertical line, on the other hand, is not about the past or the future (or your interpretations of them). This line represents what is happening in any given moment. For example, when Nelson Mandela was in prison, the world that he lived in was full of distress and threatening events (not the least was his prison cell); however, when he meditated, he went somewhere else within himself. Eventually, he taught himself to stay in the present moment without meditating; a conscious breath would bring him back to it.

Spiritual practices, mindfulness techniques, or even a short walk remind us that we are more than the events, wounds, or dramas in our daily lives. When we use our mindful practices to center ourselves in the midst of relationship drama, for example, we learn not to take things personally, such as our partner's bad mood or disappointing news. We regulate our emotional responses quickly, which allows more empathy between us rather than the blame and judgment that always take us down a lost highway into more trouble.

Recently, I spent a day with a dear friend who has stage 4 cancer — sadly, his treatment options are running out. Surprisingly, though, this friend told me he is happier now than he has ever been, and he feels more engaged in his life. He said when he thinks about what is happening to his body (and his life), he panics and quickly becomes fearful and distressed. However, when he takes a deep, slow breath, he is reminded that right here, right now, he is alive, and the panic goes away. This moment is all he has, he reminds himself, and the moment is usually a good one.

Although I live on the horizontal line and am affected by the flow of events in my life (and relationship), I am also in the current moment of my life — the "now" that Tolle refers to. To live wholeheartedly, we must find our way to this calm center within ourselves, even as life's challenges and disappointments continue to test us. This allows us to manage how we react to others with thoughtful responses instead of knee-jerk, emotional ones, and this is a key component of the emotional intelligence we've discussed in earlier chapters. Fundamentally, this work is accomplished through a mindfulness practice. It helps us see everything differently, even in the middle of turmoil and old loops.

In the words of Nelson Mandela, "There is nothing like returning to a place that remains unchanged to find the ways in which you yourself have altered."

Tool #3: The Breath and the Moment

Forget about enlightenment. Sit down wherever you are and listen to the wind that is singing in your veins. Feel the love, the longing and the fear in your bones. Open your heart to who you are, right now, not who you would like to be. Not the saint you're striving to become. But the being right here before you, inside you, around you. All of you is holy. You're already more and less than whatever you can know. Breathe out, look in, let go.

— JOHN WELWOOD, clinical psychologist and writer

Taking a breath, essential and mysterious, is the first thing we do when we are born and the last thing we do before we die. Perhaps that is why many practices look to the breath as the grounding source of centeredness. We may consciously "breathe the breath," slowing down or speeding up as we practice different forms of yoga, meditation, martial arts, and biofeedback. When we are afraid, our bodies tighten and we breathe more quickly; when we soften and relax, we breathe more slowly.

We've all heard the notion of "taking a deep breath" before reacting when we're upset, and many mindfulness teachers say we *are* the breath we inhale and exhale. It's the ground that anchors us to both the horizontal journey of our outer lives and the vertical state of staying centered in our inner lives. It helps us "be in the moment," which is the deepest meaning of mindfulness.

I find that when I start my day with a breathing exercise, I am much better prepared to meet whatever happens with calm and equanimity, two key components of wholeheartedness. Here is one of my favorites:

1. Stand up straight, with your knees slightly bent. Bend forward at the waist, allowing your arms to hang limply toward the floor.
2. Inhale deeply as you slowly roll your body up, vertebra by vertebra. Lift your head last.
3. Slowly exhale as you return to your original position.
4. Gently stretch your whole body.
5. Repeat this exercise three times.

Tool #4: The Practice of Kindness

Metta, or "loving-kindness," is a form of Buddhist meditation for sending well wishes to others, a wholehearted prayer expressing unconditional love. We extend *metta* not just to those who please us but to all beings, no matter how we feel about their actions. Variations of this sentiment can be found in most major religions in the world, including Christianity, Judaism, Hinduism, and Islam. Everywhere we look in spiritual teachings, we hear about the value of loving one another and treating others as we wish to be treated. This does not mean that any behavior is okay or that good boundaries and righteous anger don't have a place in our lives. We have the right and responsibility to protest behavior we think is unethical or hurtful. But *metta* reminds us that every action, thought, and response can be practiced with kindness.

After the 2019 attacks on a mosque in Christchurch, New Zealand, where fifty people were killed and many more injured, members of a Zen center in the town of Nelson on the South Island read the following prayer at a memorial. A friend sent me a copy of the prayer, which is the essence of kindness:

> May we awaken Buddha's compassion and wisdom. Having offered incense, flowers, candlelight, and chanting, we offer all virtue and metta to the peace, well-being, and safe passage of all those whose lives were taken in the events of that day. To the peace and well-being of all those injured and affected by these acts. To the healing of the planners and perpetrators of all destructive actions whose damaged hearts and clouded minds have created endless suffering for the present and the future. May we all, with our acts of body, speech, and mind, dedicate ourselves to peacefulness.

Notice that the perpetrator was included in the prayer for healing. No matter what, the supplication wishes peace upon all beings.

EXERCISE: Retaking the Wholehearted Love Quiz

This is a good time to go back to Chapter 1 and retake the test about Wholehearted Love to be able to appreciate all you have learned in reading *Love Skills*. Look at the way you scored at the start of this book, and look at the difference in how you have scored after it.

Reflections

Ask yourself: "What have I learned?" This may be a good time to make a list of your biggest takeaways, and take some time with your partner, if you are doing this together, to share your lists. It is also a time to appreciate yourself and one another for putting the time and care into your relationship to learn how to love smarter, braver, and more skillfully.

The Two Pillars of Wholehearted Loving:
Connection and Individuation

Love one another but make not a bond of love:
let it rather be a moving sea between the shores of your souls.

— Kahlil Gibran, Lebanese American poet, philosopher, and painter

There are many paths to wholeness, including an intimate relationship. Partnership is one of the richest, most challenging, and rewarding avenues I know. As the spiritual teacher Ram Dass writes in his classic book *Be Here Now*, "We are all just walking each other home." I hope the love skills you've picked up from this book, guided by an understanding of the Love Cycles — the enduring seasons of love — can help make that walk easier, kinder, and a lot more joyful.

Acknowledgments

I am delighted to be working once again with New World Library. Editor Jason Gardner, publicist Kim Corbin, and the staff are fountains of wisdom and practical help and the best example I know of merging the friendly with the professional. My agent, Barbara Moulton, is such a fabulous cheerleader. I am so lucky to work with all of them. Thank you.

My "offline" editors used their patience, skill, and expertise to help me bring my ideas to fruition with flow and clarity. In spite of an impossible schedule of her own, writer and editor Marian Sandmaier (The Gentle Pen) took on this project fully. Kelly Gonsalves, sex and culture writer extraordinaire, helped to shape my thoughts into workbook form and to translate theory into concrete and readable text. Thanks to Leigh Weingus and Joanne Machin for editing help.

My colleagues from the world of psychotherapy have been unfailingly generous. When I asked Harville Hendrix if I could quote him and use his exercises, he said, "Take whatever you need. No permission needed." Thanks go to authors Rita Jacobs (journaling) and Ann Gadd (the Enneagram), who generously donated their own pieces for use in this book, and to sociologist Nicholas Velotta, who wrote the first generation of quizzes on the Love Cycles, wholeheartedness, and listening.

Dr. Lori Gordon, founder of PAIRS International, was the first person to introduce me to the idea that love is based on a feeling and a healthy relationship is based on a skill set, for which I am most grateful.

When I asked Alicia Muñoz if I could quote from her book, I didn't expect to make such an amazing new friend. Her wisdom, support, and friendship have been a gift.

I also want to thank my "posse" of dear friends and supporters who have guided, laughed with, and challenged me while endlessly listening to my struggles and triumphs as I moved through the writing of *Love Skills*: Deb Lyman, Margaret Ronda, Mark Aron, Karen Randall, and Kaylene Campbell. To my Rancho La Puerta family, always an inspiration in so many ways, I thank you.

To my coteachers at Northwest Seminars and Consulting, I give deep appreciation for the twenty-plus years of bringing Love Skills to hundreds of people. Dave Long and Deb Lyman have been faithful, patient, and inspiring friends as we travel together, create together, and teach together what we are learning in our own marriages to others. *Love Skills* would not be in this world without their patience, willingness, and hours of dedicated work, and Tim and I would not be nearly as wholeheartedly together without your friendship.

I am so thankful for decades of collaborative work and friendship with Dr. Ann Ladd, developer of "The Loop," and for her generous sharing of Loopwork with me and hundreds of people throughout the years. Dale Rhodes's daylong Enneagram classes have informed and enlightened our students for decades, and I thank him for his friendship and careful reading of the Enneagram chapter in this book.

I thank my clients, who have trusted me with vulnerability and a willingness to learn new ways of being and who continue to teach me about resilience and courage. The stories in this book are based on composites of many people; they do not represent any specific person or couple. In the rare cases where I do use examples based on real people, I have changed the details so completely that it would be impossible to identify the source, with the exception of examples from my own life. In the stories from my marriage, I told it as it happened and always with the full permission of my partner, Tim.

I am so grateful to my stepfather, Martin Greenberg, writer and encourager (and 101 as of this writing!), for his interest in my work. I'm inspired by watching his long and flourishing writing career.

Most of all, however, I want to thank Tim, who remains a paragon of patience as I move from one project to another. He keeps me grounded and reminds me every day of what is essential in life.

Notes

Introduction

p. 12 *wholeness…as having the courage to be imperfect…*: Brené Brown, "The Power of Vulnerability," TEDxHouston, 2010, https://www.ted.com/talks/brene_brown _on_vulnerability.

p. 12 *"When there is nothing left to lose…"*: Elizabeth Lesser, *Broken Open: How Difficult Times Can Help Us Grow* (New York: Villard, 2005), p. 56.

Chapter 2. The Love Cycles

p. 24 *Dorothy Tennov coined the term "limerence"…*: Dorothy Tennov, *Love and Limerence: The Experience of Being in Love* (Lanham, MD: Scarborough House, 1999).

Chapter 4. Now What?

p. 45 *There are five so-called love languages…*: Gary Chapman, *The 5 Love Languages: The Secret to Love That Lasts* (Chicago: Northfield, 2015).

Chapter 5. How Did I Get Here?

p. 61 *[Genograms] contain basic data found in family trees…*: "Introduction to the Geno-gram," accessed September 17, 2019, https://www.genopro.com/genogram.

Chapter 6. Stories from Your Past

p. 79   *six key traits of strong families*...: John DeFrain and Nick Stinnett, "Creating a Strong Family: American Family Strengths Inventory," Family Strengths Research Project, University of Nebraska, https://medicalhomeinfo.aap.org/about/Documents/Nebraska.pdf.

p. 83   *three kinds of people...Islands, Waves, and Anchors*: Stan Tatkin, *Wired for Love: How Understanding Your Partner's Brain and Attachment Style Can Help You Diffuse Conflict and Build a Secure Relationship* (Oakland, CA: New Harbinger, 2011).

p. 84   *Most of us do not neatly fit*...: Stan Tatkin, "Am I an Anchor, Island, or Wave?" *PACT Institute Blog*, 2013, https://stantatkinblog.wordpress.com/2013/01/29/am-i-an-anchor-island-or-wave.

Chapter 8. Discoveries and Disclosure

p. 108   *described a 1997 lab experiment*...: Mandy Len Catron, "To Fall in Love with Anyone, Do This," *New York Times*, January 9, 2015, https://www.nytimes.com/2015/01/11/fashion/modern-love-to-fall-in-love-with-anyone-do-this.html.

p. 108   *"One key pattern associated with the development..."*: Arthur Aron, et al., "The Experimental Generation of Interpersonal Closeness: A Procedure and Some Preliminary Findings," *Personality and Social Psychology Bulletin* 23 no. 4 (April 1, 1997): 363–77 (364), https://doi.org/10.1177/0146167297234003.

p. 123   *"We've found that the positives..."*: Howard J. Markman, Scott M. Stanley, and Susan L. Blumberg, *Fighting for Your Marriage* (San Francisco: Jossey-Bass, 2010), p. 26.

Chapter 9. The Power of the Pause

p. 127   *"Practice the pause..."*: Lori Deschene, "Practice the Pause," *Tiny Buddha*, https://tinybuddha.com/fun-and-inspiring/practice-the-pause.

p. 132   *"researchers put heart monitors on dogs..."*: Helena Horton, "A Dog's Heart Beats in Sync with Its Owner's, Says New Study," *The Telegraph*, May 4, 2016, https://www.telegraph.co.uk/news/2016/05/04/a-dogs-heart-beats-in-sync-with-its-owners-says-new-study.

Chapter 10. Listening and the "And"

p. 139   *"Listening is about being present..."*: Krista Tippett, @kristatippett, Twitter, March 12, 2016.

Chapter 11. Managing Defensiveness and Speaking Smartly

p. 159   *it might be helpful to read...or watch*...: Harriet Lerner, *Why Won't You* Apologize? (New York: Touchstone, 2017); "Why Won't He Apologize?" TEDxKC, October 21, 2016, https://www.youtube.com/watch?v=5r6Y9uhmL6Y.

Chapter 13. Establishing Connection before Conflict

p. 190   *happy couples have a five-to-one ratio*…: Kyle Benson, "The Magic Relationship Ratio, According to Science," *Gottman Relationship Blog*, October 4, 2017, https://www.gottman.com/blog/the-magic-relationship-ratio-according-science.

p. 198   *we each have our own way*…: Gary Chapman, *The 5 Love Languages: The Secret to Love That Lasts* (Chicago: Northfield, 2015).

p. 204   *Use Alicia Muñoz's book*…: Alicia Muñoz, *A Year of Us: A Couples Journal: One Question a Day to Spark Fun and Meaningful Conversations* (Emeryville, CA: Zephyros, 2019).

Chapter 14. A Few Things about Sex I Know for Sure

p. 209   *millennials report fewer sexual encounters*…: Hope Reese, "Americans Are Having Less Sex, But Is That a Problem?" *Greater Good Magazine*, February 18, 2019, https://greatergood.berkeley.edu/article/item/americans_are_having_less_sex_but_is_that_a_problem.

p. 209   *"Coming out of your comfort zone*…": Manoj Arora, author of *From the Rat Race to Financial Freedom*, @ChickenSoup4theSoul, Twitter, February 19, 2019.

p. 211   *split the topic of romantic love into three categories*…: Helen Fisher, "Helen Fisher on Love, Lust and Attachment," Binghamton University, *YouTube*, July 13, 2009, https://www.youtube.com/watch?v=D8Od-bsCsFA.

p. 212   *Dr. Fisher examined brain scans*…: Helen Fisher, "Love and Hormones," TED Archive, *YouTube*, August 25, 2017, https://www.youtube.com/watch?v=PgoNoko_obg.

p. 214   *Ann Gadd details some sexual characteristics*…: Ann Gadd, *Sex and the Enneagram: A Guide to Passionate Relationships for the 9 Personality Types* (Rochester, VT: Findhorn Press, 2019).

p. 223   *So what sustains desire*…: Esther Perel, "The Secret to Desire in a Long-Term Relationship," TEDSalon NY2013, February 2013, https://www.ted.com/talks/esther_perel_the_secret_to_desire_in_a_long_term_relationship.

p. 225   *"As someone who is in the front lines*…": Michele Weiner-Davis, "Sex-Starved Wives," *HuffPost: The Blog*, December 7, 2017, https://www.huffpost.com/entry/sex-starved-wives_b_5339269.

p. 225   *believes our minds are more in charge*…: Emily Nagoski, *Come As You Are: The Surprising New Science That Will Transform Your Sex Life* (New York: Simon & Schuster, 2015).

p. 228   *Graham crackers were invented*…: Adee Braun, "Looking to Quell Sexual Urges? Consider the Graham Cracker," *Atlantic*, January 15, 2014, https://www.theatlantic.com/health/archive/2014/01/looking-to-quell-sexual-urges-consider-the-graham-cracker/282769.

p. 228   *Men fake orgasms too…*: Carla Sosenko, "More Than 30 Percent of Guys in New York Have Faked an Orgasm!" *Time Out New York*, July 9, 2014, https://www.timeout .com/newyork/sex-dating/more-than-30-of-guys-in-new-york-have-faked-orgasm.

p. 229   *In a study of 731 Italian women…*: Taryn Hillin, "New Study Says Eating Apples May Increase Sexual Pleasure in Women," *HuffPost*, August 7, 2014, https://www.huffpost .com/entry/sex-study_n_5568877?.

p. 229   *The orgasm gap, which holds that men…*: Ritch C. Savin-Williams, "Who's Most Likely to Have an Orgasm? Men and Lesbians," *Psychology Today*, April 17, 2018, https://www.psychologytoday.com/us/blog/sex-sexuality-and-romance/201804 /who-s-most-likely-have-orgasm-men-and-lesbians.

p. 229   *One study from Brown University found…*: Jeremy Adam Smith, "What's Sex Got to Do with Mindfulness?" *Mindful*, July 17, 2015, https://www.mindful.org/whats-sex -got-to-do-with-mindfulness; Maureen Salamon, "For Women, Sex May Be Improved by 'Mindfulness Meditation,'" *LiveScience*, November 15, 2011, https://www.live science.com/17040-women-sex-improved-mindfulness-meditation.html.

p. 229   *People who talk more during sex…*: Kelly Gonsalves, "Why Couples Should Talk More During Sex, According To Science," https://www.mindbodygreen.com/articles /why-couples-should-talk-more-during-sex-verbally-or-nonverbally-according-to -research.

Chapter 15. Conflict

p. 246   *Entomologists have found that insects…*: Kansas State University, "Cleaning Conflict? What Happens When Roommates, Romantic Partners Have Different Levels of Tolerance for Housework Left Undone?" *ScienceDaily*, July 24, 2012, https://www .sciencedaily.com/releases/2012/07/120724114707.htm.

p. 246   *One study has found that similar thresholds…*: Diane Mapes, "Study Reveals How a Neat Freak and a Slob Can Live in Peace," Today.com, August 3, 2012, https://www .today.com/health/study-reveals-how-neat-freak-slob-can-live-peace-924727.

p. 254   *"our tendency to pursue and believe facts…"*: Dean Yeong, "Confirmation Bias: Why We Make Poor Judgment and Bad Decision," *DeanYeong.com*, https://deanyeong .com/confirmation-bias.

p. 257   *subtle but undiagnosed "shadow" disorders…*: John J. Ratey and Catherine Johnson, *Shadow Syndromes: The Mild Forms of Major Mental Disorders That Sabotage Us* (New York: Bantam, 1998).

p. 259   *"Uncoupling is primarily a tale…"*: Diane Vaughan, *Uncoupling: Turning Points in Intimate Relationships* (New York: Oxford University Press, 1986); https://www .goodreads.com/work/quotes/628954-uncoupling-turning-points-in-intimate -relationships.

p. 261   *"Probably the wisest words that were ever uttered…"*: Laura Munson, *This Is Not the Story You Think It Is: A Season of Unlikely Happiness* (New York: Amy Einhorn Books, 2010), p. 3.

p. 262   *"When there's a big disappointment..."*: Pema Chödrön, *The Pocket Pema Chödrön* (Boston: Shambhala Pocket Classics, 2008), p. 90.

Chapter 16. Wholehearted Love

p. 267   *"Love addiction is just as real..."*: Helen Fisher, "In the Brain, Romantic Love Is Basically an Addiction," *The Crux* (*Discover* magazine blog), February 13, 2015, http://blogs.discovermagazine.com/crux/2015/02/13/love-addiction-brain /#.XWlf8y5Kjcc.

p. 269   *volunteering is even associated with direct health benefits...*: University of Exeter, "Go On, Volunteer — It Could Be Good for You!" *ScienceDaily*, August 22, 2013, https://www.sciencedaily.com/releases/2013/08/130822194451.htm.

p. 271   *"Owning our story can be hard..."*: Brené Brown, *The Gifts of Imperfection: Let Go of Who You Think You're Supposed to Be and Embrace Who You Are* (Center City, MN: Hazelden, 2010), p. 6.

Resources

The Merge

Bader, Ellyn, and Peter T. Pearson. *In Quest of the Mythical Mate: A Developmental Approach to Diagnosis and Treatment in Couples Therapy*. New York: Routledge, 1988.

Fisher, Helen. *Why We Love: The Nature and Chemistry of Romantic Love*. New York: Owl, 2005.

Halpern, Howard M. *How to Break Your Addiction to a Person*. New York: Bantam, 2004.

Tennov, Dorothy. *Love and Limerence: The Experience of Being in Love*. Lanham, MD: Scarborough House, 1999.

Relationship Skills

Brittle, Zach, and John Gottman. *The Relationship Alphabet: A Practical Guide to Better Connection for Couples*. CreateSpace, 2015.

Chapman, Gary. *The 5 Love Languages: The Secret to Love That Lasts*. Chicago: Northfield, 2015.

Hendrix, Harville, and Helen LaKelly Hunt. *Getting the Love You Want: A Guide for Couples*. New York: St. Martin's, 2019.

Muñoz, Alicia. *No More Fighting: The Relationship Book for Couples: 20 Minutes a Week to a Stronger Relationship*. Emeryville, CA: Zephyros, 2018.

Muñoz, Alicia. *A Year of Us: A Couples Journal: One Question a Day to Spark Fun and Meaningful Conversations*. Emeryville, CA: Zephyros, 2019.

Parker-Pope, Tara. *For Better: How the Surprising Science of Happy Couples Can Help Your Marriage Succeed*. New York: Dutton, 2010.

Tatkin, Stan. *Wired for Love: How Understanding Your Partner's Brain and Attachment Style Can Help You Defuse Conflict and Build a Secure Relationship*. Oakland, CA: New Harbinger, 2011.

Understanding the Self

Hollis, James. *Finding Meaning in the Second Half of Life: How to Finally, Really Grow Up*. New York: Avery, 2006.

Journaling and Inquiry

Jacobs, Rita D. *The Way In: Journal Writing for Self-Discovery*. Sharmor Editions, 2010.

The Genogram and Family History

Fitzpatrick, Sean. "Genogram Template 2." November 15, 2018. https://pdfsimpli.com/forms/form-type/template/genogram-template-2.

Genoware. "Genogram." http://www.genogram.org.

Family

Hendrix, Harville. *Keeping the Love You Find: A Personal Guide*. New York: Atria, 2003.

Hendrix, Harville, and Helen LaKelly Hunt. *Getting the Love You Want: A Guide for Couples*. New York: St. Martin's, 2019.

Johnson, Sue. *Hold Me Tight: Seven Conversations for a Lifetime of Love*. New York: Little, Brown, 2008.

Kluger, Jeffrey. *The Sibling Effect: What the Bonds Among Brothers and Sisters Reveal about Us*. New York: Riverhead, 2011.

Richo, David. *When the Past Is Present: Healing the Emotional Wounds That Sabotage Our Relationships*. Boston: Shambhala, 2008.

Sandmaier, Marian. *Original Kin: The Search for Connection Among Adult Sisters and Brothers*. New York: Plume, 1995.

The Enneagram

Baron, Renee, and Elizabeth Wagele. *Are You My Type, Am I Yours? Relationships Made Easy Through the Enneagram*. San Francisco: HarperSanFrancisco, 1995.

Daniels, David, and Virginia Price. *Essential Enneagram: The Definitive Personality Test and Self-Discovery Guide — Revised and Updated*. San Francisco: HarperOne, 2009.

Gadd, Ann. *Sex and the Enneagram: A Guide to Passionate Relationships for the 9 Personality Types*. Rochester, VT: Findhorn, 2019.

Wagele, Elizabeth. *The Enneagram of Parenting: The 9 Types of Children and How to Raise Them Successfully*. San Francisco: HarperSanFrancisco, 1997.

Sexuality

TED Talks

Nagoski, Emily. "The Keys to a Happier, Healthier Sex Life." TEDxUniversityofNevada, January 2016, video, 17:09. https://www.ted.com/talks/emily_nagoski_the_keys_to_a _happier_healthier_sex_life.

Perel, Esther. "The Secret to Desire in a Long-Term Relationship." TEDSalon NY2013, February 2013, video, 18:55. https://www.ted.com/talks/esther_perel_the_secret_to_desire _in_a_long_term_relationship?language=en.

Weiner-Davis, Michele. "The Sex-Starved Marriage." TEDxCU, April 2014, video, 17:34. https://www.youtube.com/watch?time_continue=1&v=Ep2MAx95m20.

Books

Davis, Michele W. *The Sex-Starved Marriage: Boosting Your Marriage Libido: A Couple's Guide*. New York: Simon & Schuster, 2004.

Klein, Marty. *Sexual Intelligence: What We Really Want from Sex — and How to Get It*. San Francisco: HarperOne, 2012.

Love, Patricia, and Jo Robinson. *Hot Monogamy: Essential Steps to More Passionate, Intimate Lovemaking*. CreateSpace, 2012.

Nagoski, Emily. *Come as You Are: The Surprising New Science That Will Transform Your Sex Life*. New York: Simon & Schuster, 2015.

Northrup, Chrisanna, Pepper Schwartz, and James Witte. *The Normal Bar: The Surprising Secrets of Happy Couples and What They Reveal about Creating a New Normal in Your Relationship*. New York: Harmony, 2013.

Perel, Esther. *Mating in Captivity: Unlocking Erotic Intelligence*. New York: HarperCollins, 2016.

Schnarch, David. *Passionate Marriage: Keeping Love and Intimacy Alive in Committed Relationships*. New York: Norton, 2009.

LGBT

Pink Therapy. https://www.pinktherapy.com.

Affairs

Spring, Janis A. *After the Affair: Healing the Pain and Rebuilding Trust When a Partner Has Been Unfaithful*. New York: Morrow, 2012.

Weiner-Davis, Michele. *Healing from Infidelity: The Divorce Busting Guide to Rebuilding Your Marriage After an Affair*. Woodstock, IL: Michele Weiner-Davis Training Corporation, 2017.

Mindfulness

Kabat-Zinn, Jon. *Wherever You Go, There You Are: Mindfulness Meditation in Everyday Life*. New York: Hachette, 2005.

Muñoz, Alicia. *Mindful Loving*. Amazon Digital Services LLC, 2019.

Nepo, Mark. *The Book of Awakening: Having the Life You Want by Being Present to the Life You Have*. San Francisco: Conari, 2000.

Siegel, Daniel J. *Aware: The Science and Practice of Presence — The Groundbreaking Meditation Practice*. New York: TarcherPerigee, 2018.

Wholeheartedness

The Call to Courage. Directed by Sandra Restrepo. Netflix, April 2019.

Chödrön, Pema. *When Things Fall Apart: Heart Advice for Difficult Times*. Boston: Shambhala, 2016.

Lesser, Elizabeth. *Broken Open: How Difficult Times Can Help Us Grow*. New York: Villard, 2005.

Munson, Laura. *This Is Not the Story You Think It Is . . . : A Season of Unlikely Happiness*. New York: Berkley, 2011.

Palmer, Peter J. *A Hidden Wholeness: The Journey Toward an Undivided Life*. San Francisco: Jossey-Bass, 2004.

Salzberg, Sharon. *Real Love: The Art of Mindful Connection*. New York: Flatiron, 2017.

Index

attitudes, passed-down, 66–68
attraction, 211
avoidance, 47
avoidant attachment, 83, 84
awareness: attachment styles and, 85; empathic, of others, 173–75; importance of, 9, 10; through inquiry practice, 120; of partner's relationship history, 43–44; reactivity without, 41. *See also* self-awareness; self-discovery/self-disclosure; self-knowledge

Bader, Ellyn, 15
balance, 269
Baron, Renee, 97
Be Here Now (Ram Dass), 276
beliefs: passed-down, 66–68; relationships impacted by, 72
betrayals, 258
biofeedback, 273
biology, 56
blame: breakups and, 49, 50, 261; childhood stories and, 78, 237; conflict management and avoidance of, 244, 248; disconnection resulting from, 232; emotional intelligence vs., 169; temporary comfort derived from, 261; vulnerability loops and, 237, 240
body: feelings and, 179–80; moving, 126, 127; sexuality and, 210, 222; tips for pausing/rebalancing, 128–29
body language, 161
books, 204
boredom, 262–63
boundaries, 48, 51, 56, 153, 274
Bowlby, John, 83
brain: conflict and, 256–57; defensiveness and, 154–55, 234–35; distractions and, 128; during intimate moments, 140; love addiction and, 267; during Love Cycle stages, 24–25, 26, 47, 49, 212; mindfulness and,

131; rejection and, 261; romantic love and, 211; sexuality and, 208, 225; during stress, 126–27, 155, 234–35; vulnerability loops and, 237

brainstorming, 162, 255
breakups, 49, 232, 259–63
breathing, 126, 127, 128, 158, 273–74
Breath Matching (joint exercise), 132–33
Brittle, Zach, 153
Broken Open (Lesser), 12
Brown, Brené, 12, 271
Buddhism, 274–75
"but" statements, 149, 150–51

candles, 204
care, 45
careful listening, 141, 144–45
Care of the Soul (Moore), 159
caring style, 46
case building, 254
Catron, Mandy Len, 108
Center for Nonviolent Communication, 169
change, 58
Chapman, Gary, 45, 198
childhood, 203
childhood stories: affection and, 79–81; attachment and, 81–87; balance in, 73; defensiveness and, 154–55; exercises, 74–75, 76–77, 83, 85–87; inner dialogue and, 175–76; learning, 72; lingering impact of, 71–72, 237, 267; parents and, 71–72, 73–75; red flags in, 73; self-told, 77–79; sexuality and, 207; siblings and, 75–77; wholeheartedness and owning of, 270–71
Chödrön, Pema, 262
Christianity, 274
classes, 50
codependency, 266–67
Come as You Are (Nagoski), 225
commitment, 79, 263

conflict management, 251–53; connection, 191, 197, 200, 201–4, 205; DTR, 48; emotional intelligence, 172–73, 176, 177, 178–79, 182; Enneagrams, 96–97; how to use, 9, 10–12, 58–59; identity, 57, 60–61, 65–66, 68–70, 87; mindful communication, 150–51, 155–57, 163–64; pausing, 129–31, 132–35; pillow-talk, 2, 6, 138; relationships, 88–92; self-discovery/self-disclosure, 112–16, 117, 119–20, 121–22, 123; sex, 213–14, 219–21, 225–26, 228–29; values, 112–16; Wholehearted Loving (Love Cycles stage), 275. *See also* joint exercises; quizzes

expectations, 106

experiences, lived, 56, 59

Exploring Your Values (exercise), 112–16

extroversion, 58, 232

eye contact, 173

eye gazing, 109, 122–24

Eye Gazing (exercise), 123

facial expressions, 161

families: criticism from, 154; emotional expression and, 182; resources, 288; romantic codependency and, 267; strong, 79; values taught by, 110

family history: affection in, 79–81; exercises, 68–70, 87; family tree for, 60–61; genograms for, 61–66; resources, 288; self-knowledge through understanding of, 58–59; sharing (joint exercise), 87; stories, 66–68, 71–72, 87

family rules, 59, 66, 67–68

family stories, 66–68, 87

family themes, 69–70

family tree, 60–61

family values, 207

Faraway Nearby, The (Solnit), 71

Fast Facts (exercise), 228–29

fear, 47, 129, 181, 273

feelings: defined, 179–80; labeling, 181; observing, 41; recognizing, 183–84; "rules" about, 182; truths about, 183. *See also* emotions

Fences (Wilson), 71–72

Fifty Shades of Grey (film trilogy), 209

fighters, 155, 234–35

fight/flight/freeze response, 154–55, 234–35

Fighting for Your Marriage (Markman, Stanley, and Blumberg), 123–24

financial infidelity, 258

Fisher, Helen, 211, 267

5 Love Languages, The (Chapman), 198

flee-ers, 155, 235

flexibility, 56

food waste, 244

foreplay, 204

forgetfulness, 248

forgiveness, 10, 262

freezers, 155, 234

friends, 50, 262–63, 267

frontal lobe, 127, 234

future dreams, 194

Gadd, Ann, 97

gay men, 229

gender stereotypes, 179

generosity, 45, 56

genetics, 56

genograms, 61–66, 73, 288

genopro.com, 61–62, 65

Germaine, Sister, xiv, xv

Getting the Love You Want (Hendrix), 251, 266

gifts, 45, 46, 199, 200

Gifts of Imperfection, The (Brown), 271

Gilbert, Elizabeth, xiii

Givers (personality type), 98–99, 215

Goleman, Daniel, 177, 186

goodbye kisses, 196

good will, 45, 47

Google, 133
Gordon, Lori, 6, 184
"Gossip" (children's game), 68
Gottlieb, Lori, 1
Gottman, John, 190
gratitude, 255
grief, 261

habits, annoying, 244–46, 256–57, 263
half-heartedness, 267–68
happiness, 181
head nodding, 173
heart, troubles of, 266–68
heartbreak, 261
Hendrix, Harville, xv, 6, 31, 44, 88, 200, 250,
    251, 266
Hesse, Hermann, 129
Hidden Wholeness, A (Palmer), 265
Hinduism, 274
hobbies, 50
home, connection rituals for leaving/returning,
    196
hope, 207
hopelessness, 262
hugging, 197, 210
humor, 51
Hunt, Helen LaKelly, xv, 6, 88, 250, 251

Idealists (personality type), 97–98, 214–15
identity: exercises, 57, 60–61, 65–66, 68–70;
    family stories and, 66–68; family tree and,
    60–61; genograms and, 61–66; nature vs.
    nurture and, 55–59; personality and, 93;
    resources, 288; romantic codependency
    and, 267; understanding, 55, 59. *See also*
    childhood stories; family history; self-
    discovery/self-disclosure
"if" statements, 159
Imago Dialogue, 251–53, 255
Imago relationship therapy, xv, 6, 88–92, 200,
    251

immigrants, 68
imperfection, acceptance of, 29
impulsivity, 50
"In Blackwater Woods" (poem; Oliver), 260
indifference, 28
individuation, 29, 276
infatuation, 3, 4, 25, 44, 45
infidelities, 258
inner dialogue, 175–77
inner noise, 128
Inner Self-Description (exercise), 176
inquiry, practice of, 120–22, 254, 288
interruptions, 173
intimacy, 108–9, 210, 276
introversion, 56, 58, 232
irritability, 248
"ish-ness," 84–85
Islam, 274
Islands (attachment style), 83–85, 191
"It's Just the Way I Am!" (exercise), 57

Jacobs, John, 55
Jacobs, Rita D., 118, 119
jealousy, 56
Jenner, Father, 110
Johnson, Catherine, 259
joint exercises: conflict management, 251–53;
    connection, 194, 202–4; emotional intelli-
    gence, 184–85; family history, 87; pausing,
    132–35; speaking skillfully, 166–67; values,
    117
journaling, 43, 118–20, 288
Journaling for Self-Discovery (exercise),
    119–20
Judaism, 274
Jung, C. G., 17
justifications, 175, 248

kindness, 45, 210, 274–75
kisses, 196, 210

relationships (*continued*)
improving, 15; leaving, 49, 259–63; marriages vs., 1; necessary elements of, 3; new, after breakups, 261–63; open, 253; partner's history of, 43–44; personality types and, 97–104; polarization in, 149; positive vs. negative interaction ratio for, 190; reconnecting in, 187–90; repairing of, 248–50, 258–59; resources, 287–88; sexuality and, 207–8, 222; sibling, 75–77; as skill set, 82; stages of, 3, 8, 24–30; values and, 112; wholeness and, xvi, 276; work required for, 195. *See also* partners

relationship skillfulness, 16, 18–19

relationship therapy, xv, 6, 11. *See also* Imago relationship therapy

Replacing "But" with "And" (exercise), 150–51

requests, 224

resentment, 261

resources, 256, 287–90

respect, 162, 207

Retaking the Wholehearted Love Quiz (exercise), 275

Rhodes, Dale, 93

Richards, Suzanne, 269

"rightness," need/desire for, 7, 10, 67, 135–36, 148, 157, 250, 251, 254, 255

rituals, 192–97

Road Back to You, The (Cron), 105

Romantics (personality type), 100–101, 215

Rosenberg, Marshall B., 169

rubbing, 210

sadness, 181

sarcasm, 44–45

Satir, Virginia, 193

Schwartz, Pepper, 212, 213

secure attachment, 83, 84

selective listening, 141

self-awareness, 118, 133, 247. *See also* mindful self-awareness; self-discovery/self-disclosure

self-care, 49–50, 51, 269

self-compassion, 59

self-contemplation, 109, 118–22

self-discovery/self-disclosure: author's experience, 107–9; conflict and, 232, 263; exercises, 112–16, 117, 119–20, 121–22, 123; eye gazing for, 122–24; intimacy created by, 108–9; self-contemplation for, 118–22; tips for, 109–10; of values, 110–17; Wholehearted Loving stage and, 29

self-knowledge, 55, 58, 210

self-love, 269

self-protection, 48–49, 154–55

self-reflection, 58

self-reflectivity, 48

self-regulation, 171–73

self-talk, 175–77

separations, 28

serotonin, 211

service, acts of, 45, 199, 200

sex/sexuality: accelerators/brakes, 225–26; cultural ambivalence about, 208–9; differing desires for, 198, 212; Enneagrams and, 97, 209, 214–17; exercises, 213–14, 219–21, 225–26, 228–29; exploring, 230; foreplay for, 204; Love Cycles model and, 30, 209, 211–14; mindful, 227; mindful communication about, 209, 222–25, 227; resources, 289; same-gender, 229; truths about, 210; as universal human aspect, 207–8, 210; values and, 209, 217–22

Sex and the Enneagram (Gadd), 97

Sexual Accelerators and Brakes (exercise), 225–26

sexual intelligence, 224, 227

shadow disorders, 256–58

Shadow Syndromes (Ratey and Johnson), 259

About the Author

Linda Carroll, MS, LMFT, has practiced psychotherapy since 1981 and recently obtained life-coach certification. She believes that wholehearted relationships are the foundation to a good life, and she teaches her clients the skills to maintain them. She wrote *Love Skills* as a companion to her first book on relationships, *Love Cycles: The Five Essential Stages of Lasting Love*, published by New World Library in 2014. Linda teaches Love Skills to couples all over the United States, in her hometown of Corvallis, Oregon, and online.

Linda grew up in San Francisco during the conventional 1950s and came of age during the countercultural 1960s. She preserves faith in the importance of service, mystery, and reverence for all living things. Since her early flower-child leanings, she has believed in looking to unexpected sources for approaches to healing.

Linda is an inner-fitness coach at Rancho La Puerta, in Tecate, Mexico, and a founder of Just One Story at a Time (justoneatatime.org), a nonprofit that brings education, relief, and music to migrant refugees, immigrants, and the poor living at the Mexican border.

Linda lives in Corvallis with her veterinarian husband, Tim Barraud, and their dog, an Australian labradoodle named Jackson. She has five children and nine grandchildren.

To learn more about her work, visit her website, LindaACarroll.com.